RESILIENCE AND AGEING
Creativity, culture and community

Edited by
Anna Goulding, Bruce Davenport
and Andrew Newman

First published in Great Britain in 2018 by

Policy Press
University of Bristol
1-9 Old Park Hill
Bristol
BS2 8BB
UK
t: +44 (0)117 954 5940
pp-info@bristol.ac.uk
www.policypress.co.uk

North America office:
Policy Press
c/o The University of Chicago Press
1427 East 60th Street
Chicago, IL 60637, USA
t: +1 773 702 7700
f: +1 773-702-9756
sales@press.uchicago.edu
www.press.uchicago.edu

© Policy Press 2018

British Library Cataloguing in Publication Data
A catalogue record for this book is available from the British Library

Library of Congress Cataloging-in-Publication Data
A catalog record for this book has been requested

978-1-4473-4091-1 hardback
978-1-4473-4092-8 paperback
978-1-4473-4093-5 ePdf
978-1-4473-4095-9 ePub
978-1-4473-4096-6 Mobi

The rights of Anna Goulding, Bruce Davenport and Andrew Newman to be identified as editors of this work has been asserted by them in accordance with the Copyright, Designs and Patents Act 1988.

All rights reserved: no part of this publication may be reproduced, stored in a retrieval system, or transmitted in any form or by any means, electronic, mechanical, photocopying, recording, or otherwise without the prior permission of Policy Press.

The statements and opinions contained within this publication are solely those of the author and not of the University of Bristol or Policy Press. The University of Bristol and Policy Press disclaim responsibility for any injury to persons or property resulting from any material published in this publication.

Policy Press works to counter discrimination on grounds of gender, race, disability, age and sexuality.

Cover design by Clifford Hayes
Front cover image: kindly supplied by Anna Goulding
Printed and bound in Great Britain by CMP, Poole
Policy Press uses environmentally responsible print partners

Contents

List of figures, tables and boxes — v
Notes on contributors — vii
Series editors' foreword — xiii

Introduction — 1
Anna Goulding

one   Setting the field: older people's conceptualisation of resilience and its relationship to cultural engagement — 19
Anna Goulding

two   Ages and Stages: creative participatory research with older people — 43
Miriam Bernard, Jill Rezzano and the Ages and Stages Theatre Company

three   Social connectivity and creative approaches to dementia care: the case of a poetry intervention — 65
Kate de Medeiros and Aagje Swinnen

four   Narrative identity and resilience for people in later life with dementia living in care homes: the role of visual arts enrichment activities — 87
Andrew Newman, Bruce Davenport and Teri Howson-Griffiths

five   After the earthquake: narratives of resilience, re-signification of fear and revitalisation of local identities in rural communities of Paredones, Chile — 111
Cynthia Meersohn Schmidt, Paulina Osorio-Parraguez, Adriana Espinoza and Pamela Reyes

six   Integrating sense of place within new housing developments: a community-based participatory research approach — 129
Mei Lan Fang, Judith Sixsmith, Ryan Woolrych, Sarah L. Canham, Lupin Battersby, Tori Hui Ren and Andrew Sixsmith

seven	Ageing in place: creativity and resilience in neighbourhoods *Cathy Bailey, Rose Gilroy, Joanna Reynolds, Barbara Douglas, Claire Webster Saaremets, Mary Nicholls, Laura Warwick and Martin Gollan*	157
eight	Crafting resilience for later life *Jackie Reynolds*	181
nine	Oral histories and lacemaking as strategies for resilience in women's craft groups *Anna Sznajder and Katarzyna Kosmala*	203
ten	Objects of loss: resilience, continuity and learning in material culture relationships *Helen Manchester*	227
eleven	Later-life gardening in a retirement community: sites of identity, resilience and creativity *Evonne Miller, Geraldine Donoghue, Debra Sullivan and Laurie Buys*	249
Index		267

List of figures, tables and boxes

Figures
3.1	Average frequencies by week for five observation categories	75
4.1	Pose by respondent ND34	101
4.2	Pose by respondent ND36	102
5.1	Body awareness workshop	116
5.2	Collage workshop	120
6.1	Conceptual framework for an inclusive, participatory redevelopment strategy for seniors transitioning into new housing	135
6.2	An older-adult participant shows her Bible	143
7.1a,b	Visual representations of group conversations	165
9.1a,b	Charming Threads workshop	209
9.2	Fifteenth anniversary of Charming Threads, November 2014	213
9.3	Zofia Sienicka and Olga Szerauc discussing a lace pattern during an ethnographic interview/conversation	216
9.4	Charming Threads logo in 2015, incorporating the monogram of King Kazimierz	220
9.5	Collected laces of Zofia Dunajczan during the exhibition in Kraków, 2015	221

Tables
1.1	Groups/organisations/charities through which participants were recruited	26
3.1	Response categories and definitions	74
4.1	Baseline characteristics of the study sample from care homes in North East England	96
6.1	Purpose and use implications of the five qualitative methods selected for the study	137
6.2	Data analysis matrix of information captured through a storytelling session with an older-adult participant	140
6.3	Key discussion topics and associated quotes from the deliberative dialogue sessions	146
6.4	Activities, services and other social and physical design features identified by participants to enhance ageing in place	149
7.1	Workshop 1: conversations about significant people, places and facilities	166

| 7.2 | Distilling the findings of the conversations | 171 |
| 8.1 | Craft group participants | 186 |

Boxes
1.1	Interview questions related to forms of participation	27
1.2	Interview questions related to cultural engagement	27
2.1	Questions on Ages and Stages	50
2.2	Questions on interview technique and cultural value	50
7.1	Synopsis of 'Doorbells of Delight'	172

Notes on contributors

Cathy Bailey, PhD, is an Associate Professor in Ageing at the Department of Nursing, Midwifery and Health, Northumbria University, Newcastle upon Tyne, UK. Her interests broadly encompass participatory approaches to working with older people to develop preventative, enabling and cost-effective services and supports. She has managed and supported international and national research projects including those focusing on: health technologies and older adults; social aspects of falls and older adults; creating dementia-friendly communities and intergenerational understanding of health and well-being. Cathy has collaborated within large multi-disciplinary and cross-sector research teams and her work is widely published.

Miriam Bernard is Professor of Social Gerontology at Keele University and a former President (2010–12) of the British Society of Gerontology. Her research career has been distinguished by a commitment to inter- and multi-disciplinary perspectives and much of her written work combines social scientific research with insights drawn from literature and the arts. She has long-standing interests in women's lives as they age, in intergenerational relationships and in environmental gerontology. Since 2009, Miriam has been privileged to lead the successive multi-research council-funded Ages and Stages projects. This continuing collaboration with the New Vic Theatre in Newcastle-under-Lyme has seen the establishment of the Ages and Stages Theatre Company and the now annual Live Age Festival. Miriam currently leads the Leverhulme-funded Ageing of British Gerontology project (2015–17) charting the evolution of the discipline through archival work and filmed interviews with 'senior' gerontologists.

Bruce Davenport is a Research Associate in Media, Culture, Heritage in the School of Arts and Cultures at Newcastle University. Before this he worked as an educator in museums and galleries in the North East of England. Bruce has worked on a variety of projects exploring the impact of older people's engagement with cultural heritage, either as participants in formal activities or as volunteers. He is also interested embodied approaches to exploring how people interact with each other and with museum/gallery objects to create meanings.

Adriana Espinoza, PhD, is Assistant Professor in the Department of Psychology at the University of Chile. She teaches postgraduate qualitative methodology courses. Her methodological interests include the development of innovative research interventions from creative and art-based approaches. Her research explores transgenerational transmission of trauma, collective memory processes and psychosocial trauma in the context of socio-natural disasters and political violence.

Mei Lan Fang is a Research Associate at the STAR Institute, Simon Fraser University, Vancouver, Canada and an Academic Fellow in Communications and Community Engagement with AGE-WELL NCE (a Canadian technology and ageing network). At AGE-WELL she works with the transdisciplinary-working research team, focusing on generating and disseminating knowledge on how large networks can work more collaboratively to facilitate real-world impact. She leads a Vancouver Foundation-funded community-based research project, Place-Making with Seniors, working closely with local stakeholders to capture the place-based needs of older adults transitioning into affordable senior housing. Mei Lan is also a PhD candidate at Heriot-Watt University, Scotland, where she investigates how individual experiences and histories shape place transitions and impact on unique fluctuations in social isolation and connectedness in older adults.

Rose Gilroy is Professor of Ageing, Policy and Planning and Director of Engagement at the School of Architecture, Planning and Landscape at Newcastle University, UK. Her research explores the impact of the ageing population, particularly in relation to planning and housing. Her concerns embrace the home and the lines of attachment that radiate from it into neighbourhood, city and region. Her research explores how place supports everyday life in later life. As a planner, she is interested in the transactional relationship between people and their environment.

Anna Goulding is a Research Associate at the Institute of Health and Society, Newcastle University, UK. Before this she was a Research Fellow at the Manchester Institute for Collaborative Research on Ageing, University of Manchester. This book proposal developed out of the research project The Role of Creative Interventions in Fostering Connectivity and Resilience in Older People (AHRC Connected Communities Programme), on which she was principal investigator. Anna has worked as a co-investigator on a range of research council-funded projects exploring the processes and outcomes of engagement with art gallery programmes on older people. These include: Contemporary Visual Art and Identity Construction – Wellbeing amongst Older People; and Dementia and Imagination: Connecting Communities and Developing Well-being through Socially Engaged Visual Arts Practice.

Teri Howson-Griffiths is a Lecturer at Liverpool John Moores University specialising in contemporary and applied performance. Her research and practice focuses on socially and community engaged participatory and immersive forms. Within her work she is particularly interested in exploring memory, self, and notions of illness and wellness.

Katarzyna Kosmala, PhD, is Professor of Culture, Media and Visual Arts, Research and Enterprise Development Lead for Culture and Creativity at the School of Media, Culture and Society, the University of the West of Scotland, a curator and art writer. In 2011–10 she was a Visiting Research Fellow at GEXcel, Institute of Thematic Gender Studies, Linköping University and Örebro University, Sweden and Visiting Professor at the Getulio Vargas Foundation in Rio de Janeiro, Brazil. She researches cultural labour and discourses of creativity, identity and community in the context of a globalising network society, heritage and participation, art production and enterprise, arts-run projects, as well as gender and politics of representation. Her most recent publication is a co-edited volume, *Precarious Spaces: The Arts, Social and Organizational Change*). She also writes regularly about video and new media art in international art journals and catalogues.

Helen Manchester is a Reader in Digital Inequalities and Urban Futures at the University of Bristol. Helen is interested in sociotechnical change, digital exclusion, material cultures and the challenges of 21st-century urban living. She develops methodologically innovative approaches to research, working across disciplines to collaborate on research projects with artists, technologists, young and older people, community organisations and policy makers. Helen has led a number of Research Councils UK-funded projects, including Tangible Memories: Community in Care (AHRC Digital transformations and Connected Communities award) and Parlours of Wonder (AHRC Follow on Fund).

Kate de Medeiros is Associate Professor of Gerontology and a Research Fellow at the Scripps Gerontology Center at Miami

University, Oxford, Ohio, USA. Her research includes work on meaning making, the arts and dementia; narrative gerontology, to include the use of multiple genres in life stories work; friendships and social connectivity among people living with dementia; and generativity in later life.

Cynthia Meersohn Schmidt has been based at Durham University since 2017 and has previously held posts at the University of Chile and the London School of Economics. Cynthia's primary area of research is ageing and the life course. She has been involved in projects addressing quality of life and well-being in older populations; changing social networks in widowhood; the resilience to natural disasters of older individuals in rural communities; the life trajectories and social class identification of British, precarious mid-life individuals; and the transitions from mid-life to later life of individuals in Chile. Besides these projects, Cynthia also has experience in research on neighbourhoods, communities and collective memory. Cynthia is also an enthusiast for innovative research methods such as – but not limited to – combining arts-based research with network analysis, or using cluster analysis of text for making sense of large amounts of archival information.

Evonne Miller is an environmental psychologist and Director of the QUT Design Lab at Creative Industries, Queensland University of Technology, Australia. She has over 90 publications and A$1.5 million dollars in competitive research grant funding for projects exploring the interrelationships between people and their built, technical and natural environments. As a qualitative researcher, Evonne uses participatory design, visual and creative art (for example, poetry, photovoice) approaches to explore and enhance the ageing experience.

Andrew Newman is Professor of Cultural Gerontology at Newcastle University. His research applies the arts, in terms of both subject and methodologies, to current questions in gerontology. He is also interested in how social and cultural policy is constructed and practice regulated. His work responds to the challenges faced by ageing populations in areas such as loneliness, social-economic disadvantage, bereavement, life transitions and negative societal meta-narratives that can affect health. He has been involved in a number of research projects funded by AHRC, ESRC and MRC, the most recent of which explores the engagement of older people with dementia with the arts.

Jackie Reynolds is a Research Impact Manager at Staffordshire University. She is particularly interested in public engagement as a pathway to impact and was previously Keele University's first-ever Public Engagement (with Research) Fellow, undertaking research on a range of community-focused projects. Jackie was also the Research Associate on the Leverhulme-funded Ageing of British Gerontology project (2015–17), and as Senior Researcher at Staffordshire University led an AHRC-funded Cultural Value project in 2014 investigating the value of arts and culture in relation to empathy, compassion and understanding.

Jill Rezzano is Head of Education at the New Vic Theatre, Newcastle-under-Lyme. She is responsible for managing New Vic Education's workshop and participatory programme, which provides accessible opportunities for the whole community to learn through theatre. Since 2009, Jill has been collaborating with Keele colleagues on the Ages and Stages projects, exploring the impact of theatre on our ideas about ageing. She is Artistic Director of the Ages and Stages Theatre Company; Co-Director of the annual Live Age Festival; and Co-Director (with Jackie Reynolds) of the new (2017–19) Arts Council England/Baring Foundation-funded Meet Me at Live Age project – a year-round programme of commissioned arts events and performances created with and for older people. Jill has also written for theatre and organised workshops for new writers.

Aagje Swinnen, PhD, is an Associate Professor in the Department of Literature and Art at Maastricht University and Endowed Socrates Chair in International Humanism and the Art of Living at the University of Humanistic Studies in Utrecht. Her study of ageing includes research into representations of dementia in literature and film as well as meanings of literature in arts-based approaches to dementia care. She has published on these topics in *The Gerontologist*, *Journal of Aging Studies* and *Dementia*. Her research has been funded by the Netherlands Organization for Scientific Research and for Health Research and Development, by Fulbright and by the Dutch Cultural Participation Fund. Swinnen is co-founder of the European Network in Aging Studies and co-editor of *Age, Culture, Humanities*.

Anna Sznajder is a freelance researcher. Anna obtained her PhD at the School of Media, Culture and Society, University of the West of Scotland. Her research interests include history of lace-making in Central and Eastern Europe, women's work strategies, traditional crafts and the anthropology of ageing. Anna is a member of the International Bobbin and Needle Lace Organization and the Polish Ethnological Society.

Claire Webster Saaremets is the Artistic Director of Skimstone Arts. Skimstone Arts collaborates with artists, researchers, individuals and communities, nationally and internationally. Together, they create multi-disciplinary touring theatre, music and exhibitions that reflect the current social narratives, challenges and inspirations faced in today's diverse society. As Artistic Director and performer, Claire has professional practice, in 20 years' work, of over 50 collaborative artistic projects/commissions with more than 5,000 people of all ages, both regionally and internationally. Claire is a strong proponent of enabling research participants both to engage with research activity in meaningful ways and to shape how what they have contributed is shared, presented and further developed more widely.

Ryan Woolrych is an Associate Professor in Urban Studies at Heriot Watt University, Edinburgh, Scotland and an Adjunct Professor at the Gerontology Research Centre, Simon Fraser University, Vancouver, Canada. Ryan has expertise of working on funded research in the UK and internationally, working with vulnerable and marginalised groups, undertaking participatory research alongside older adults and applying visual methodologies to understanding the relationship between people and place. Ryan has expertise in training local residents to act as co-researchers, developing older-adult advisory teams and ensuring that the community are partners in the dissemination process. He has published widely in ageing, housing and community journals. Ryan is currently principal investigator on a three-year cross-national ESRC project (Place-Making with Older Adults: Towards Age-Friendly Communities) bringing together local government, community groups and older adults in a process of collaborative planning.

Series editors' foreword

Around the globe, communities of all shapes and sizes are increasingly seeking an active role in producing knowledge about how to understand, represent and shape their world for the better. At the same time, academic research is increasingly realising the critical importance of community knowledge in producing robust insights into contemporary change in all fields. New collaborations, networks, relationships and dialogues are being formed between academic and community partners, characterised by a radical intermingling of disciplinary traditions and by creative methodological experimentation.

There is a groundswell of research practice that aims to build new knowledge, address longstanding silences and exclusions, and pluralise the forms of knowledge used to inform common sense understandings of the world.

The aim of this book series is to act as a magnet and focus for the research that emerges from this work. Originating from the UK Arts and Humanities Research Council's Connected Communities programme (www.connected-communities.org), the series showcases critical discussion of the latest methods and theoretical resources for combining academic and public knowledge via high-quality, creative, engaged research. It connects the emergent practice happening around the world with the longstanding and highly diverse traditions of engaged and collaborative practice from which that practice draws.

This series seeks to engage a wide audience of academic and community researchers, policy makers and others with an interest in how to combine academic and public expertise. The wide range of publications in the series demonstrate that this field of work is helping to reshape the knowledge landscape as a site of democratic dialogue and collaborative practice, as well as contestation and imagination. The series editors welcome approaches from academic and community researchers working in this field who have a distinctive contribution to make to these debates and practices today.

Keri Facer, Professor of Educational and Social Futures,
University of Bristol

George McKay, Professor of Media Studies,
University of East Anglia

Introduction

Anna Goulding

Introduction

This book is unique in bringing together researchers from multiple disciplines to address the relationship between taking part in different forms of creative and cultural practice and the development of resilience in older people. It makes a distinctive contribution to a strong body of research on the role of the arts in sustaining well-being (Walker, 2014; APPG, 2017) by articulating the role of culture in helping people to thrive. This edited collection arises from an UK Arts and Humanities Research Council's Connected Communities programme Follow-on Fund award, The Role of Creative Interventions in Fostering Connectivity and Resilience in Older People.[1] Critical reflection on a range of projects from across the Connected Communities portfolio and beyond prompted innovative ways of thinking about the relationship between creative engagement and resilience. Through discussions during the series of workshops, it became clear that resilience was an integral yet distinct component of well-being and quality of life, which we wanted to investigate further. Workshop participants were invited to submit chapter proposals and a call was made via the Connected Communities programme mailing list and other social media channels. By examining the role of a broad range of international and UK-based projects, this book adopts a holistic cross-sector approach towards suggestions for facilitating active ageing and resilience.

The link between resilience and creativity may at first glance seem tenuous, as both terms come from such different disciplinary paradigms. Added to this, both terms are applied to multiple and contrasting contexts. Resilience can be used in relation to how communities cope with macro-level natural disasters such as earthquakes, right down to individual personality traits such as having a sense of humour helping people to navigate life. Similarly, creativity can be an original idea that carries value (Robinson, 1999), or associated with everyday problem solving. We view resilience as a combination of 'both environmental and individual factors' (Wild, Wiles and Allen, 2013, p 144) and as a 'negotiated process', rather than as a trait that some people are fortunate enough to possess (Wild et al, 2013, p 144). The distinction we have made is important, as the book aims to investigate what forms of cultural engagement make a difference for people in later life, with implications for the development of interventions. The book draws from a wide range of creative and cultural practices including gardening, housing design, craft and reading. The range of practices chosen reflects our preferred definition of creative activity as a process whereby the individual seeks an original solution to a problem or challenge at hand (Mariske and Willis, 1998). We examine the cultural means through which people make sense of the normal transitions and experiences associated with ageing, alongside more acute stresses.

Rather than focusing on mitigating risk factors, this book examines how older people can bounce back despite adversity, and perhaps even because of it. There are significant challenges associated with old age and, as a response, policy initiatives have been developed which focus on reducing social isolation,[2] improving well-being and creating dementia-friendly communities.[3] The chapters in this book provide crucial support for such initiatives by reporting findings that enhance understanding of how cultural engagement can develop both individual and community resilience (Windle, 2011). In the UK political context, where the retrenchment of the welfare state has implications for health and social care in older age (Age UK, 2012; Age UK, 2014; Loopstra et al, 2016; Scharf and Shaw, 2017), and reduced public spending on the arts has implications for arts and health or outreach work (Knell and Taylor, 2011; Hebron and Taylor, 2012), we consider two key questions.

- How does the act of engagement with culture enable older people to thrive in the face of everyday adversities and life transitions associated with older age, as well as severe, traumatic stressors?
- How can older people apply the creative skills they have developed to other areas of their life, making them more able to cope with life challenges (Fisher and Specht, 1999)?

Through critically examining the meaning and value of creative engagement in later life, this book brings vital new understandings to the field of cultural gerontology. We consider research where the creative activity is the focus of the study and where the creative activity is part of the research methodology (Hope, 2016). Participatory methods have been used to ensure that older people's voices shape and direct arguments about ways of conceptualising and fostering resilience (Gattuso, 2003; Wild et al, 2013).

Central themes

Creativity

We include a broad range of creative practices, including those not necessarily associated with the arts, partially reflecting the current interest in an examination of the significance of everyday life (Neal and Murji, 2015; Conner et al, 2016). Critically, because we examine how people might apply thought processes or problem-solving strategies generated by creative activity to other aspects of their life, it is imperative to include a range of activities requiring different skills. The more conventionally recognised art forms (APPG, 2017) included in the book are the visual and performing arts (participatory theatre), crafts (lace making), film, literature (reading privately and as part of a group). While the book does not make sectional claims for one art form over another, the chapters do interrogate what engagement with each specific art form brings to the experience. Crucially, the book does not make a distinction between the production and consumption of the arts, but incorporates both (O'Brien and Oakley, 2015). One notable omission from the book is research with a focus on music and singing, which merely reflects the chapter contributions received.

A crucial aspect of researching the value of cultural engagement concerns the aesthetic encounter: what it feels like to have an aesthetic experience and the meaning and purpose derived from that experience (Hanquinet, 2013; Varriale, 2016; Goulding, 2018). We examine what is specific to different artistic encounters. For example, Bernard et al's chapter (Chapter Two) looks at participatory theatre. It has been argued that drama, as a form of creative engagement, depends in its essence on the dialogical creation and exchange of meanings; it is a performative art that engages and integrates voice, body and imagination (Bernard et al, 2014). The role of social interaction in the act of engagement is also part of the process examined throughout the book. We also look at the sense of enjoyment gained from creative engagement. In Chapter Three de Medeiros and Swinnen emphasise the importance of play in a poetry intervention with people with dementia, an aspect that the authors argue is rarely given enough attention. Similarly, Miller et al (Chapter Eleven) look at the pleasure gained from gardening.

Looking at conventionally recognised art forms, chapters include both fine art and craft skills. Risatti (2007) explores how different domains (for example, contemporary fine art compared with contemporary craft and traditional crafts) value technical mastery as compared to creative expression, with crafts placing greater emphasis on technical mastery and in-depth understanding of material qualities. Seen in this light, traditional crafts such as those explored in Chapters Eight and Nine, create opportunities for creative self-expression on a foundation of technical skills (see also, Sennett, 2009). The patterns of engagement for these sorts of activities are quite distinct from activities involving abstract, expressive fine art forms, such as those used in Chapters Four and Five.

The other creative forms of engagement include gardening, which is now more widely considered an art form (APPG, 2017). Miller et al (Chapter Eleven) explicitly explore artistic pleasure as one potential aspect of gardening through the purposeful arranging and layering of plants in terms of colour, texture and pattern. Approaching everyday creativity from another angle, Manchester's chapter (Chapter Ten) looks at everyday creative choices by exploring the importance of personal objects in care home settings. Chapters Six and Seven use participatory approaches to generate decisions about housing and the development of age-friendly environments. Finally, Meersohn Schmidt et al (Chapter Five) explore the potential of creative expressive arts to help people deal with acute stress by researching a psychosocial intervention (Forsman et al, 2011) specifically designed to support people in overcoming the trauma of an earthquake.

Making creative choices is linked strongly to people's sense of self. Chapters demonstrate how older people use engagement to maintain or reinterpret their sense of identity. In Chapter Ten, Manchester explores the relationship between older people with dementia and objects. She examines the degree to which the objects that matter to individuals are imbued with meanings over time, and how such meanings are expressed through how people care for and display them. In Chapter Eleven, Miller et al explore the experience of gardening in later life, focusing on how people who move to a retirement community maintain or reinterpret their gardening identity. Goulding (Chapter One) looks at how engaging in culture contributed to participants' cultural identity, with meanings of gender, class and ethnicity made in acts of cultural consumption. In reading about other lives, participants made sense of other groups and cultures and simultaneously communicated their own identity (Pitcher, 2014). Both Newman et al (Chapter Four) and de Medeiros and Swinnen (Chapter Three) look at communication and personhood in dementia. De Medeiros and Swinnen found that participatory arts programmes provided opportunities for people to be reminded of their 'humanness' and value as human beings. The authors argue that through imaginative play people can enact important aspects of meaning and personhood that might otherwise go unacknowledged in the care environment. Newman et al (Chapter Four) show how arts enrichment activities supported the personhood of those in later life, living with dementia in care homes, through facilitating narrative expression. Through both language and embodied forms of communication respondents were communicating a sense of self that was not consciously autobiographical. In Chapter Five, Meersohn Schmidt et al reveal how, in post-earthquake Chile, creative expression and imagination were fundamental in the re-conceptualisation of local community identity. The authors argue that engaging in the psychosocial creative intervention allowed the reconstruction of individual and collective well-being. Through engagement, participants were able both to accept ambiguous emotions towards past events and to find a safe outlet for trauma.

Creative problem solving as a component of creative engagement is a theme that the book sets out to explore. In Chapter One people draw from literature to put their own problems in perspective and to engage in processes of life review (Westerhof et al, 2010). Another example of the ways that people think around problems is in Miller et al's chapter (Chapter Eleven), where gardeners find ways of adapting to downsizing, diminishing energy and restricted mobility. Bernard et al (Chapter Two) found that older people were motivated to take part in participatory theatre due to the 'challenge', which supports positive psychological research on the optimum levels of difficulty of a task (Csikszentmihályi, 1990). Reynolds (Chapter Eight) found that people's enthusiasm for adapting their skills, problem solving and developing new craft skills was an important motivating factor, which supports findings on the importance of mastery as a mental health resource (de Beurs et al, 2005). The social science and creative practice methods used here reveal how participants cite problem solving and challenging capabilities as an important draw of creative engagement. They articulate the link between challenge, mastery and resilience in terms of these aspects providing them with a sense of meaning and purpose (Chapters One and Eleven). This is a facet which warrants further investigation, and discipline perspectives from the medical sciences would provide further insight.

Resilience

The relationship between creative engagement and resilience was first proposed by McFadden and Basting (2010). Drawing on empirical work by Cohen et al (2006), they argue that creativity fosters emotional experiences and social interactions that contribute to a person's resilience. Chapter findings make a major advance to research on resilience in older age (Wild et al, 2013) by providing qualitative data on older people using creative engagement to bounce back from adversity, whether extreme (Chapter Five) or more everyday (Chapters One, Three, Eight and Ten). Chapters throw light on how people have negotiated and adapted to life transitions associated with ageing, highlighting the importance of adopting a lifecourse approach when studying resilience (Zautra et al, 2008). Goulding (Chapter One) draws from Wild et al's (2013, p 151) contextualised framework, which recognises resilience as operating across a number of different areas of life. Their framework incorporates different domains across which resilience can occur that include psychological, mobility, financial, environmental, physical, social and cultural areas of resilience. Concentrating on more severe risk factors, Chapter Five looks at how psychosocial interventions can be used to mediate the effects of acute stress, trauma and chronic adversity (Southwick et al, 2014) in the form of the aftermath of an earthquake.

Engaging in cultural forms of participation is shown to help people thrive, as opposed to merely cope and survive (Bauman et al, 2001). Miller et al (Chapter Eleven) make suggestions for designing retirement communities that encourage residents to garden together as a means of supporting pleasure and resilience. De Medeiros and Swinnen (Chapter Three) argue that the arts offer a style of communication and self-expression that is particularly suited to capitalising on the emotional and social capabilities of people with dementia. This book makes an essential contribution to social gerontology by showing how, as the population ages, understanding how older people maintain, adapt and reinterpret participation in creative leisure activities, despite declining health and mobility, is a critical part of supporting continued flourishing in later life.

Throughout the book, the participatory methods used ensure that older people's voices direct arguments about ways of conceptualising and fostering resilience, addressing the absence of older people's accounts in the literature (Gattuso, 2003; Wild et al, 2013). The first chapter sets the scene by asking older people for their perspectives on the relevance of the term to their lives. Responses to the questions highlighted the unequal playing field that the formal research interview setting presents, with some participants apologising for not understanding the meaning of the term resilience. Different methods resulted in further differences of emphasis in the data – while the book set out to shift thinking away from seeing resilience as a personality trait, in individual interviews people focused on personality traits or strategies used by individuals to cope when faced with challenges. However, in group exercises conducted as part of a cultural animation workshop, participants articulated the support that they gained from their local community.

Narrative agency in people with dementia and its relationship to resilience is a key theme (Randall, 2013). Changes in opportunities to express oneself through language have been found to affect self-expression (Blair et al, 2007) and threaten personhood (Sabat and Harre, 1992). Both Newman et al (Chapter Four) and de Medeiros and Swinnen (Chapter Three) show how the personhood of a person living with dementia might be supported or enhanced (Kitwood, 1997) through engagement in arts-based interventions. They examine the role of arts enrichment activities and a poetry intervention in supporting narrative agency and expression. Manchester's research in a care home setting (Chapter Ten) involved residents in bringing personal objects and telling their stories. She observed that objects and their stories were found or rediscovered and that people who had previously considered themselves bereft of tales found themselves with things of interest to share with a wider audience.

The relationship between well-being and resilience

The arts and health field is well established, with the Age of Creativity network[4] showcasing exemplary practice and recent policy-focused research culminating in the All-Party Parliamentary Group report (APPG, 2017). Resilience is viewed here as an aspect of well-being. Creative engagement has been shown to contribute to identity processes and promote a sense of belonging, self-esteem and self-confidence; facilitate the development of supportive social networks; build skills, broaden horizons and challenge capabilities; and support involvement during times of transition such as retirement and widowhood (Bazalgette et al, 2011; Richards et al, 2012; Newman et al, 2013; Walker, 2014; Bernard et al, 2014).

The field of arts and older-people practice has grown rapidly since the late 2000s, with claims made for contributions to participants' health and well-being. However, it has been argued that the benefits claimed for engagement are not well articulated or understood (Clift et al, 2009). Furthermore, the pressure on research to fulfil an uncritical advocacy role (Belfiore and Bennett, 2010) limits the scope for exploring the broader meanings attached to engagement. Moreover, caution has been expressed over policy-focused research solely conceptualising engagement through the prism of health and well-being (Twigg and Martin, 2015). The book's focus on resilience contributes to such debates. Aware that resilience is at risk of becoming the latest emancipatory buzzword (Luthar et al, 2000), the chapters do not take an uncritical stance.

Cultural value

The opportunity to engage is not equal. There are different levels of engagement in different forms of cultural participation according to class, gender, ethnicity, sexuality and age (DCMS, 2017). The field of cultural class analysis explores how forms of cultural engagement are both defined by, and define, social class identities as intersected by other demographic markers. None of the chapters explicitly addresses inequality of opportunity according to social class, as other research projects are currently addressing such questions (Miles and Gibson, 2016). Other seminal studies have addressed cultural participation in terms of social class and education among working-age populations (Bennett et al, 2009), while emergent work looks more closely at how class and education levels intersect with age (Goulding, 2018). As socio-economic status and education correlate with health (Marmot et al, 2010), which in turn impacts on resilience, the correlations cannot be ignored. In the first chapter, in which older people from the UK define resilience, the study set out to learn from participants with a broad range of life experiences, including those who have experienced adversity in the form of socio-economic disadvantage (Lowenstein, 2009), bereavement (Bennett, 2010) and health challenges such as depression and physical frailty (Grenier, 2005). The other chapters throw light on the role of age, gender and class on cultural practices, but do not explicitly use social bases as a starting point for framing research questions or sampling strategies. For example, through their interest in older women engaging in craft, both Reynolds (Chapter Eight) and Sznajder and Kosmala (Chapter Nine) draw conclusions specific to the place-based experience of women from working-class backgrounds in Europe. In Chapter Five, through the lens of a psychosocial creative intervention, Meersohn Schmidt et al expose the post-earthquake challenges faced by people from lower socio-economic groups in

Chile. Another marker of potential exclusion of particular importance to critical gerontology is cognitive decline. This important theme is addressed by the three chapters looking at dementia, communication and personhood by de Medeiros and Swinnen (Chapter Three), Newman et al (Chapter Four) and Manchester (Chapter Ten).

Social relationships

In exploring community resilience, all the chapters address the role of social relationships in the creative process. This enables us to articulate what is specific to engaging the arts as opposed to other activities involving social interaction (Miles and Sullivan, 2012). The social contexts of cultural participation are particularly important when looking at older populations (Scherger, Nazroo and Higgs, 2011). Reynolds (Chapter Eight) uses the construct of social capital, which has been defined as the range of social contacts that give access to social, emotional and practical support (Gray, 2009). Her study was prompted by a lack of qualitative insights into how social capital is actually *experienced* (Blackshaw and Long, 2005), with gender differences and the social capital of older women in particular as largely neglected in the literature (O'Neill and Gidengil, 2006). Reynolds highlights the ways in which women's relationships and widowhood have impacted upon their later life participation. Similarly in Chapter Nine, Sznajder and Kosmala confirm the value of craft activities as both creative and social experiences that contribute towards participants' resilience. Unlike studies that have shown the importance of cultural engagement in fostering the development of supportive friendships, Goulding (Chapter One) found that cultural engagement provided a focus for loose-tie relationships. Being able to talk about the art form, as opposed to personal information, was a relief for participants experiencing difficulties such as later-life divorce or for those who wanted to pursue activities independently, outside of the marital relationship. The chapters provide insights into the distinctive nature of arts-generated social capital, with networks of support and reciprocity arising from arts engagement. They consider how the development of different types of social relationships contributes towards both individual and community resilience.

Place

The importance of place identity and community is explored, with case studies drawing from experiences of ageing in Chile, Australia,

Canada, the US, Poland and the UK. Place is an important constituent part of cultural identity and, as argued here, community resilience. This theme builds on Rowles' (1993) influential work on the importance of place identity to older populations and is a response to the lack of research understanding the relationship between place and cultural consumption (Gilmore, 2013; Jones, 2014). In some chapters the specific geographic location informs the creative context, most clearly in Chapter Five, where a psychosocial intervention is used to help an ageing rural community in Chile to develop community resilience post-earthquake. Similarly, Sznajder and Kosmala's ethnographic study (Chapter Nine) in Poland revolves around lacemaking and the oral history accounts generated by these older, female lacemakers. The chapter shows how the women reconstituted traditional practices and grounded them in the wider cultural heritage of Kraków, their home city. In some chapters, the context of a community's living environment is more generalisable, for example, Miller et al (Chapter Eleven) look at people moving into a retirement community. Similarly, Fang et al (Chapter Six) capture sense-of-place as experienced by older people transitioning into an affordable housing development. Fang et al develop practical guidelines and make recommendations for supporting the place-based needs of older adults. In Chapter Seven Bailey et al examine older people's preferences around ageing in place, which include adapting housing and ensuring that local amenities are accessible by affordable public transport. Both Goulding (Chapter One) and Reynolds (Chapter Eight) found that engaging in culture contributed to participants' cultural identity, with meanings of gender and class made in acts of cultural production and consumption. Participants enjoyed exhibits in museums or art galleries that related to their life experiences. For some participants, discussion of the exhibits helped participants to communicate their own identities as working-class women and the pride they felt in their region.

Participatory methods

Participatory methods that involve older people co-creating research, from the initial design to delivery, analysis and dissemination of findings, have become increasingly common in gerontological work (Barnes, 2007; Ray, 2007; Ward et al, 2012). In Chapter Two, Bernard employed creative participatory methods to turn a theatre programme's members into a company of researchers. Fang et al (Chapter Six) explore the potential of a community-based participatory research approach in capturing the distinct viewpoints of local stakeholders involved in the redevelopment of an affordable housing community in Canada. They test the applicability of qualitative methods, including narrative inquiry techniques, storytelling, photovoice (Wang and Burris, 1997) and mapping exercises (Corbett, 2009). Similarly, Bailey et al's use of the World Café method (Brown and Isaacs, 2002) was used to connect diverse perspectives on developing age-friendly places (Chapter Seven). Sznajder and Kosmala's ethnographic approach (Chapter Nine) developed as they began investigating craft making in Poland. They found that the cultural artefact, in this particular case lace, could be used to facilitate oral history narratives. Goulding (Chapter One) found that a cultural animation exercise (Kelemen et al, 2015) provided participants with non-verbal means to articulate their viewpoints around individual and community resilience. Meersohn Schmidt et al's research team (Chapter Five), with disciplinary backgrounds spanning social anthropology, community psychology and art therapy, used action research to develop a psychosocial (Forsman et al, 2011) creative intervention. They found that the creative expression and imagination generated through the intervention was fundamental in the re-conceptualisation of local community identity. Fang et al and Meersohn Schmidt et al argue that participatory methods have an emancipatory effect on participants that can lead to social change, an aspect of the debate where academics need to show moderation in the claims they make.

The authors discuss the advantages and disadvantages of their chosen participatory methods and reflect more widely on the challenges of working in these creative and collaborative ways. They outline the risk involved when outcomes are not defined from the outset, and the need to trust and place faith in colleagues and participants representing different stakeholder perspectives. Academics experimenting with different participatory methods demonstrate a willingness to try new ways of working and the ability to relinquish control over some aspects of the process. When participatory research results in a final public performance or exhibition, the academics involved have an ethical responsibility towards participants who may be affected in different unforeseen ways. Future research would benefit from a greater criticality of participatory methods. To do this, the research community needs to provide more detail on how different approaches are executed, including the time frames involved, so that the applicability of methods to research questions can be tested. For example, how are people who have difficulties with verbal communication encouraged to contribute? How long does it take for everyone around the table to feel comfortable expressing their opinions and how do we stop certain voices from dominating? How is iterative reflection built in to projects when deadlines for outputs are predetermined? In aiming to break down traditional notions of expert versus layperson and to value different kinds of experiential knowledge, how do we ensure that scientific knowledge is still valued and informs the dialogue?

The chapters are grouped according to the themes that they have in common. The first two chapters use participatory methods and are centred on officially- and widely-recognised cultural forms – participatory theatre, reading groups and film (categories used in the Taking Part household survey which collects data in England on cultural engagement).[5] Chapters Three and Four both interrogate creative activities using expressive fine art forms with people with dementia. They both consider the impact of creative interventions on personhood. The following three chapters are grouped together as they use research methods as a tool for community action. Interestingly, they are all centred on the built environment and neighbourhood, which suggests something about the particular applicability or acceptability of participatory methods being used in this context. Chapters Eight and Nine both involve studies of craft activities – perhaps unsurprisingly, in both cases the participants are mainly women, which has interesting implications for collective, gendered identity and community resilience. The book finishes with two chapters looking at more everyday forms of creativity – the importance of personal objects and of gardening in fostering resilience in later life.

Acknowledgements

We would like to thank the AHRC Connected Communities programme and all the research participants who gave their time.

Notes

[1] https://blogs.ncl.ac.uk/annagoulding/.
[2] For the campaign to end loneliness see www.campaigntoendloneliness.org/.
[3] For dementia-friendly communities see www.alzheimers.org.uk/site/scripts/documents_info.php?documentID=1843.
[4] For the Age of Creativity network see http://ageofcreativity.co.uk/about/.
[5] Taking Part is a household survey in England and measures engagement with the cultural sectors. The data are widely used by policy officials, practitioners, academics and charities. https://www.gov.uk/guidance/taking-part-survey.

References

Age UK (2012) *Care in crisis: Seven building blocks for reform*, London: Age UK.

Age UK (2014) *Age UK inquiry submission APPG on hunger and food poverty inquiry*, London: Age UK.

APPG (All-Party Parliamentary Group on Arts, Health and Wellbeing) (2017) *Creative health: The arts for health and wellbeing*. Available at: www.artshealthandwellbeing.org.uk/appg-inquiry/Publications/Creative_Health_Inquiry_Report_2017_-_Second_Edition.pdf.

Barnes, M. (2007) *Involving older people in research: examples, purposes and good practice*, Brighton: HSPRC, University of Brighton.

Bauman, S., Adams, J.H. and Waldo, M. (2001) 'Resilience in the oldest-old', *Counseling and Human Development*, 34(2): 1–19.

Bazalgette, L., Holden, J., Tew, P., Hubble, N. and Morrison, J. (2011) '*Ageing is not a policy problem to be solved...*': *Coming of age*, London: Demos. Available at: https://www.demos.co.uk/files/Coming_of_Age_-_web.pdf.

Belfiore, E. and Bennett, O. (2010) 'Beyond the "toolkit approach": Arts impact evaluation research and the realities of cultural policy-making', *Journal for Cultural Research*, 14(2): 121–42.

Bennett, T., Savage, M., Silva, E., Warde, A., Gayo-Cal, M. and Wight, D. (2009) *Culture, class, distinction*, London: Routledge.

Bennett, K. (2010) 'How to achieve resilience as an older widower: Turning points or gradual change?', *Ageing and Society*, 30(3): 369–82.

Bernard, M., Rickett, M., Amigoni, D., Munro, L., Murray, M. and Rezzano, J. (2014) 'Ages and Stages: The place of theatre in the lives of older people', *Ageing and Society*, doi: 10.1017/S0144686X14000038.

Blackshaw, T. and Long, J. (2005) 'What's the big idea? A critical exploration of the concept of social capital and its incorporation into leisure policy discourse', *Leisure Studies*, 24(3): 239–58.

Blair, M., Marczinski, C.A., Davis-Faroque, N. and Kertesz, A. (2007) 'A longitudinal study of language decline in Alzheimer's disease and frontotemporal dementia', *Journal of the International Neuropsychological Society*, 13(2): 237–45.

Brown, J. and Isaacs, D. (2002) *The World Café book: Shaping our futures through conversations that matter*, San Francisco, CA: Berrett-Koehler

Clift, S.M., Chapman, P., Clayton, G., Daykin, N., Eades, G., Parkinson, C., Secker, J., Stickley, T. and White, M. (2009) 'The state of arts and health in England', *Arts and Health*, 1(1): 6–35.

Cohen, G.D., Perlstein, S., Chapline, J., Kelly, J., Firth, K.M. and Simmens, S. (2006) 'The impact of professionally conducted cultural programs on the physical health, mental health, and social functioning of older adults', *The Gerontologist*, 46(6): 726–34.

Conner, T., DeYoung, C.G. and Silvia, P.J. (2016) 'Everyday creative activity as a path to flourishing', *The Journal of Positive Psychology*, 13(2), 181–89, doi: 10.1080/17439760.2016.1257049.

Corbett, J. (2009) *Good practices in participatory mapping: A review prepared for the International Fund for Agricultural Development (IFAD)*, Rome, Italy: International Fund for Agricultural Development.

Csikszentmihályi, M. (1990) *Flow: The psychology of optimal experience*, New York, NY: Harper and Row.

de Beurs, E., Comijs, H., Twisk, J.R., Sonnenberg, C., Beekman, A.T. and Deeg, D. (2005) 'Stability and change of emotional functioning in late life: Modelling of vulnerability profiles', *Journal of Affective Disorders*, 84: 53–62.

DCMS (Department for Culture, Media and Sport) (2017) *Taking Part 2016/17: Quarter 4 statistical release*, London: DCMS. Available at: https://www.gov.uk/government/statistics/taking-part-201617-quarter-4-statistical-release.

Fisher, B. and Specht, D. (1999) 'Successful aging and creativity in later life', *Journal of Aging Studies*, 13(4): 457–72.

Forsman, A.K., Nordmyr, J. and Wahlbeck, K. (2011) 'Psychosocial interventions for the promotion of mental health and the prevention of depression among older adults', *Health Promotion International*, 26(1): supplement 1: i85–i107

Gattuso, S. (2003) 'Becoming a wise old woman: Resilience and wellness in later life', *Health Sociology Review*, 12(2): 346–48.

Gilmore, A. (2013) 'Cold spots, crap towns and cultural deserts: The role of place and geography in cultural participation and creative place-making', *International Journal of Cultural Policy*, 22(2): 86–96.

Goulding, A. (2018) 'The role of cultural engagement in older people's lives', *Cultural Sociology*, online first (22 February 2018), doi: 10.1177/1749975518754461.

Gray, A. (2009) 'The social capital of older people', *Ageing & Society*, 29(1): 5–31.

Grenier, A.M. (2005) 'The contextual and social locations of older women's experiences of disability and decline', *Journal of Aging Studies*, 19(2): 131–46.

Hanquinet, L. (2013) 'Visitors to modern and contemporary art museums: Towards a new sociology of "cultural profiles"', *The Sociological Review*, 61: 790–813.

Hebron, D. and Taylor, K. (2012) *A new age: An examination of the changing state of health funding for arts activity with, by and for older people in England*, London: London Arts and Health Forum.

Hope, S. (2016) 'Bursting paradigms: a colour wheel of practice-research', *Cultural Trends*, 25(2): 74–86.

Jones, P. (2014) 'Where's the capital? A geographical essay', *The British Journal of Sociology*, 65(4): 721–35.

Kelemen, M., Mangan, A., Phillips, M., Moffat, S. and Jochum, V. (2015) *Untold stories of volunteering: A cultural animation project*, AHRC Connected Communities programme report. Available at: https://www.keele.ac.uk/media/keeleuniversity/ri/risocsci/events/untoldstories/Untold%20Stories%20Final%20Report.pdf.

Kitwood, T. (1997) *Dementia reconsidered: The person comes first*, Buckingham: Open University Press.

Knell, J. and Taylor, M. (2011) *Arts funding, austerity and the big society: Remaking the case for the arts?* London: Royal Society of the Arts.

Loopstra, R., McKee, M., Katikireddi, S.V., Taylor-Robinson, D., Barr, B. and Stuckler, D. (2016) 'Austerity and old-age mortality in England: A longitudinal cross-local area analysis, 2007–2013', *Journal of the Royal Society of Medicine*, 109(3): 109–16.

Lowenstein, A. (2009) 'Elder abuse and neglect – "Old phenomenon": New directions for research, legislation, and service developments', *Journal of Elder Abuse and Neglect*, 21(3): 278–87.

Luthar, S., Cicchetti, D. and Becker, B. (2000) 'The construct of resilience: A critical evaluation and guidelines for future work', *Child Development*, 71(3): 543–62.

Mariske, M. and Willis, S.L. (1998) 'Practical creativity in older adults' everyday problem solving: Life span perspectives', in C.E. Adams-Price (ed) *Creativity and successful aging: Theoretical and empirical approaches*, New York, NY: Springer, pp 73–113.

Marmot, M., Allen, J., Goldblatt, P., Boyce, T., McNeish, D., Grady, M. and Geddes, I. (2010) *Fair society, healthy lives: The Marmot review*, London: University College London.

McFadden, S.H. and Basting, A.D. (2010) 'Healthy aging persons and their brains: Promoting resilience through creative engagement', *Clinical Geriatric Medicine*, 26: 149–61.

Miles, A. and Gibson, L. (2016) 'Everyday participation and cultural value', *Cultural Trends*, 25(3): 151–7.

Miles, A. and Sullivan, A. (2012) 'Understanding participation in culture and sport: Mixing methods, reordering knowledges', *Cultural Trends*, 21(4): 311–24.

Neal, S. and Murji, K. (2015) 'Sociologies of everyday life: Editors' introduction to the special issue', *Sociology*, 49(5): 811–19.

Newman, A., Goulding, A. and Whitehead, C. (2013) 'How cultural capital, habitus and class influence the responses of older adults to the field of contemporary visual art', *Poetics*, 41(5): 456–80.

O'Brien, D. and Oakley, K. (2015) *Cultural value and inequality: A critical literature review*, Swindon, UK: Arts and Humanities Research Council: Swindon.

O'Neill, B. and Gidengil, E. (eds) (2006) *Gender and social capital*, London: Routledge.

Pitcher, B. (2014) *Consuming race*, London: Routledge.

Randall, W. (2013) 'The importance of being ironic: Narrative openness and personal resilience in later life', *The Gerontologist*, 53(1): 9–16.

Ray, M. (2007) 'Redressing the balance? The participation of older people in research', in M. Bernard and T. Scharf (eds) *Critical perspectives on ageing societies*, Bristol: Policy Press, pp 73–87.

Richards, N., Warren, L. and Gott, M. (2012) 'The challenge of creating "alternative" images of ageing: Lessons from a project with older women', *Journal of Aging Studies*, 26(1): 65–78.

Risatti, H. (2007) *A theory of craft: Function and aesthetic expression*, Chapel Hill, NC: University of North Carolina Press.

Robinson, K. (1999) *All our futures: Creativity, culture and education*, London: Department for Education and Employment. Available at: http://sirkenrobinson.com/read/all-our-futures/ (accessed 23 March 2018).

Rowles, G.D. (1993) Evolving images of place in aging and "aging in place"', *Generations*, 17(2): 65–70.

Sabat, S. and Harre, R. (1992) 'The construction and deconstruction of self in Alzheimer's disease', *Ageing and Society*, 12(4): 443–61.

Scharf, T. and Shaw, C. (2017) *Inequalities in later life*, London: Centre for Ageing Better.

Scherger, S., Nazroo, J. and Higgs, P. (2011) 'Leisure activities and retirement: Do structures of inequality change in old age?', *Ageing and Society*, 31(1): 146–72.

Sennett, R. (2009) *The craftsman*, London: Penguin.

Southwick, S.M., Bonanno, G.A., Masten, A.S. Panter-Brick, C. and Yehuda, R. (2014) 'Resilience definitions, theory, and challenges: interdisciplinary perspectives', *European Journal of Psychotraumatology*, 5(1), doi: 10.3402/ejpt.v5.25338

Twigg, J. and Martin, W. (2015) *Routledge handbook of cultural gerontology*, Abingdon: Routledge.

Varriale, S. (2016) 'Beyond distinction: Theorising cultural evaluation as a social encounter', *Cultural Sociology*, 10(2): 160–77.

Walker, A. (ed) (2014) *The new science of ageing*, Bristol: Policy Press.

Wang, C. and Burris, M.A. (1997) 'Photovoice: Concept, methodology, and use for participatory needs assessment', *Health Education and Behavior*, 24(3): 369–87.

Ward, L., Barnes, M. and Gahagan, B. (2012) *Well-being in old age: Findings from participatory research*, Brighton: University of Brighton and Age Concern Brighton, Hove and Portslade. Available at: www.brighton.ac.uk/sass/older-people-wellbeing-and-participation/.

Westerhof, G.J., Bohlmeijer, E. and Webster, J.D. (2010) 'Reminiscence and mental health: A review of recent progress in theory, research and interventions', *Ageing and Society*, 30: 697–721.

Wild, K., Wiles, J. and Allen, R. (2013) 'Resilience: Thoughts on the value of the concept for critical gerontology', *Ageing and Society*, 33(01): 137–58.

Windle, G. (2011) 'What is resilience? A review and concept analysis', *Reviews in Clinical Gerontology*, 21: 152–69.

Zautra, A., Hall, J. and Murray, K. (2008) 'Resilience: A new integrative approach to health and mental health research', *Health Psychology Review*, 2(1): 41–64.

ONE

Setting the scene: older people's conceptualisation of resilience and its relationship to cultural engagement

Anna Goulding

Editorial introduction

This chapter uses a 'cultural animation method' which involves deploying a range of creative activities to elicit responses from participants. As such, this and the following chapters are examples of creative techniques being used as part of a research methodology. By the end of the chapter, it remains an open question whether these techniques provide insights that are different from traditional techniques. Nonetheless, they are used to successfully draw out participants' own understandings of resilience and the personal, social and cultural factors that shape their resilience across the life span.

Introduction

This chapter produces new understandings of the relationship between cultural engagement and resilience in older age. It uses data from a cultural animation (Kelemen et al, 2015) workshop and qualitative interviews with a range of older people to understand their conceptualisation of resilience and the strategies they have used to overcome challenges experienced throughout the lifecourse. Findings develop the field of cultural gerontology by revealing how cultural participation, as defined by the participants themselves, can foster psychological, social and cultural resilience (Wild et al, 2013).

In contrast to the successful ageing paradigm (Foster and Walker, 2015), the notion of resilience comes with an acceptance that older people will face adversity, and that such challenges are a normal part of life (Wild et al, 2013). The concept is particularly applicable to understanding older people's lives because, while people face extreme life adversity, the term also encompasses the negotiation of more normal upheavals associated with normal 'life transitions' (Bauman et al, 2001). Mindful of how resilience is in danger of becoming the 'new emancipatory buzzword' (Luthar et al, 2000), this chapter charts how engagement may inform the everyday processes, the 'ordinary magic' (Masten, 2001) of human adaptation.

Older people's voices are missing from arguments shaping the conceptualisation of resilience (Gattuso, 2003; Wild et al, 2013). This study used creative methods to stimulate and articulate the challenges that older people faced and how they addressed them. A facilitated cultural animation approach (Kelemen et al, 2015) was used, as the method has been argued to place the day-to-day experiences of ordinary people at the heart of the inquiry. Twelve older people participated in the workshop, and themes emerged that were explored further through qualitative interviews with a larger sample. The study draws from participants with a broad range of life experiences, including those who have experienced adversity in the form of socio-economic disadvantage (Lowenstein, 2009), bereavement (Bennett, 2010) and health challenges such as depression and physical frailty (Grenier, 2005).

The study provides a multi-dimensional and contextualised examination of how cultural participation functions. Therefore, from the outset, what was considered as culture was not limited to official or legitimate forms (Bennett et al, 2009; Miles and Sullivan, 2012). Also, participants were not asked to distinguish between producing and consuming culture, precisely because traditionally both are treated separately in academic research (O'Brien and Oakley, 2015). Therefore, using participants' own conceptualisations of culture, the study includes: reading privately and as part of a book group; independent or facilitated group visits to cultural venues such as art galleries, museums and music venues; institutionally provided choral and musical programmes; lifelong learning classes in independent/arthouse cinema, art history and literature; painting; taking photographs; and listening to music at home. The forms of participation that participants referenced bridged those taking place in public spheres, those brokered by institutions, and those practised individually in the home. Significantly, participants only described and referenced official and legitimate forms of participation.[1]

The chapter explores the 'aesthetic encounter', which has been described as the interaction between the participant and the aural, visual and narrative properties of the cultural object (Varriale, 2016).

This is necessary to articulate what is specific to engaging the arts as opposed to other activities involving social interaction (Miles and Sullivan, 2012). Engagement with the arts has been found to aid personal reflection and provide pleasure, appreciative experience and the development of knowledge (Crossick and Kaszynska, 2016). Data examines to what extent such outcomes might foster resilience across psychological, social and cultural areas of life (Wild et al, 2013).

Literature review

Arts engagement, well-being and resilience in older age

Cultural engagement has been found to benefit older people's lives through sustained subjective well-being, increased social activity and involvement in the community (Walker, 2014). The same can be argued for other forms of social participation (Adams et al, 2011). Outcomes specific to cultural engagement include the development of new musical (Varvarigou et al, 2012), acting (Bernard et al, 2014) or artistic skills (Richards et al, 2012). Goulding (2013) argues for the development of analytical skills, while Rumbold (nd, cited in Crossick and Kaszynska, 2016) found that engagement with the arts aided personal reflection. Turning to how such outcomes may relate to resilience, Gattuso (2003) looks at how older people use storytelling, especially narratives about coping with loss, as a way of constructing a sense of self as resilient. Related to this, 'meaning making' has been found to be important for older populations (Westerhof et al, 2010). The use of arts to facilitate reflection, which some older adults find difficult to achieve, therefore has implications for interventions aimed to encourage life review. This chapter examines to what extent personal reflection, pleasure, appreciative experience and the development of knowledge stimulated by engagement may impact on an individual's resilience.

One of the challenges inherent to researching the relationship between cultural engagement and resilience is that engagement in 'official' or 'legitimate' culture such as art galleries, museums or classical concerts (Bennett et al, 2009) is related to class and education, which in turn correlates with health (Marmot et al, 2010). While engagement among working-age populations is well documented (Bennett et al, 2009), research is lacking on how cumulative advantages and disadvantages intersect with cultural practices in later life (Scherger et al, 2011). This study gains perspectives from a sample of participants from different socio-economic classes (with education level and former professional occupation used as proxy for class) and ethnic backgrounds, who also had different experiences of cultural engagement.

Resilience

In the social sciences, research on resilience stems from developmental psychology and tends to focus on survival and adaptation in overcoming risk (Luthar, Chicetti and Becker, 2000; Wild et al, 2013). Adversity in older age has been found to be typified by functional limitation; poor health, increased stress and decline in general living circumstances; and people experiencing a negative life event. The resilient tended to report fewer multiple adversities (Hildon et al, 2009). While identifying and reducing risk is part of the equation, avoidance of adversity is not universally possible. Early research tended to concentrate on the personality characteristics of individuals that helped them to cope with difficulty. More recently, researchers have begun to investigate the processes and mechanisms that can facilitate the development of resilience (Hildon et al, 2009; Bennett, 2010). This development ties in with recommendations for the need of community-based approaches to be researched and highlighted, as the prevalent 'successful ageing' discourse places too much emphasis on individual agency, as opposed to organisational and societal actions (Foster and Walker, 2015).

Looking at research examining the processes through which people develop resilience, Bennett (2010) used qualitative interviews to explore resilient behaviour among widowers. She found that personal characteristics had been particularly important for those who had been consistently resilient, but that both informal and formal social support had been important for widowers who had become resilient more gradually and after turning points. Many of the turning points were associated with joining clubs or going to concerts and other social activities. Another example she gave, of a turning point triggered by an internal trait, was of one participant who viewed widowhood as a job to be undertaken – he could be seen to be applying his lifelong work ethic to overcoming this personal challenge. Bennett's findings are important, as they reveal how a combination of both personal characteristics and external support operate within a time frame.

Hildon et al (2009) used questionnaire data to identify the characteristics of resilient individuals and the factors that can help to reduce adversity. Having good-quality relationships and integration in the community were found to be important. Hildon et al (2009) argue that resilience can be actively encouraged through providing ways for people to develop social relationships and to participate in civic life through voluntary and paid work. This study builds on these findings by using a qualitative approach to provide a multi-dimensional and contextualised examination of how cultural participation functions. It examines how the contexts in which arts engagement occurs can play a role in providing formal and informal social support (Bennett 2010), and the tailoring of this to different individuals.

Wild et al (2013, p 151) recognise resilience as operating across a number of different areas of life. Their contextualised framework incorporates different domains across which resilience can occur: psychological, mobility, financial, environmental, physical, social and cultural. The different areas overlap or interact; for example, a person may be financially but not emotionally resilient. Psychological, social and cultural resilience are the focus of this chapter as they relate to research findings on the well-being outcomes of engagement with cultural forms.

To describe the three different forms of resilience, first, psychological resilience is an individual's capacity to adapt to life tasks in the face of social disadvantage or other adverse conditions (Reich et al, 2012). Here a person's individual character traits, outlook or beliefs may influence their ability to cope. For example, whether someone is optimistic or pessimistic, how they apply their sense of humour or perspective to challenging situations, or whether a sense of faith guides or reassures them. This chapter will investigate whether meaning making and the development of knowledge and understanding stimulated by cultural engagement contributes towards psychological resilience.

Second, social resilience moves away from the individual to look at how relationships between people can contribute to resilience. This category encompasses social relations, social capital and social networks and how individuals and communities harness or mobilise these entities to adjust to or cope with environmental and social threats (Sapountzaki, 2007). Social capital has been defined as the range of social contacts that give access to social, emotional and practical support (Gray, 2009). Studies looking at social support for older people have pointed towards declining family care and the increasing dependence of older people on friends (Gray, 2009). The social contexts of cultural participation are particularly important when looking at older populations, with Scherger et al (2011) calling for further research on whether cultural activities are pursued alone or with other people. Integral to researching these three areas of resilience is an examination of the changing social roles (Minkler and Holstein, 2008) that older people occupy and to what extent creative engagement plays a role in facilitating or creating these new identities.

Third, cultural resilience can be viewed as a culture's ability to maintain and develop cultural identity, cultural knowledges and practices (Reich et al, 2012). Cultural identity encompasses a range of intersecting social bases including class, gender, ethnicity, disability, age and sexuality. When viewed as a relational social process, cultural consumption can be seen to help constitute community identity (Miller, 2010). Material culture has been argued to determine and define categories of cultural identity such as gender and race. For example, Cann (2013) showed how young readers found gendered values in texts. Looking at race, Pitcher (2014) argues that the meanings of race are made in acts of creative consumption – through what people read, the television programmes they watch and the food they eat. He argues that in understanding race through depictions in art and media, we make sense of other groups and cultures and communicate our own identities (Pitcher, 2014). Also, what is valued by one community may be rejected by another. Place is another important constituent part of cultural identity, as demonstrated in Rowles' (1993) work on the importance of place identity to older populations. Currently, however, there is a lack of research understanding the relationship between place and cultural consumption (Gilmore, 2013). The development of flagship cultural venues as part of the regeneration of urban areas was identified as an important factor in older people's feelings of exclusion from official cultural institutions (Goulding, 2013).

It is important to consider these three areas as dynamic and not static. Furthermore, while we are aware of the physical barriers to engagement in older age, such as transport and mobility (Keaney and Oskala, 2007), we need further understanding of the complex psychosocial barriers to participation, motivation, processes and outcomes of engagement.

In summary, the chapter investigates how cultural aspects of life may contribute to older people's resilience across social, cultural and psychological domains. It starts off by examining older people's conceptualisation of resilience and strategies used to overcome challenges faced throughout the lifecourse. It then explores how and in what ways cultural participation might function to help develop individual and community resilience.

Methods

The study took place in the North East of England. The first stage of the project involved using creative methods to stimulate and articulate participants' experiences of the challenges they had faced and how they had overcome them. A charity that develops art and older-people projects was approached and, through it, various contacts at sheltered accommodation units were made. The arts charity facilitated contact with a group it had been working with for three years who were considered as currently engaging with cultural organisations. To capture the responses of those not currently engaging with official cultural practices, residents at one of the sheltered accommodation units were approached by the research team. After gaining informed consent, a total of 12 participants were assembled together and invited by the research team on an accompanied visit to a local authority museum. Transport and refreshments were provided. Participants were accompanied by the research team and the charity organiser. At the museum, they were given a guided tour by an education officer and then given time to go around exhibitions on their own.

A few weeks later, participants were assembled at the sheltered accommodation unit lounge, where they took part in a facilitated participatory theatre activity led by an outreach officer. The workshop, using a cultural animation approach, was used to articulate the difficulties participants faced and how they addressed them. A cultural animation approach was chosen as it has been argued to place the everyday experiences of ordinary people at the heart of the inquiry (Kelemen et al, 2015). Integral to the method is validating the language used by community members to describe their experiences (Dworakowska et al, 2011; Kelemen and Rumens, 2013). During the two-hour workshop, participants explored what resilience meant to them using various creative methods. They worked together in small groups to create mimes and tableaux, wrote poems as individuals, read the poems aloud to the group and compiled a group poem that the facilitator read out. Throughout the session, participants discussed the theme as a group while the researchers made field notes about the content of the discussions.

A few weeks later all participants were invited to the university to participate in the seminar series.[2] Participants from the cultural animation workshop gave a presentation to an audience of academics and voluntary sector professionals about their conceptualisation of resilience and attended the following workshops in the series.

A month later the lead researcher returned to interview the participants about their understanding and experience of resilience and how cultural participation or creative engagement might contribute to developing resilience in older age. The research team met and compared notes and drew out key themes from the cultural animation workshop, seminars and interviews. The link between cultural engagement and resilience was felt to be salient enough to investigate further. At this stage the research team decided to widen out the study to gain perspectives from a sample of participants from different socio-economic classes (with education level and former professional occupation used as proxy for class) and ethnic backgrounds who also had different experiences of cultural engagement. The study aimed to draw from participants who had experienced adversity in the form of socio-economic disadvantage (Lowenstein, 2009), bereavement (Bennett, 2010) and health challenges such as depression and physical frailty (Grenier, 2005; Braudy Harris, 2008).

Purposive sampling was used to recruit a further 40 participants (21 male, 19 female). To capture the responses from participants with a range of experiences of cultural engagement, participants were recruited through reading, film, lifelong learning groups and choirs. Further participants were recruited through a befriending charity for South Asian elders, a Catholic lunch club and a charity providing social activities to help reduce social isolation and assist people to live at home in the community. Participants from these groups either had ceased to engage with culture or had visited cultural venues only when facilitated by the charities.

Semi-structured interviews were conducted with participants on the topic of resilience and how their everyday activities and practices and relationships contributed to the development of resilience. Participants were asked about what activities they participated in and what they enjoyed doing. To capture both official and unofficial forms of culture, participants were initially asked what they did in their leisure time, before questions about cultural participation and their

Table 1.1: Groups/organisations/charities through which participants were recruited

Group	Age and gender
Lifelong learning organisation	69 (1 male)
Cinema group	67–69 (1 male, 1 female)
Non-formal literature class	64–68 (1 male, 3 female)
Choir	64–77 (3 female)
Sheltered accommodation unit	74–85 (4 female)
Live at Home scheme volunteers	67–79 (3 male)
Live at Home scheme	67–87 (6 male)
Live at Home scheme	87–91 (4 male)
Catholic lunch club	77–98 (4 male)
Chinese befriending scheme	72–86 (1 male, 2 female)
South Asian befriending scheme	60–90 (6 female)

conceptualisations of culture. They were then asked about other forms of social participation and educational experiences.

Box 1.1: Interview questions related to forms of participation

- What do you do in an average week? Could you describe the things you do or activities you take part in on an average week? What do you do for enjoyment? What are the things you do that are important to you? Why do you do these things? Why are they important? What do you get out of doing these things?
- Has what you do changed with ageing? In what ways?

Box 1.2: Interview questions related to cultural engagement

- Can you describe the cultural activities you participate in on an average week? Is there anything else you do more infrequently?
- Why do you engage with culture? What do you get out of it?
- Does engaging with culture relate to other areas of your life?
- Do you apply anything learnt to other areas of your life?

Results and discussion

Participants' conceptualisations of resilience

Participants were asked what being resilient meant to them. Representative responses from participants from the live-at-home scheme, Catholic lunch club and sheltered accommodation unit were as follows:

> "I got a dictionary and I looked it up ... and it was ... exactly what we'd said ... bouncing back from terrible things." (Female, age 79, punch card operator, sheltered accommodation)

> "I can't say it." (Female, age 78, shop assistant, sheltered accommodation)

"'Up and at it!' My English is very poor, words are not my thing. I blame the teachers." (Male, age 98, factory worker, lunch club)

There was a common consensus, with 14 people defining resilience as having the ability to bounce back from adversity. Other participants gave definitions such as "A bit cautious" (male, age 80, Live at Home scheme). Participants from these three groups noted that it was not a term that they thought about or was relevant to their lives:

"It's not a word that you use a lot is it? It's not it's not a word I hear a lot in conversation." (Male, age 80, Live at Home scheme)

Three participants from the lunch club explicitly stated that they did not know what the term meant, demonstrating how in the interview situation some participants are disadvantaged. Participants' responses do not necessarily mean that the concept of resilience is not relevant to their lives. However, their apologetic answers highlight the difficulties inherent in developing policy directives when the terms being used are not necessarily recognisable or used in everyday speech. Public consultation and co-produced research is necessary to ensure that policy directives are relevant (Buffel et al, 2012). Ensuring a representative sample of older people who feel able to voice their perspectives requires the development of a trusting professional relationship between researcher and participant, which takes considerable time to build. This small example of responses also cautions against using popular buzzwords, which may have a very short life span (Luthar et al, 2000), with the aim of setting longer-term policy initiatives.

In contrast to the responses above, participants who had higher linguistic capital, which also correlated with higher educational qualifications and former professional occupations, were more able to articulate different aspects of resilience. They distinguished between emotional and practical forms, although they did not describe the role of social relationships in the process. The following quote comes from a 79-year-old former social worker. She is widowed and has physical health problems. She describes coping as being distinct from resilience:

"I think because my son had cancer and my first daughter had to have a pacemaker fitted when she was 21 and the second daughter had anorexia. I think when you've got children and getting through those illnesses – I'm not sure whether that's resilience or just knowing that you've got to get through. Just coping." (Female, age 79, social worker)

Her response is suggestive of passive survival as opposed to a sense of active agency. Looking at resilience in older age, it reveals the importance of adopting lifecourse perspectives, as it was her children's illnesses over 40 years ago, as opposed to her own current health problems, which she views as formative (Zautra et al, 2008).

Two participants reflected on innate personality traits that might enable some individuals to cope more than others:

"How do some people go through such dreadful things in life and cope with them? There must be such a thing as a kind of in-built ability to overcome huge difficulties. People seem to have it in varying degrees, and then there's a question about whether you can learn some of it." (Female, age 68, librarian)

The quotation raises the relative significance of the adversity people face, and whether resilience is something that can be developed. The participant went on to define resilience as having the ability to rethink one's life according to changing circumstances and adapt, citing the example of giving up work to care for an elderly parent. This reflection is important, as it points to the need to explore the processes that explain how people become resilient (Hildon et al, 2009).

Participants considered how their resilience might be tested in the future. They expressed anxiety in anticipation of having to cope with adversity such as widowhood or becoming socially isolated. The following participant has a self-perception as not being strong enough:

"I've always suspected that I don't have much of it. ... I have this thing of going into a spiral of worry. ... You're not sure until you're tested ... but ... I think it is a useful term because ... all of us are going to encounter some big difficulties ... and if you can be more resilient they're going to do you less damage and you're going to recover more quickly." (Female, age 65, widowed, academic)

In the individual interviews, participants focused on psychological resilience and how the individual copes in the face of external tests such as children's illnesses or caring for parents. Having resilience is perceived as a personal trait, albeit one that can be developed. This counters the concern in the literature over too much emphasis being placed on individual agency, as opposed to organisational and societal actions (Foster and Walker, 2015). The idea of not being able to cope in the future is a source of anxiety, showing the importance of future projection impacting negatively on current psychological states.

Proving resilience

Resilience across the lifecourse

Participants described a range of life events that had proved – that is, tested and consequently developed – their resilience. They noted significant adverse events that had happened throughout the lifecourse.

Male participants aged over 80 referred to cohort effects associated with the Second World War such as National Service (n=1) and being evacuated during the war (n=1), while the females of equivalent age referred to the experience of post-war rationing (n=5). In the cultural animation workshop, the participants who had experienced the Second World War felt that difficulties encountered during the war had both tested and contributed to their resilience. They discussed a community spirit fostered during those years that they felt had remained with their generation.

Younger participants who had not experienced the war cited the following examples of life events that had required, tested and developed their resilience. These included having children (n=1), children leaving home (n=1), death of parents (n=1), death of spouse (n=3), children's serious illnesses (n=1), children's death (n=2), retirement (n=2), ill health (n=4), moving into sheltered accommodation (n=1), work (n=1).

Resilience as specific to old age

In terms of challenges associated with later life, participants in the lunch club and the live-at-home scheme noted declines to their or their partner's physical health. One had become a carer to his spouse and one had only recently stopped caring for his spouse with Alzheimer's disease, as she had moved into a care home three months before the interview. One described being dependent on professional carers since having a stroke and becoming paralysed. Five participants referenced the day-to-day resilience needed to cope with a lack of purpose without work. Only one participant felt resilience was not particular to ageing.

Strategies and resources used to develop resilience

During the cultural animation workshop participants articulated strategies that they had developed to overcome challenges. The resources they brought to bear included knowledge of how they had overcome problems in the past, and an increasing sense of control over their lives that had developed as they had aged. They also talked about the role of supportive communities, including other residents in the sheltered accommodation unit. They discussed cultural traditions, such as the Durham Miners' Gala, which gave them a sense of pride in their region. This idea then led to a discussion of the visit to the museum, and participants recounted being particularly interested in exhibits that they could relate to their own life experiences – for example, photographs of the shipyards on Tyneside or an iron lung. They described having enjoyed an exhibition at a local authority art gallery that consisted of life-sized knitted everyday objects such as bicycles, baking ingredients and rubbish bins that were produced by older women from the same region. They liked the exhibition because they identified with the knitters and liked the fact that they had captured recognisable aspects of everyday life. The reminiscence prompted by the exhibitions could be seen to reinforce a sense of cultural identity, with pride expressed at being North Eastern working-class women.

These results demonstrate the importance of the lifecourse and how resources for resilience change and develop over time. One participant, aged 79, from the sheltered accommodation unit, went on to describe how she coped with being widowed. Reflecting Bennett's (2010) findings on older male widowers, she described a turning point in her bereavement:

> "My friends invited me on holiday after two years of being widowed. I came home and thought 'I've got to get on with it'." (Female, aged 79, punch card operator, sheltered accommodation)

She attributed the social support from her friends, coupled with a determined personality trait, as helping her to rebuild her life and maintain hope for the future. She also described how she kissed a photograph of her late husband every night before she went to sleep and recounted her daily activity to him, rather like keeping a diary. This personal ritual appears to be the way in which the participant keeps a sense of continuity in her life – she derives comfort from maintaining a dialogue with her late husband.

One participant from the Live at Home scheme described how providing support to others had helped him to become more resilient. He felt that volunteering and helping people with Alzheimer's "made you slow down and become more adaptable" (male, 87, painter and decorator, Live at Home scheme). This shows the importance of reciprocal relationships in the process of developing resilience.

The following section focuses on a married man aged 81 from the lunch club. Describing tests to his resilience, he describes his youngest son being killed 24 years ago, noting: "You don't get over it, you learn to live with it." Turning to his later life, for the previous seven years he had nursed his wife who had Alzheimer's. Four months before the interview she had been moved into a care home. Following her admission, he had himself been admitted to hospital after acute anxiety and psychological distress. He described how, since leaving hospital, he was organising his financial affairs by seeing a financial adviser. He had been attending the lunch club for two months but noted that he had not been on the visits as "that's not me. I've got my car and I still drive." He is keen to maintain his independence, and driving allows him to do this. It also suggests that he wants to control his level of engagement in the lunch club. He is not seeking intimate friendships, but is instead looking for acquaintances. Asked about whether he is engaged in any creative or cultural activities, he notes that he has bought an iPad and is teaching himself how to use it. He talks about how he makes dolls' house furniture and intends to do more of this in the future. He describes teaching his cleaner woodworking skills and, probed further on why he does this, he replies, "It's just one of the things you do." At different times in the interview he states, "I'll sail through it I expect", and, "We just live life as it is". One of the things he intends doing as the weather improves is to visit his children and grandchildren, who live in the south of England.

The data is important in demonstrating the complicated range of challenges individuals have coped with throughout the lifecourse and the resourcefulness and stoicism they display. He attributes a combination of personal interests (making dolls' house furniture and teaching himself how to use the iPad), close network ties (children living four hours away, whom he communicates with on the phone regularly) and loose network ties (cleaner, lunch club facilitator, financial adviser) as helping him to cope with everyday life without his wife. There is a reciprocity to the relationships, as he is teaching his cleaner how to make dolls' house furniture. The understated way in which he describes how he is coping suggests that he has an acceptance of his situation. He has experienced significant negative life events, yet there is a calm control in the way he describes his circumstances and attitude to events. The stoical framing of his situation may contribute towards the development of his psychological resilience.

Other participants drew inspiration from how other people had coped with difficulties. A former head teacher, aged 67, described how she used her father's calm acceptance of dying as an example to live by:

> "Towards the end when things got incredibly difficult for him he seemed to acquire this sort of calm acceptance of the difficulties that he was facing, didn't get upset, didn't get angry just said 'Well you know I'll have to cope with this, it's horrible, it's hard but there you go'." (Female, age 67, head teacher)

She described consciously adopting his calm, stoical attitude when she herself had to cope with a number of negative life events simultaneously, happening post-retirement:

> "I needed to be resilient because I moved, my marriage broke up, my mother died, I retired in six weeks, so yes, I did need to be resilient. ... It was really hard going but ... a lot of my friends have faced things. ... It's scary, retirement, if you live on your own. But it's also got great possibilities, so you just have to look at it that way. So now I do Italian once a week ... and I'm now reading Italian novels so I do that and then because English was my thing I'm in a book group. ... I have done art courses, I'm not talented at art but I do enjoy it and it's quite therapeutic and my cinema is my big thing and I adore going to the cinema." (Female, age 68, deputy head teacher)

In recounting their narratives of resilience, all participants ended their descriptions by turning to the positive. Finding herself post-retirement living in a new location, divorced and bereaved, the opportunities the head teacher actively pursued were cultural pursuits in social contexts – for example, language classes, reading groups, and art classes. She also reads on her own and goes to the cinema. She has planned a timetable of sociable activities focused around the arts.

Resilience and learning in older age

Participants defined cultural engagement in terms of learning. One female participant, aged 64, who was formerly a university tutor described how an awareness of her own mortality was motivating her to make the most of her time:

> "Mortality plays a role and for many people, myself included, until you reach a certain age you never are really dealing with health issues for yourself or other people. … That's the sort of the spectre that haunts us all which gives added pleasure because you know you're living each day in itself. … You feel very mortal when you're older so it changes your whole framework." (Female, age 64, academic)

She described this awareness as propelling her to lead a productive life, with cultural engagement in the form of a reading group being an important part of this:

> "I don't know if the appetite for learning [is] something that you're given as a gift and you pursue it … and a lot of people are too lazy … to do it and I've never been able to find out the answer to that. … So resilience – I personally because it's a set of values and those are the values I live by; it's incredibly important. If I go away on holiday or am taken out of my world where I'm choosing what I want to do for any period I start to feel dried up, I love to come back to what is my sandbox as it were and I would be very distressed if I was taken away from it." (Female, age 64, academic)

She discusses individual agency as opposed to structural inequalities in terms of people being motivated to learn. For her, pursuing learning is described as a value fundamental to her life. She also notes the habitual importance of structuring or timetabling her learning activities.

The participant described earlier, who had experienced later-life divorce and bereavement, articulated why she read:

> "It enriches the mind, it deepens your understanding of the world around you and also yourself. … For me it was a way of experiencing things that I couldn't possibly experience, other worlds. When I was in my very early teens, I wanted to be either a French Foreign Legionnaire, a Knight of the

Round Table or a North American Indian. ... I haven't exactly lost that and it's part of me. Education shapes the person and develops the person and gives them resources to fall back on in their private life in their spare time as a human being. I haven't talked about education taking it to career progression. ... What I'm talking about to me is more important." (Female, age 68, deputy head teacher)

She views learning not as important in terms of career progression, but as having a more fundamental existential impact. She goes on to describe a book she recently read as part of an informal literature class:

"Nadine Gordimer made me think about what it's like for black people in a place like South Africa to be always being rescued by heroic white people in novels and their story. They must get really fed up with that and I think that's probably true of in Africa – lots of films about white people heroically rescuing black people, the slave line and everything like that and to a certain extent there were reasons for that but also it's too much skewed that way and they did make me think that, definitely." (Female, age 68, deputy head teacher)

Here she can be seen as using material culture to determine and define categories of cultural identity such as gender and race. Drawing from Pitcher (2014), here meanings of race are being constructed in acts of creative consumption. In understanding race through depictions in literature, the participant is making sense of other groups and cultures and simultaneously communicating her own identity (Pitcher, 2014).

One participant made direct comparisons between situations depicted in literature and his own life:

"you could see ... parallels and ... that ... helps to enable you to deal with certain things in your own life. Even if it was written two hundred years ago ... those ... things don't change ... you reflect on something that you've read ... and you say well it's not as bad as this ... they could get over it or ... I'm very lucky ... you can use it to reinforce positively your behaviour." (Male, age 68, town planner)

Literature provides him with a sense of perspective and continuity. Reading about people or characters who have experienced universal life challenges helps him to make downward comparisons, which he finds reassuring.

Developing knowledge of wider subjective experiences was used by other participants to aid personal reflection. One participant, aged 77, noted how the ideas presented in films and plays stimulate discussion with others:

> "It's become so much part of my life that ... it's just absorbed ... when I've seen a good play or a good film I would naturally want to talk about it to people. It wouldn't be something that I would keep in. Like the other day seeing the Turing film [*The Imitation Game*] ... you realise how much politically and socially ... we've become much better as far as homosexuality is concerned. ... It does affect you seeing and doing and reading things." (Female, age 77, social worker)

She uses the content of art forms to debate societal issues with friends, which informs the construction of her value frameworks. Significantly, this practice of assimilation is so embedded that she does it unconsciously. The way she articulates the aesthetic encounter is as an interaction between the psychological, social and cultural – participants are collectively negotiating and coming to a collective consensus over key values. Reflecting on alternative subjectivities in relation to their own lives contributes towards processes of self-actualisation. Since participants choose to negotiate moral responses collectively, this suggests the importance of co-constructing value judgements.

Social relationships

While academic literature has described the importance of friendships developed through cultural participation – particularly important for widows (Bernard et al, 2014), for example – the following section focuses on the development of less intimate relationships that may be particularly important to older people experiencing life transitions such as retirement or later-life divorce. The participants in the Live at Home schemes and lunch club did not meet with other members outside these groups. Two participants from the literature class, one of whom had experienced later-life divorce, described how they were not seeking to make friends through the cultural activities they participated in:

"If you have a friend then there's a certain degree of shared knowledge of one another, if you've got an acquaintance then you can just dump all that and just be the person who's interested in similar literature." (Female, aged 64, learning manager)

"I'm not looking for close friendships, acquaintanceships I think are wonderful because again that's another side of stimulation. You are friends with those people because of the common interest so when you meet them on the street you have something to talk about which is really lovely but you don't have to then get, you know, personal." (Female, age 68, deputy head teacher)

Participants wanted to focus discussion on the common interest of the art form as opposed to their own life circumstances. Additionally, two participants described engaging in culture as something they did separately from their partners since they had retired, providing them independence outside of the home and relationship.

Conclusion

This chapter has argued that cultural engagement contributes to the psychological, social and cultural aspects of older people's resilience. Framed in terms of learning, cultural engagement was cited as crucial in developing the self and, in turn, helping participants to become more resilient. Participants observed that as they had aged they were more motivated to learn and had become more conscious of their own mortality.

First, participants used the aesthetic encounter to contribute to meaning-making processes. The arts provided invaluable insights into human experience and presented alternative subjectivities. Participants actively drew from the experiences faced by characters in novels to make downward comparisons with the challenges they faced in their own lives, which was found to be reassuring.

Second, learning with others co-produced knowledge and understanding, which helped to develop collective consensus over key morals and values. Significantly, this chapter has drawn attention to the role of cultural engagement in facilitating loose-tie social networks: participants who had experienced later-life divorce and those who wanted independence from their spouse post-retirement were not seeking friendships. Instead, they welcomed discussions focused on the content of the art form, as opposed to enquiries about their wider lives.

Third, engaging in culture contributed to participants' cultural identity, with meanings of gender, class and ethnicity made in acts of cultural consumption. Participants enjoyed exhibits in museums or art galleries that related to their life experiences. For some participants, discussion of the exhibits helped them to communicate their own identities as working-class women, and the pride they felt in their region. For another participant, in reading about apartheid she made sense of racial discrimination and the problematic positioning of White people as 'saviours' in film and literature.

Participants felt that resilience was a useful term to describe their response to challenges that they had encountered throughout the lifecourse. Tests specific to ageing included becoming carers to partners, decline in physical health, widowhood and retirement. Participants distinguished between emotional and practical resilience and tended to see it as an individual trait, albeit one that could be developed. A distinction was made between active agency in the face of adversity and passive coping. Participants expressed anxiety when anticipating whether they would be equipped to cope with challenges in the future. Discussions about strategies that participants used to overcome difficulties were particularly revealing. Reciprocal social relationships were important, with supportive communities and the ability to help others cited as important. The resources that participants brought to bear included knowledge of how they had overcome problems in the past, and an increasing sense of control over their lives as they had aged. In terms of bereavement, participants noted the importance of turning points, coupled with social support from friends, supporting Bennett's (2010) findings. Participants also maintained their own private rituals as a way of maintaining a sense of continuity in their lives. These results demonstrate the importance of the lifecourse and how resources for resilience change and develop over time. Past and future perceptions of self all fed into participants' current-day perceptions of resilience.

In contrast to the data gathered through interviews, using cultural animation methods provided a way for participants who were less confident or less able to express themselves verbally in a formal interview format to articulate their perspectives on resilience. This method placed the day-to-day experiences of ordinary people at the heart of the inquiry (Kelemen et al, 2015), and feedback from those involved was positive. Using different creative forms of expression including mime, poetry and group role-play offered the opportunity for participants to articulate their opinions in non-verbal ways. On the strength of a two-hour workshop the study cannot make claims for this method of eliciting responses that could not be gained from other participatory methods. However, the method was particularly effective in facilitating group dialogue. This is particularly important in light of calls to move away from looking at developing individual resilience to developing community resilience, which would involve groups of individuals working together to develop solutions. Significantly, it was during the group exercise that participants discussed the importance of social relationships in facilitating resilience, whereas in individual interviews participants tended to focus on individual responses.

Notes

[1] A broad range of cultural forms are recognised and funded by Arts Council England and therefore considered 'legitimate' or 'official'. For example, in terms of music, they support different musical genres and experiences, in both traditional venues like concert halls and unconventional spaces like car parks. The organisations they fund range from independent music producers and venues to large scale opera companies and orchestras, as well as music education for children and young people (https://www.artscouncil.org.uk/what-we-do/supporting-arts-museums-and-libraries). The Department for Digital, Culture, Media and Sport's 'Taking Part' household survey measures engagement with the cultural sectors (and therefore informs funding decisions) and collects data on engagement in arts, museums and galleries, archives, libraries, heritage and sport. The survey asks questions about both participation and attendance across a wide range of art forms and activities, for example, attending a play in a theatre to taking part in a carnival (https://www.gov.uk/guidance/taking-part-survey).

However, despite a largely recognised democratisation of culture since the 1960s, there remains a recognisable notion of 'highbrow' and 'lowbrow' cultural practices with different status correspondingly attached. Culture considered as establishment or legitimate can translate to cultural forms which are prioritised in terms of funding. But notions of status also influence what people feel included or excluded from and how they say they spend their free time. The volume therefore considers a broad range of creative practices, including those not necessarily associated with the arts, partially reflecting the current interest in an examination of the significance of everyday life (Neal and Murji, 2015).

[2] https://blogs.ncl.ac.uk/annagoulding/2014/05/08/everyday-creativity-everyday-resilience/.

References

Adams, K.B., Leibbrandt, S. and Moon, H. (2011) 'A critical review of the literature on social and leisure activity and wellbeing in later life'. *Ageing and Society*, 31(4): 683–712.

Bauman, S., Adams, J.H. and Waldo, M. (2001) 'Resilience in the oldest-old', *Counseling and Human Development*, 34(2): 1–19.

Bennett, K. (2010) 'How to achieve resilience as an older widower: Turning points or gradual change?', *Ageing and Society*, 30(3): 369–82.

Bennett, T., Savage, M., Silva, E., Warde, A., Gayo-Cal, M. and Wight, D. (2009) *Culture, class, distinction*, London: Routledge.

Bernard, M., Rickett, M., Amigoni, D., Munro, L., Murray, M. and Rezzano, J. (2014) 'Ages and Stages: The place of theatre in the lives of older people', *Ageing and Society*, 35(6): 1–27.

Braudy Harris, P. (2008) 'Another wrinkle in the debate about successful aging: the undervalued concept of resilience and the lived experience of dementia', *The International Journal of Aging and Human Development*, 67(1): 43–61.

Buffel, T., Phillipson, C. and Scharf, T. (2012) 'Ageing in urban environments: Developing "age-friendly" cities', *Critical Social Policy*, 32(4): 597–617.

Cann, V. (2013) 'Appropriate articulations: The (re)production of gender in contemporary youth taste cultures', unpublished PhD thesis, University of East Anglia.

Crossick, G. and Kaszynska, P. (2016) *Understanding the value of arts and culture: The Arts and Humanities Research Council project*, Swindon: AHRC.

Dworakowska, Z., Jackson, B., Kurz, I., Litwinowicz, M., Piwowarska, D., Ptak, A., Reksnis, D., Rogozińska, A., Sosnowski, J. and Zięba, J. (2011) *Culture animation now!* Warsaw: Stowarzyszenie Katedra Kultury.

Foster, L. and Walker, A. (2015) 'Active and successful aging: A European policy perspective', *The Gerontologist*, 55(1): 83–90.

Gattuso, S. (2003) 'Becoming a wise old woman: Resilience and wellness in later life', *Health Sociology Review*, 12(2): 346–48.

Gilmore, A. (2013) 'Cold spots, crap towns and cultural deserts: The role of place and geography in cultural participation and creative place-making', *International Journal of Cultural Policy*, 22(2): 86–96.

Goulding, A. (2013) 'How can contemporary art contribute toward the development of social and cultural capital for people aged 64 and older', *The Gerontologist*, 53(6): 1009–19.

Gray, A. (2009) 'The social capital of older people', *Ageing and Society*, 29: 5–31, doi: 10.1017/S0144686X08007617.

Grenier, A.M. (2005) 'The contextual and social locations of older women's experiences of disability and decline', *Journal of Aging Studies*, 19: 131–46.

Hildon, Z., Montgomery, S.M., Wiggins, R.D. and Netuveli, G. (2009) 'Examining resilience of quality of life in the face of health-related and psychosocial adversity at older ages: What is "right" about the way we age?', *The Gerontologist*, 50(1): 36–47.

Keaney, E. and Oskala, A. (2007) 'The golden age of the arts? Taking Part survey findings on older people and the arts', *Cultural Trends*, 16(4): 323–55.

Kelemen, M., Mangan, A., Phillips, M., Moffat, S. and Jochum, V. (2015) *Untold stories of volunteering: A cultural animation project*, AHRC Connected Communities programme report. Available at: https://www.keele.ac.uk/media/keeleuniversity/ri/risocsci/events/untoldstories/Untold%20Stories%20Final%20Report.pdf.

Lowenstein, A. (2009) 'Elder abuse and neglect – "old phenomenon": New directions for research, legislation, and service developments', *Journal of Elder Abuse and Neglect*, 21(3): 278–87.

Luthar, S.S., Ciccheti, D. and Becker, D. (2000) 'The construct of resilience: A critical evaluation and guidelines for future work', *Child Development*, 71(3): 543–62.

Marmot, M., Allen, J., Goldblatt, P., Boyce, T., McNeish, D., Grady, M. and Geddes, I. (2010) *Fair society, healthy lives: The Marmot review*, London: University College London.

Masten, A.S. (2001) 'Ordinary magic: Resilience processes in development', *American Psychologist*, 56(3): 227–38.

Miles, A. and Sullivan, A. (2012) 'Understanding participation in culture and sport: Mixing methods, reordering knowledges', *Cultural Trends*, 21(4): 311–24.

Miller, D. (2010) *Stuff*, Cambridge: Polity Press.

Minkler, M. and Holstein, M.B. (2008) 'From civil rights to … civic engagement? Concerns of two older critical gerontologists about a "new social movement" and what it portends', *Journal of Aging Studies*, 22(2): 196–205.

Neal, S. and Murji, K. (2015) 'Sociologies of everyday life: Editors' introduction to the special issue', *Sociology*, 49(5): 811–19.

Newman, A. (2013) 'Imagining the social impact of museums and galleries: Interrogating cultural policy through an empirical study', *International Journal of Cultural Policy*, 19(1): 120–37.

O'Brien, D. and Oakley, K. (2015) *Cultural value and inequality: A critical literature review*, Swindon: Arts and Humanities Research Council.

Pitcher, B. (2014) *Consuming race*, London: Routledge.

Reich, J.W., Zautra, A.J. and Hall, J.S. (2012) *Handbook of adult resilience*, New York, NY: Guilford Press.

Richards, N., Warren, L. and Gott, M. (2012) 'The challenge of creating "alternative" images of ageing: Lessons from a project with older women', *Journal of Aging Studies*, 26(1): 65–78.

Rowles, G.D. (1993) 'Evolving images of place in aging and "aging in place"', *Generations*, 17(2): 65–70.

Sapountzaki, K. (2007) 'Social resilience to environmental risks: A mechanism of vulnerability transfer', *Management of Environmental Quality: An International Journal*, 18(3): 274–97.

Scherger, S., Nazroo, J. and Higgs, P. (2011) 'Leisure activities and retirement: Do structures of inequality change in old age?' *Ageing and Society*, 31(1): 146–72.

Varriale, S. (2016) 'Beyond distinction: Theorising cultural evaluation as a social encounter', *Cultural Sociology*, 10(2): 160–77.

Varvarigou, M., Hallam, S., Creech, A. and McQueen, H. (2012) 'Benefits experienced by older people who participated in group music-making activities', *Journal of Applied Arts and Health*, 3(2): 183–98.

Walker, A. (ed) (2014) *The new science of ageing*, Bristol: Policy Press.

Westerhof, G.J., Bohlmeijer, E. and Webster, J.D. (2010) 'Reminiscence and mental health: A review of recent progress in theory, research and interventions', *Ageing and Society*, 30: 697–721.

Wild, K., Wiles, J. and Allen, R. (2013) 'Resilience: Thoughts on the value of the concept for critical gerontology', *Ageing and Society*, 33(1): 137–58.

Zautra, A., Hall, J. and Murray, K. (2008) 'Resilience: A new integrative approach to health and mental health research', *Health Psychology Review*, 2(1): 41–64.

TWO

Ages and Stages: creative participatory research with older people

Miriam Bernard, Jill Rezzano and the Ages and Stages Theatre Company

Editorial introduction

This chapter provides insight into a long-running programme of research exploring the value for people's sense of well-being and resilience of being involved in theatre. The project represents a successful example of a creative, participatory research programme. The authors focus mainly on the process of the research and their reflections on that process. None the less, the chapter also indicates that taking part in such a research programme may have consequences that arise out of the act of participation.

Introduction

Ages and Stages is a continuing collaboration between researchers at Keele University and colleagues at the New Vic Theatre, Newcastle-under-Lyme.[1] Funded initially by the national, cross-council New Dynamics of Ageing programme (Oct 2009–July 2012) and, subsequently, by the Arts and Humanities Research Council (AHRC)'s Follow-on Funding Scheme (2012–13) and Cultural Value Project (2013–14), we have explored historical representations of ageing within the New Vic's well-known social documentaries; examined the role that the theatre has played – and continues to play – in the creative lives of older people living in the Potteries; devised and toured four different theatre pieces to date; developed, delivered and evaluated a pilot inter-professional training course; and established the Ages and Stages Theatre Company. In this chapter, we focus primarily on one of our two awards under the AHRC's Cultural Value Project in which we employed creative participatory methods to turn Ages and Stages' members into a 'company of researchers'. The aim of the award was to co-explore the cultural value that members place on their experiences of theatre-making (Bernard, Rezzano and the Ages and Stages Company, 2014). Here, we describe the design and conduct of this project; discuss how the research findings were turned into performance; and reflect on the challenges of working in these creative and collaborative ways. In doing so, we show how our approach and findings add to earlier Ages and Stages work that has already highlighted the benefits of theatre engagement for older people in terms of: enhancing identity, belonging, well-being, self-esteem and self-confidence; challenging deficit, negative and stereotypical views of ageing and late-life creativity; promoting dialogue between, and facilitating the inclusion of, both older and younger people; building supportive social networks, trust and reciprocity; extending skills, widening horizons and challenging capabilities; and supporting involvement during times of transition such as retirement and widowhood (Bernard and Munro, 2015; Bernard et al, 2015; Bernard and Rickett, 2017; Bernard et al, 2018). We would contend that outcomes such as these resonate strongly with the central ideas in this book around promoting resilience in later life (Centre for Policy on Ageing, 2014), demonstrating the value of applied and socially engaged theatre practice at both individual and group levels (McCormick, 2017).

The academic context

For the purposes of this chapter, we briefly draw attention to three areas of literature that provide pertinent background to the work of the project we go on to discuss. We consider the growing international literature about the benefits of arts engagement in general for older people, and of theatre and drama in particular; current understandings around the cultural value of such engagement; and the use of creative participatory research methodologies.

The pioneering work of Gene Cohen, a US-based psychiatrist who published extensively on the subject of creativity and ageing before his death in 2009, provided early evidence about the benefits of arts participation. The research of Cohen and his colleagues focused largely on health and well-being: on understanding the physiological and psychological effects of arts participation. It also challenged deficit models of ageing by drawing attention to the potential – as opposed to the problem – of ageing in relation to creativity (Cohen, 2006). Yet, while the evidence base on arts and ageing has increased exponentially in recent years (Bernard and Rickett, 2017), at the time when we began developing the original Ages and Stages project (from 2007 onwards) there was little UK research examining the value of engaging in theatre and drama specifically, and none that considered overtly how it may promote and enhance resilience. Even by the time of the Mental Health Foundation's evidence review of the impact of participatory arts on older people in 2011, only five of the 31 included studies were in its 'drama' category. By contrast, our critical review of Ageing, Drama and Creativity a few years later (Rickett and Bernard, 2014) demonstrates a sharp increase from the year 2010 onwards, with a third (n=25 or 32.5%) of the 77 documents selected for inclusion having been published between 2010 and 2014.

Our own and others' work has also demonstrated that theatre and drama are rewarding areas both for examining the artistic outputs of older people and for uncovering some of the ways in which the arts may construct, perpetuate or challenge conceptions and experiences of ageing (Mangan, 2013; Bernard and Munro, 2015). For example, in 2010, the Bristol Old Vic staged the radical *Juliet and her Romeo*, which, by recasting Shakespeare's play with well-known older actors in the lead roles, and by setting it in a care home called 'Verona', deliberately plays with our expectations about ageing. Also in 2010, UK theatre companies Fevered Sleep and the Young Vic together developed *On Ageing*: a production focused on the experiences of growing older in which the words of the older people who had been interviewed were spoken, on stage, by a cast of children. Evaluation of the production echoes the resilience literature in that it facilitated reflection for participants and audience members, and encouraged people to question assumptions about ageing (Johnson, 2011).

Historically too, theatre is a cultural arena in which older people actively participate as audience members, employees and volunteers. By contrast, participation opportunities as co-creators and performers are far more limited – apart, that is, from involvement in specific senior theatre groups. Such groups are much more common in North America than in the UK. Bonnie Vorenberg, one of the pioneers of the senior theatre movement, compiled the very first directory of information, at which time there were some 79 senior theatre groups in the US (Vorenberg, 1999); by 2011, there were over 800 registered groups (Vorenberg, 2011). In addition, research on both sides of the Atlantic now provides compelling evidence of the benefits of engaging in theatre and drama work: it has demonstrable cognitive, social, physical and emotional benefits (Basting, 1998, 2009; Schweitzer, 2007, 2010; Vorenberg, 2011; Noice et al, 2013); positive effects on intergenerational relations and intergenerational learning (Hafford-Letchfield et al, 2010; Johnson, 2011) and on the wider community (Schweitzer, 2007; Cutler, 2009; Magic Me, 2009); and enhances older people's skills and learning ability, improves confidence and self-esteem and supports the development of new social connections and friendships (Pyman and Rugg, 2006). All these, it could be argued, are also mechanisms through which resilience can be developed both individually and collectively.

Researching the benefits of engagement, however, is not necessarily the same thing as assessing the value of participation. Indeed, in the UK, the 'value' of the arts in general, and 'cultural value' in particular, tends to be concerned more with the impacts of cultural engagement in policy terms, rather than being related to – and drawing from – the experiences of individuals (Crossick and Kaszynska, 2016). Although Holden (2004, 2006) argued over a decade ago that research and analysis should focus on affective experiences as well as on quantifiable social and economic impacts and outcomes, we are still bedevilled by the tendency of many cultural institutions to write off the myriad and varied capabilities of older people – including creative and cultural ones – which in turn constrains their opportunities to build resilience and engage in, develop and share the cultural capital they may have accumulated over a lifetime (Goulding, 2012). Moreover, simply focusing on health and well-being, as much arts work with older people still does (AHRC, 2014), both reinforces stereotypical notions of what later life might offer and presents a reductionist assessment of the potential cultural value of older people's participation in arts activities (Fraser et al, 2015).

In their final report of the national Cultural Value Project, of which our work was a part, Crossick and Kaszynska (2016, p 7) reassert the need 'to reposition first-hand, individual experience of arts and culture'. They go on to explain how, between them, the projects have identified a range of components of cultural value, some of which are familiar and some of which have been too little acknowledged. In our critical review of the field of ageing, creativity and drama, we uncovered three familiar dimensions of cultural value which, perhaps unsurprisingly, echo some of the existing literature around benefits and, indeed, the underlying components of resilience (Rickett and Bernard, 2014). Cultural value was viewed and conceived of in terms of health and well-being; in the development of group relationships; and in learning and creativity. The fourth area, which was only starting to emerge in the literature, concerned the aesthetic value and quality of older people's drama: what it feels like to have an aesthetic experience and the meaning and purpose people derive from that experience. Our conclusion and contention was that this dimension was important for understanding the cultural value provided *by* older people, rather than just the value they derive *from* their participation. Moreover, the experience of producing cultural value, and being valued for it, may in turn contribute positively to changing older people's views of themselves, their circumstances and capabilities, and to challenging negative societal expectations of what may be possible in later life. Thus, in the case of our research with the Ages and Stages Company, which we present later, we were particularly interested in trying to get at what older members felt about their theatre-making experiences - especially given that many of them had never set foot on stage before.

Theoretically and practically, it was also important for us to continue to work – as we have done for many years – with creative and participatory research methodologies. Participatory methods that involve older people in co-creating research from initial design through to execution, analysis and dissemination of findings have become increasingly common in gerontological work (Barnes and Taylor, 2007; Ray, 2007; Ward et al, 2012), even if they are less accepted or familiar ways of researching in other disciplines. Participatory research tends to focus on work with groups or communities, with the aim of benefiting and enriching participants as well as researchers (Bhana, 2006; Wassenaar, 2006). More recently, Helen Kara's (2015) practical guide to creative methods in the social sciences presents participatory research as one aspect of what she terms 'transformative research frameworks'. The other creative techniques and approaches that she discusses include arts-based research; research using technology; and mixed-methods research. In her typology, our work is located at the intersection of arts-based and transformative approaches.

The creative context

We now turn our attention to the creative context against which our Cultural Value project was developed, providing a broad-brush picture of the original Ages and Stages project and the work that has followed from it. For the very first Ages and Stages project (2009–12), we brought together a large interdisciplinary research team with backgrounds in social gerontology, cultural theory and history, social and health psychology, social anthropology and theatre studies (Bernard et al, 2018). Together, we set out to examine historical representations of ageing within the New Vic's ground-breaking documentaries and docu-dramas (produced between 1964 and 1995) and to explore the recollections and experiences of older people who are, or had been, involved with the theatre in different ways. Employing a conventional mixed-method case study research design, we worked in the theatre's archive, housed at Staffordshire University, and also conducted over 100 individual and group interviews.

The archival strand focused on the 11 pioneering social documentaries and five docu-dramas developed under the artistic directorship of the late Peter Cheeseman during his 36-year tenure at the Victoria and New Vic Theatres (1962–98). Between them, these social documentaries chart social, economic and political changes in the Potteries over a 40-year period. They are based on a variety of source materials, including a remarkable collection of tape-recorded interviews with members of the community. For our interview strand, we managed to track down a number of these people and re-interview them, together with three other groups of older people: long-standing audience members; current or former theatre volunteers; and theatre employees and actors who continue to live in the area. In the individual interviews, participants spoke about how they had come to be involved with the theatre, and what part it had played – and continues to play – in their lives; and recalled their memories of, and involvements with, the social documentaries. The group interviews focused on three emerging themes: ageing, intergenerational relationships and the place of the theatre in the community and in individual lives. As noted in the introduction, the interviews that we conducted yielded a series of findings that resonate with the resilience literature and demonstrate the value of participation at both individual and group levels.

In the third and final strand we departed from our conventional research design and, instead of then analysing and writing up our findings, extended an invitation to everyone who had been interviewed to come back and help us draw together the archival and interview materials into what became the Ages and Stages Exhibition and a new, hour-long, intergenerational documentary drama *Our Age, Our Stage*. We deliberately avoided asking people to 'come and perform' and, in the event, 16 older people (aged 59–92) joined nine 'senior' members (aged 16–19) of the New Vic Youth Theatre to help with both the production and the exhibition. Under the directorship of the New Vic's Head of Education and research team member Jill Rezzano, a series of weekly workshops were held at the theatre between September 2011 and May 2012 during which the whole group (participants, researchers and artistic director) shaped the materials into the documentary piece. As the weeks went by, those who were interested in performing began to emerge and, in the end, 10 people became the main cast: six older participants and four Youth Theatre members. Following an intensive two-week rehearsal period in June 2012, *Our Age, Our Stage* toured to the local borough council, a school, a college and a retirement community before playing to a capacity audience on the theatre's main stage in early July. This final performance was attended by families and friends of everyone who had taken part, members of the project's Advisory Group, and delegates to the British Society of Gerontology's annual conference, being hosted that year at Keele University. The performance was filmed and turned into a DVD; over 700 people saw the productions and engaged in discussions with the cast, crew and research team after each performance; and the parallel exhibition ran for a month at the theatre, from 25 June to 20 July 2012.

Having 'got the acting bug', the group were understandably reluctant to disband. Fast-forward two years to 2014 and we found – through a series of other funded projects – that we had been able to transform the group into the Ages and Stages Company. A year of 'follow-on' funding from the AHRC supported this development, alongside increasing requests and opportunities for the Company to create and perform other pieces. These developments included: the Company working further with the research team on the existing research materials to devise and tour a new interactive, 40-minute-long, forum theatre piece, *Happy Returns*; their involvement in helping deliver a pilot inter-professional training course, which we devised and evaluated (Reynolds, 2013); scoping out, with a range of partners, the potential for holding a Creative Age Festival in Stoke-on-Trent and North Staffordshire; and, late in 2013, an invitation from the Royal Exchange Theatre in Manchester to take part in its Truth about Youth programme (for details of this see: Bernard, Rezzano and the Ages and Stages Company, 2014).

Set against these developments, the main aim of the project that we discuss later was to then co-explore and co-research the Company's theatre-making experiences over the previous four years. Our intention was for members to work collaboratively with the project team (in this case one researcher and the artistic director) to identify the benefits, drawbacks and cultural value of what they had been engaged in. As with the earlier projects, a key element was that the Company would also be supported to show to us and others, through live performance, any new piece or pieces that arose from the work. In other words, we would again be using the medium we work in – theatre and drama – to directly convey research findings by performing the pieces as part of an invited symposium at the conclusion of the project.

Creating a company of researchers – researching the company

At its heart, this project sought to analyse the experiences, meanings and value that Company members attach to their engagement with the arts as seen through their involvement with a notable cultural institution (the New Vic Theatre) and a particular ongoing project (Ages and Stages). As we have seen, Company members were already theatre makers but, in this instance, our intention was to move away from academic-driven research agendas about cultural value and to support them to work with us as co-researchers to explore the following research questions:

Box 2.1: Questions on Ages and Stages
- What has the experience of being involved with Ages and Stages been like?
- How has participants' involvement helped to shape them as people?
- How has their involvement helped to shape their understandings of ageing?
- What value/benefits have they derived from being involved with Ages and Stages?

As a first step, in late November 2013, 10 core members of the Company agreed to participate in a research skills training day at the University facilitated jointly by us. Three weeks ahead of the training day, we asked Company members to begin to think about their experiences of undertaking interviews and/or being interviewed and to come prepared to share their thoughts. Specifically, we asked them to consider the following questions:

Box 2.2: Questions on interview technique and cultural value
- What makes for a good interview?
- What makes for a bad interview?
- Is there an interviewer – or interviewers – you particularly admire? If so, what is it about her/him/them that you think is so good?
- What does the phrase 'cultural value' mean to you?'

The training day was structured around six sessions, beginning with an introduction to the overall Cultural Value Project, a reminder of the aims and objectives of our own award and what we were all hoping to achieve by the end of the day. We also gave out a pack of information for everyone to take away, which included background information about research interviewing, as well as literature introducing participants to notions of 'resourceful ageing' and ideas about social and cultural capital (see, for example, Putnam, 2000; Daly, 2005; Field, 2005; Reynolds, 2011). 'Resourceful ageing' contrasts with the problematic concepts of 'successful' or 'active' ageing (influenced by bio-medical perspectives and critiqued for their prescriptive nature) and acknowledges that later life cannot be understood in isolation from other phases of the lifecourse. It also resonates with ideas about social and cultural capital and is especially useful in challenging the tendency in existing literature to focus on older people as consumers, rather than generators, of social and cultural value and capital.

In the next session we spent an hour discussing the 'homework' questions we had set. This resulted in a lively discussion of who were good interviewers and what it is that good interviewers do to make a good interview. The most frequently mentioned names were familiar TV and radio personalities such as Michael Parkinson, Jenni Murray, Kirsty Young, John Humphrys and the late David Frost. Company members identified the qualities of a good interviewer as: being well prepared and listening; showing interest, respect and being non-judgemental; not talking too much themselves but being able to adapt and respond to what was being said; and being able to establish a warm and pleasant relationship which would draw people out.

Next, we then compared these responses with selected research methodology literature. Specifically, we looked together at Kvale's (1996) 10 criteria for what makes a successful research interviewer, plus two additional criteria derived from Bryman (2008) that emphasise the importance of 'balance' (not talking too much and not talking too little) and being 'ethically sensitive' (ensuring that the interviewee appreciates the purpose of the research and that his/her responses will be treated confidentially). Although the language used in research methods texts may be somewhat different from everyday speech it was evident that, between them, Company members had drawn out a very comprehensive set of interview strategies, displaying considerable understanding and insight into how to go about undertaking an interview.

However, it is one thing to appreciate the theory behind good interviewing, another to be able to actually do it. In the third and last session of the morning, therefore, the Company were invited to put the theory into practice. Working in threes (one interviewer, one interviewee and one observer) – and with the interview topic being 'your best holiday ever' – each interviewer had 10 minutes in which to try to get the interviewee's story. The roles were then revolved around the group so that each person had the opportunity to fulfil all three at different points. The interviewers were encouraged to play with the interview strategies everyone had identified earlier, and the observers made notes and provided feedback about the kinds of questions that worked best, what didn't work so well and what was happening in terms of body language and other non-verbal aspects. Back in the larger group, we discussed what the experience of being both an interviewer and an interviewee had been like, what kinds of questions people wished they had asked but hadn't and what they had learned from this (brief) exercise. This enabled us, together, to begin to collate and draw up a set of pointers/guidelines for the conduct of the interviews that the Company would be undertaking with each other and, potentially, with one or two family members and younger people with whom they had worked on Ages and Stages productions.

The afternoon was devoted to the technicalities of constructing an interview guide and the practicalities of who was going to do what, with whom, when and where. It was essential to the project that Company members would not just carry out interviews but that they would also decide what questions needed to be asked and co-design the guide. We began the first of the afternoon's sessions by revisiting the project's four main research questions, to which we added two others: 'What impacts has being involved with Ages and Stages had on participants (emotionally, cognitively, physically, reflexively)?' and 'What impacts has being involved with Ages and Stages had on others (families, friends, the younger people you have performed with)?'

Working in pairs, members discussed what detailed questions one might need to ask in an interview to get answers to these bigger research questions. Each pair focused on just one of the first five research questions and, if they ran out of ideas, they then discussed the sixth and final question. Each pair gave feedback to the whole group and discussed what to prioritise and include. We concluded the session by comparing the form of the draft interview questions that we had generated with Kvale's (1996) nine types of research interview questions. This enabled participants to see something of the process that they had been through to turn questions into a workable schedule and accompanying guidance, which they would then be comfortable using.

The last two sessions explored and discussed a range of other issues, including the pros and cons of being an 'insider' or 'outsider' researcher. Here, we stressed the importance of not assuming that, because Company members had a shared experience of Ages and Stages, they would necessarily view that experience in the same way. Ethical issues were also discussed, especially the fact that we needed to (re)seek consent for these interviews. We talked too about how best to support each other through the fieldwork and debrief after all the interviews were completed; a date was also arranged to get everyone back together early in the New Year to co-evaluate the research process.

All 10 core Company members agreed to be interviewed and, with one exception, everyone volunteered to try their hand at being an interviewer. The research team were also to be involved in conducting these interviews. Names were drawn to decide who would interview whom; contact details were exchanged so that people could set up the interviews with each other; and details were passed on of other family members who were willing to be interviewed. Finally, we tried out the digital recording equipment and agreed that we would try to complete as many interviews as possible before Christmas.

Immediately following the training day, the draft interview schedule and guidance was tidied up and finalised. In addition to the final schedule, we produced two variations, as we were aware that one or two Youth Theatre members who had worked with us on previous productions, as well as some family members, were also agreeable to being interviewed. The core Company members were already in possession of the project's information sheet and had consented to research discussions, workshops, evaluation sessions and performances being audio and video documented. Other potential interviewees were sent the final paperwork and consent forms.

In total, 16 interviews were carried out: 11 were undertaken by Company members (10 with each other and one with a family member); and five by us (one with a Company member; two with Youth Theatre members; and one with a family member). The interviews varied between 30 minutes and an hour and a half; all were digitally recorded and then transcribed. Most interviews took place in participants' own homes, although some were carried out at the theatre when this was more convenient.

Reflections on the creative participatory research process

Towards the end of January 2014, we devoted one of our regular Monday workshops to a recorded group discussion about what Company members had made of the research-skills training they had undergone, and what their experiences of co-designing and interviewing each other had been like. Each member was sent copies of their transcripts in advance so that they could see and read their interview/s and reflect on what they had done and how they had done it.

Without exception, everyone said how much they had enjoyed the training day and how valuable they had found the preparation. However, being asked by their peers to reflect back on their experience was challenging. This was despite their having all been interviewed for the first Ages and Stages project (2009–12), and having worked closely together over the previous three years. In the following discussion, for example, Company members express concerns about being the interviewee; reflect on what seeing a written transcript is like; and have a new-found appreciation for what is involved in research interviewing.

> A&S2: I was very hesitant to give answers ... a bit like a rabbit in the headlights and I actually kept switching off the machine because I thought I can't leave a 10-minute gap while I try and think of something to say, which proved to be a bit of a problem for the little machine, but still.
>
> A&S9: I found it more difficult being interviewed.
>
> MB: Why was that?
>
> A&S9: I wasn't terribly sure what I wanted to say, which sounds pathetic. ...
>
> A&S2: And also I didn't want to let you down by just talking drivel.
>
> A&S1: Yes!
>
> A&S6: That's part of it, yes ... that's what I did all the time: kept going off the point and thinking out loud while I was trying to form my answers. ...
>
> A&S7: I was like that. Several times I'd started a sentence and I stopped because a new idea had come into my head. ...
>
> A&S6: That's right.
>
> A&S7: And then I'd just start a new sentence half way through another one. And what I found when I read through the transcript was I didn't realise I said 'you know' quite so many times.
>
> A&S6: Oh, we're all the same. [Overtalking]
>
> A&S4: That was my problem when I looked through the transcript. I said 'you know' so many times it was unbelievable, you know ... [overtalking and

laughter] ... You don't realise you're doing it ... And ... I mean, we were prepared and we'd read it ... read the questions through. ...

A&S6: Yes, that's right.

A&S2: And we'd sort of thought about answers and I'd made one or two notes, but when it's the actual interview, it's a totally different experience.

While some members found it difficult being the interviewer, others preferred this to being the interviewee, as illustrated in the following exchange:

A&S2: I prefer to be the interviewer than to be interviewed, because I felt very hesitant every time I had to think of an answer. But listening to A&S1's answers, I could then build on that and sort of concoct my next sentence ... next question to match what she'd already said, you know. ...

A&S1: I was the other way round and I thought being the interviewer was very hard work. I'd looked at the sheets beforehand and I was anxious about timing, which of course I didn't keep to, but I was so fascinated by A&S2's answers that I did find asking questions possible, but I'm not sure that they were as good as they could have been. And I think on the whole I prefer being interviewed because I just rabbit on then.

Sometimes too, there were unavoidable delays (at most a week or two) between the training day and carrying out the actual interviews, which meant, as this Company member observes: "by the time we came to it, I'd forgotten everything we'd done on the day ... I could have done a lot better if I'd been more prepared" (A&S7). However, others enjoyed both roles as this member comments:

"I did three interviews as the interviewer and I found the first one kind of a bit dry because I was just going through it. ... And then as I got into the second and third ones, I found it quite relaxing ... depending on who I was talking to: if they were kind of quite rolling along, led by you, you could kind of delve a little bit more whereas on others you just kind of like stuck to the set questions really." (A&S8)

They also commented on how interesting it had been to hear one another talk about their experiences. Even if they thought they knew each other well - and one or two members had been good friends before becoming involved with Ages and Stages – the interviews uncovered things they did not know and stimulated them to think in different ways about what they had been doing. These two comments, from different points in the group discussion, are illustrative:

> "I found ... because I interviewed A&S7 first, that she was saying things and I was thinking, 'Oh, I never thought about that' ... 'Oh that's good!' ... 'Oh my God, that's intellectual'. I hadn't thought of anything in that depth." (A&S9)

> "Something else I wanted to say ... was that during the interview an idea occurred to me that hadn't occurred to me beforehand, and I think that was part of the process: that it actually did stimulate me to put things together and have new thoughts." (A&S7)

Company members also felt that, given time, they would become more practised and comfortable, the more interviews they were able to do. Some said they would like to have gone back and repeated their interviews – especially when they saw their transcripts; others were very positive about the possibility of doing more in the future. As one member unequivocally said, "Well, I'm not going to say no to anything" (A&S7).

Participatory creative research: reflecting back findings

Using the transcribed interviews, discussions from the research skills training day and the reflections noted earlier, a programme of devising workshops were held between 13 January and the end of April 2014. The workshops mixed drama exercises, debates and discussions, exploring further the Company's experiences of their time with Ages and Stages. As always, we worked gently and gradually, looking first at the research findings around 'beginnings' and at 'motivations' for taking part. To give one example of the devising process, we selected 12 contrasting quotations from the transcripts illustrating how people had got involved and what stood out for them. In small groups, the Company discussed which quotations struck a particular chord, and which they thought would sound best to an audience. We then 'heard' and listened as each member spoke in turn around a circle, deciding together which quotations went with each other; which cut across one another; and whether any jumped out. We then amended and rearranged the circle to hear them again in a different order. The next step was to find a way to visually reflect what the Company does week in, week out. Reflecting what happens at the start of every workshop, it was agreed that one member would come on and make a circle of chairs; each person would then enter, one by one and speak their line before taking their place in the circle. Over successive weeks, this scene was refined further and became the opening of the first performance piece.

Under the generic title of *Out of the Box*, the content of what it was decided would be three short pieces gradually took shape in this way, through the active and full involvement of everyone. The title had come from a comment made on the research-skills training day by one Company member who spoke about how her thinking had been altered by the experience of taking part in Ages and Stages. It seemed, therefore, a particularly pertinent title for a series of theatre provocations that aimed to challenge an audience. We also wanted each provocation to be shaped differently and to engage the audience in different ways, rather than just performing each piece followed by a question-and-answer session. One illustration of how we did this will have to suffice.

Once we had a draft script for the first piece, the Company were invited to look at what they had helped to create and to think about the major themes coming from it. Here, we were borrowing from dramatic techniques, but also reflecting the process of analysis that we apply to qualitative research data. The Company drew out 12 key themes, including, for example, friendship, loyalty, surprise, challenge, feeling valued and curiosity. Through a voting process, they settled on 'challenge' as the one theme to be explored further with the audience. They then worked in small groups to come up with a series of questions to ask the audience about challenge. This led to further lively debate and discussion, ranging from the challenge of coming along to Ages and Stages in the first instance, through to wider concerns about challenging conventional stereotypes of ageing and old people and whether and how we should be challenged throughout our lives. All the questions about challenge were gathered together and were returned to later in the rehearsal process when we firmed up how, exactly, we intended to manage the interactions with the audience on the day of the symposium. Each piece – and the associated interactions with the audience - was developed, devised and shaped through this collaborative and iterative process. They were subsequently performed at the concluding symposium attended by a very mixed audience of some 60 people. The performances and the audience's responses were all captured on film and turned into a DVD.

Creative participatory research: benefits and challenges

The Cultural Value Project award enabled us to treat Ages and Stages as a case study and to consider what the experience of participating in theatre making has been like for a group of older people and what it has meant to them; what their perceptions and understandings of 'cultural value' are; and, methodologically, what is involved in undertaking co-created and cooperative research. Creative participatory research of this nature has a number of benefits and challenges, three of which we highlight here by way of conclusion.

First, this kind of research places older people very much at the centre as opposed to simply being respondents to surveys and interviews. Although the award was driven by pre-set research questions, these were derived from the collaborative work that we had done with the Company over a number of years. Thus, members' experiences were the basis for the project and we – and they – were aware from the start that our aim was to see if we could transform the Company into a 'Company of researchers', if only for a while. The project, and the research we undertook as an integral part of it, was therefore co-constructed, collaboratively undertaken, co-produced and co-evaluated; it also built on the strengths, connectedness, trust and resilience that the group had already developed.

Second, using the artistic medium in which we were working – namely, theatre and drama – to 'show' rather than just describe or write up the research findings was, for us, a logical approach to take. After all, it was what we had been doing since the initial Ages and Stages project. What we had not fully appreciated was how unusual an approach this was. Indeed, our companion critical review (Rickett and Bernard, 2014) found only two projects with older people that had explicitly used arts-based methods to convey research findings: an evaluation of Anne Basting's Penelope Project, set in a Wisconsin nursing home in the United States (Mello and Voigts, 2013); and an evaluation of a 10-week drama intervention for older people in Coventry in the UK, delivered by a theatre company (Savin-Baden et al, 2013; Wimpenny and Savin-Baden, 2013). In our own case, the performance pieces and scripts that we co-produced arose directly from our research; encapsulated and communicated the knowledge that, together, we had generated over the project; and, we would also argue strongly, are valid as research outputs in themselves.

Third, there are, of course, challenges for everyone involved: the whole process is a risky one, requiring trust and faith in colleagues; a willingness to try new ways of working; and the ability to relinquish control over at least some aspects of the process. For an academic or researcher, this can sometimes be very hard to do. Working together over a long time, as we have all done, is helpful; the further challenge here is to ensure that we continue to be reflexive and self-critical. Moreover, in the event that presenting findings in these ways is not well received in a public forum, there is also a huge responsibility to be aware of how this might affect participants, not just ourselves as academics and professional theatre-makers.

In conclusion, a small case study such as this has limitations and we make no claims for the generalisability of what we did, or what we found and presented. However, to date, there is comparatively little work on older people's participation in theatre and drama that explores some of the resilience-building mechanisms that we have touched on here, or that has been carried out using a creative participatory research methodology. Our aim was not to privilege any one viewpoint over another; instead, the approach we adopted was in keeping with our roots in critical gerontology and in participatory drama-based practice: its benefit is that it recognises, acknowledges and enhances the skills and abilities that older people have; captures and conveys some of the less tangible aspects of experience and participation; and shows audiences something of the actual creative process: what happens 'in the moment' and how participants feel and respond. In this vein, it seems fitting to leave the last word to Company member Colin Ramsell. Every time we get towards the conclusion of a project, Colin pens a poem for us all; this project was no exception.

Etruria Rd. 598a
    Curious:
Well that's why we're here.
An *invitation to talk*
Is where it began.
Memories of theatre shared
And views expressed,
Their words taken down
verbatim.

Would they come to a workshop?
Not a place where materials,
Clay or metal, wood or cloth
Are thrown shaped or formed.
The materials here are words,
Ideas, expressions, which are
Woven, cast or hammered into shape.
      Another *challenge*
Share with a younger generation!
It took some time
Finding what makes them tick,
Their reaction to us,
Their energy and perspective.
But together we worked it out.
Then by request to Manchester
To strut the Royal Exchange.
[Well it was in the Studio at least]
And weren't we chuffed.
      Cultural Value:
      Discuss.
Oh dear what's this,
Semantics and philosophy.
But by degrees we ventured
Into the *unknown*.
And past *experience*
And the *loyalty* of the team
The words and ideas
Gained form and shape.
With a nudge from Jill
And a prompt from Mim
A scenario emerged
And tackled with *enthusiasm*
Our theatre making
Does have a cultural value.
Can we convince an audience?
In *anticipation*
We await your verdict.

Note

[1] Readers interested in exploring other aspects of what we have done together are invited to visit the Ages and Stages website (www.keele.ac.uk/agesandstages), and the

Live Age Festival website (www.liveagefestival.co.uk), which showcases the work of the Company and their participation in this now annual event.

References

AHRC (2014) *The value of arts and culture to people and society: An evidence review*, Swindon: Arts and Humanities Research Council.

Barnes, M. and Taylor, S. (2007) *Involving older people in research: Examples, purposes and good practice*, ERA-AGE European Research Area in Ageing Research, Brighton: University of Brighton. Available at: http://eprints.brighton.ac.uk/5365/

Basting, A. (1998) *The stages of age*, Ann Arbor, MI: University of Michigan Press.

Basting, A. (2009) *Forget memory: Creating better lives for people with dementia*, Baltimore, MD: John Hopkins University Press.

Bernard, M. and Munro, L. (2015) 'Theatre and ageing', in J. Twigg and W. Martin (eds) *Routledge handbook of cultural gerontology*, Abingdon: Routledge, pp 61–8.

Bernard, M. and Rickett, M. (2017) 'The cultural value of older people's experiences of theater-making: A review', *The Gerontologist* 57(2): e1–e26, doi: 10.1093/geront/gnw093

Bernard, M., Rezzano, J. and the Ages and Stages Company (2014) *Ages and Stages: The cultural value of older people's experiences of theatre making*, Swindon: Arts and Humanities Research Council. Available at: www.keele.ac.uk/csg/research/theculturalvalueofolderpeoplesexperiencesoftheatremaking/Bernard_Rezzano.pdf.

Bernard, M., Rickett, M., Amigoni, D., Munro, L., Murray, M. and Rezzano, J. (2015) '*Ages and Stages*: the place of theatre in the lives of older people', *Ageing and Society*, 35(6): 1119–45, doi: 10.1017/S0144686X14000038 (online 10 March 2014).

Bernard, M., Amigoni, D., Basten, R., Munro, L., Murray, M., Reynolds, J., Rezzano, J. and Rickett, M. (2018) 'The place of theatre in representations of ageing', in A. Walker (ed) *The new dynamics of ageing, Vol 2*, Bristol: Policy Press, pp 285–306.

Bhana, A. (2006) 'Participatory action research: A practical guide for realistic radicals', in M. Terre Blanche, K. Durrheim and D. Painter (eds) *Research in practice: Applied methods for the social sciences* (2nd edn), Cape Town: UCT Press, pp 429–42.

Bryman, A. (2008) *Social research methods* (3rd edn), Oxford: Oxford University Press.

Centre for Policy on Ageing (2014) *Resilience in older age*, London: Centre for Policy on Ageing. Available at: www.cpa.org.uk/ information/reviews/CPA-Rapid-Review-Resilience-and-recovery. pdf.

Cohen, G. (2006) 'Research on creativity and aging: The positive impact of the arts on health and illness', *Generations*, 30(1): 7–15.

Crossick, G. and Kaszynska, P. (2016) *Understanding the value of arts and culture: The AHRC Cultural Value Project*, Swindon: Arts and Humanities Research Council.

Cutler, D. (2009) *Ageing artfully: Older people and professional participatory arts in the UK*, London: The Baring Foundation.

Daly, S. (2005) *Social capital and the cultural sector: Literature review prepared for the Department of Culture, Media and Sport*, London: Centre for Civil Society, London School of Economics.

Field, J. (2005) *Social capital and lifelong learning*, Bristol: Policy Press.

Fraser, K.D., O'Rourke, H.M., Wiens, H., Lai, J., Howell, C. and Brett-MacLean, P. (2015) 'A scoping review of research on the arts, aging, and quality of life', *The Gerontologist*, 55(4): 719–29.

Goulding, A. (2012) 'How can contemporary art contribute toward the development of social and cultural capital for people aged 64 and older?' *The Gerontologist*, 53(6): 1009–19.

Hafford-Letchfield, T., Couchman, W., Webster, M. and Avery, P. (2010) 'A drama project about older people's intimacy and sexuality', *Educational Gerontology*, 36(7): 604–21.

Holden, J. (2004) *Capturing cultural value: How culture has become a tool of government policy*, London: Demos.

Holden, J. (2006) *Cultural value and the crisis of legitimacy: Why culture needs a democratic mandate*, London: Demos.

Johnson, R. (2011) *'On Ageing' case study: Evaluation report*, Southampton: University of Southampton.

Kara, H. (2015) *Creative research methods in the social sciences: A practical guide*, Bristol: Policy Press.

Kvale, S. (1996) *InterViews: An introduction to qualitative research interviewing*, Thousand Oaks, CA: Sage.

Magic Me (2009) *Our generations: Report on a three year programme of intergenerational arts projects in Tower Hamlets, East London April 2006– June 2009*, London: Magic Me.

Mangan, M. (2013) *Staging ageing: Theatre, performance and the narrative of decline*, Bristol: Intellect.

McCormick, S. (ed) (2017) *Applied theatre: Creative ageing*, London: Bloomsbury Methuen Drama.

Mello, R. and Voigts, J. (2013) *The Penelope Project: Using the power of myth to transform long term care*, programme evaluation report. Available at: www.thepenelopeproject.com/links/materials/penelope-program-evaluation.

Noice, T., Noice, H. and Kramer, A. (2013) 'Participatory arts for older adults: A review of benefits and challenges', *The Gerontologist*, advance access (December 2013) doi: 10.1093/geront/gnt138.

Putnam, R. (2000) *Bowling alone: The collapse and revival of American community*, New York: Simon Schuster.

Pyman, T. and Rugg, S. (2006) 'Participating in a community theatre production: A dramatherapeutic perspective', *International Journal of Therapy & Rehabilitation*, 13(12): 562–71.

Ray, M. (2007) 'Redressing the balance? The participation of older people in research', in M. Bernard and T. Scharf (eds) *Critical perspectives on ageing societies*, Bristol: Policy Press, pp 73–87.

Reynolds, J. (2011) 'Creative ageing: exploring social capital and arts engagement in later life', doctoral thesis, Keele University.

Reynolds, J. (2013) *Ageing, drama and creativity: Inter-professional training course evaluation report*, Ages and Stages Project. Available at: www.keele.ac.uk/agesandstages/outputs/.

Rickett, M. and Bernard, M. (2014) *Ageing, drama and creativity: A critical review*, Swindon: Arts and Humanities Research Council. Available at: www.keele.ac.uk/csg/research/ageingdramaandcreativity/Rickett_Bernard.pdf.

Savin-Baden, M., Brady, G., Wimpenny, K. and Brown, G. (2013) *Final evaluation report: The Belgrade Theatre creative gymnasium project, Coventry*, Coventry: University of Coventry.

Schweitzer, P. (2007) *Reminiscence theatre: Making theatre from memories*, London: Jessica Kingsley Publishers.

Schweitzer, P. (2010) 'Experience shared and valued: Creative development of personal and community memory', in J. Bornat and J. Tetley (eds) *Oral history and ageing*, London: Centre for Policy on Ageing/Open University, pp 57–77.

Vorenberg, B.L. (1999) *Senior theatre connections: The first directory of senior theatre performing groups, professionals and resources*, Portland, OR: ArtAge Publications.

Vorenberg, B.L. (2011) 'The new senior theatre survey: A reflection of what's happening in community theatres', *AACT Spotlight*, November/December. Available at: www.seniortheatre.com/A_New_Senior_Theatre_Survey_article.pdf.

Ward, L., Barnes, M. and Gahagan, B. (2012) *Well-being in old age: Findings from participatory research*, Brighton: University of Brighton and Age Concern Brighton, Hove and Portslade. Available at: www.brighton.ac.uk/sass/older-people-wellbeing-and-participation/.

Wassenaar, D.R. (2006) 'Ethical issues in social science research', in M. Terre Blanche, K. Durrheim and D. Painter (eds) *Research in practice: Applied methods for the social sciences* (2nd edn), Cape Town: UCT Press, pp 60–79.

Wimpenny, K. and Savin-Baden, M. (2013) 'Using theatre and performance for promoting health and wellbeing amongst the 50+ community: An arts-informed evaluation', *The International Journal of Social, Political, and Community Agendas in the Arts*, 8(1): 47–64.

THREE

Social connectivity and creative approaches to dementia care: the case of a poetry intervention

Kate de Medeiros and Aagje Swinnen

Editorial introduction

This chapter draws together four concepts – resilience and flourishing, creativity and play – to explore the impact of poetry interventions in the lives of people with dementia living in a care facility. As in other chapters, the impact of the creative interventions is linked to the way that they encourage and enable social interactions that (in turn) support the personhood of the participants. In this chapter, these processes are drawn out through careful observations of interactions during the poetry sessions.

Introduction

This chapter continues the exploration of the proposition that arts offer a means of communication and self-expression that is particularly able to capitalise on the emotional and social capabilities of people living with dementia. The broad term 'dementia' (now referred to in the DSM-5[1] as 'neurocognitive disorders') describes a variety of chronic cognitive conditions whose etiologies, time of onset, speed of progression, associated symptoms and characteristics, and duration differ – although all feature problems with memory and learning (Blazer, 2013). Regardless of the type of dementia, however, language is an important way for memory and learning to be expressed and assessed through conversations, diagnostic interviews, formal testing and other interactions (Saunders et al, 2011). The social use of language, both verbal and non-verbal, and its interpretation are therefore a central component of our inquiry. The phrase 'social use' is meant to distinguish our inquiry from linguistic studies on language change in dementia, since our focus is not on the ways in which language itself might change with disease progression but, rather, on how changes in opportunities to express oneself through language affect self-expression (Blair et al, 2007) and potentially threaten personhood (Sabat, 2006).

For people living in unrestricted environments (for example, a home in the community where one can come and go at will), there are multiple ways to use and engage others with language such as talking to a friend or neighbour in person, on the phone or through the internet, making small talk with a shopkeeper, and so on. In a restricted environment, such as a secure dementia care ward, residents are limited in how they can engage with others and with whom. Since residents cannot come and go at will, they are, at best, limited to communication with other residents, staff and visitors within the ward. These are potential conversational partners in whose selection they likely have little choice. As such, self-expression or sharing one's thoughts, ideas or feelings may also be difficult in such a setting, depending on the opportunities that a resident is given to communicate with others (for example, through structured activities versus spontaneous communication, through staff-mediated dialogues versus uninterrupted conversations with other residents) (Moore, 1999). Other considerations include additional potential restrictions such as a resident's personal mobility or ability to freely move from one location (such as one's room) to another (such as the dining room), visual impairment, communicative ability or even barriers within the facility itself (for example, lack of appropriate space to socialise) that create additional challenges to communication and social interaction (Doyle et al, 2011; Campo and Chaudhury, 2012). In the face of such restrictions, we argue that new opportunities for language and meaningful expression can enable residents living with dementia to counter many of the barriers they may be experiencing and to reaffirm their personhood.

In this chapter, we explore language and communication in the context of resilience, creativity and, ultimately, 'flourishing'[2] via a poetry intervention for people living with dementia in a long-term care facility. We build on previous work in a variety of disciplines to consider opportunities for people living with dementia to experience continued well-being, using an illustrative case study of a poetry intervention. In doing so, we seek to further examine how such participation can be linked to increased opportunities for social interaction, engagement and connectivity through the use of language and 'play'.

Background

One of the challenges in multi-disciplinary work is that commonly shared terms can hold very different meanings depending on one's perspective and the research context in which shared terms are applied. We therefore provide a brief overview of insights into the participatory arts; social interaction, engagement and connectivity; resilience and creativity; 'flourishing'; play; and selfhood and personhood.

Participatory arts

The participatory arts in dementia care describe collaborations between trained facilitators and participants that feature engagement with new forms of expression (for example, creative storytelling, poetry and dance) (Foundation, 2011; de Medeiros and Basting, 2013). Key features of the participatory arts include: the active involvement of the participants, compared to passive interventions such as listening to music; the use of imagination as opposed to memory (Jennings, 2009); interactions with others; and a focus on valuing all contributions, regardless of how seemingly minimal (Basting, 2009). In the context of dementia care, participatory arts programmes (for example, theatre, poetry and music) have gained attention as potentially low-cost alternatives to pharmacological treatments for a variety of outcome areas such as reducing negative 'behaviours' (for example, aggression, agitation, depression) and increasing cognitive performance, although there has been little evidence to support these outcomes (de Medeiros and Basting, 2013). We argue that the participatory arts provide important opportunities and outcomes that have not been widely studied, mainly opportunities for social interaction, engagement and connectivity that are otherwise not self-evident in long-term care settings.

Social interaction, engagement and connectivity

As mentioned in the previous section, one of the potential benefits of the participatory arts is their ability to foster social interaction, engagement and connectivity. Campo and Chaudhury (2012, p 402) define a social interaction as 'a dynamic interplay between two or more individuals, where the participants interpret and react to one another's actions'. They further explain that this may include verbal and non-verbal communication such as facial expressions, gestures and body posture.

We note that there is an extensive literature in the epidemiology of ageing that describes social engagement as the product of one's social network (for example, close friends and family) and participation in activities (for example, going to the grocery store, attending church) (Jang et al, 2004; Glass et al, 2006). However, as many of these studies note, this definition fails to capture any qualities of engagement; it provides the 'who' and 'what' but not the 'what does it mean?' Anja Machielse (2015) has attempted to gain a better understanding of social isolation in older adults living in the community by suggesting two isolation categories (situational and structural) and coping strategies for each. Situational isolation is the result of a circumstance or event. Structural isolation describes people who have been socially isolated for some time but without a clear identifiable event to mark its beginning. She also suggests that there are various action orientations (that is, motivation and desire to participate socially) and coping strategies that people employ to become more socially engaged. She ultimately argues that, for older isolated individuals, re-embedding in social networks implies that the social world is open to accepting people who are less sociable, able and independent. We thus suggest that social engagement implies a slightly deeper connection than 'interaction', 'network' or 'activity'.

Social connectivity, then, is stronger than social engagement. It describes actual or perceived support and recognition by others (Cornwell and Waite, 2009). Social connectivity implies a friendliness that may involve the actual formation of friendships but that also may provide an avenue for familiarity and trust that extends beyond a social interaction or being socially engaged with another. In dementia care, social connectivity is often assumed to exist between the person living with dementia and a staff or family member but not typically another resident living with dementia because of memory loss or other functional challenges expressed through language (de Medeiros and Sabat, 2013; Keyes et al, 2016). As we later argue, not only is social connectivity possible for people living with dementia in long-term care, but participatory arts interventions help in facilitating such important social connections.

Resilience, creativity and 'flourishing'

At the heart of the argument about social connectedness and the arts are the concepts of resilience and creativity. Phyllis Harris has defined resilience in the context of dementia as 'the ability to bounce back, to overcome negative influences that block achievement. Resilience is conceptualized as a process and not a personality trait. Thus people display resilience in their behaviour; it is an observable pattern' (Harris, 2008, p 45). Moving away from conceptualisations of resilience built on the observations of children who are able to thrive despite challenging circumstances, Harris rethinks what resilience means for people living with dementia. She notes, as we have discussed earlier, that risk of social isolation is a major challenge for people living with dementia. Although her work focuses on people living in the community in the early stages of their disease, the same thought can be applied to people living in long-term care. If resilience is a 'doing' rather than a 'being', participatory arts interventions can be conceptualised as approaches that support practices of resilience within the dementia care context.

Along with resilience comes the notion of creativity. In discussing creativity in later life, Gene Cohen wrote that

> it's not a matter of whether you have or you don't have the 'right stuff'. The right stuff – those aspects of human nature and human behaviour that can make a difference – becomes activated at different times and under differing circumstances. Until such circumstances or life events occur, you may not even know you had the capacity to mobilize them. (Cohen, 2001, p 20)

For Cohen, creativity broadly refers to one's ability to adapt to new realities by applying creative skills that are newly developed. Although his work on creativity did not focus on people living with dementia, his central premises certainly do apply, since creativity can be seen as a type of liberation from 'decline' or behaviour that departs from what is expected from people with dementia in a specific 'hypercognitive' cultural setting (Post, 2002). Participatory arts approaches may show that people living with dementia have even greater potential and need for these creative skills than others who are not living with dementia.

With regard to language and social connectivity for people living with dementia in long-term care, we argue that resilience can be seen as the ability to 'bounce back' from the restrictions of the physical and social environment through expressive engagement. In other words, engaging in opportunities for meaningful expression and connection with others may provide the mechanism through which one can overcome the negative aspects of his or her environment and/or situation. Together, resilience and creativity point to the notion of 'flourishing'.

'Flourishing' is a term that has gained renewed interest in positive psychology as a way to acknowledge that the absence of symptoms for a given mental health disorder (for example, depression) does not mean that a person is necessarily functioning well. For example, in discussing 'flourishing' in the context of middle-aged adults and clinical depression, psychologist Corey Keyes (2002) writes the following:

> To be flourishing, then, is to be filled with positive emotion and to be functioning well psychologically and socially ... languishing may be conceived of as emptiness and stagnation, constituting a life of quiet despair that parallels accounts of individuals who describe themselves and life as 'hollow', 'empty', 'a shell' and 'a void'. (Keyes, 2002, p 210)

Within the dementia literature, 'flourishing' is often conceptualised as engagement, meaningful involvement, and participating in positive relationships (Clarke et al, 2016). Along this line of thinking, Jennings (2009), in conceptualising the concept of 'flourishing' in people living with dementia, writes that

> healing, wholeness, and human flourishing, even in the labyrinth of dementia, come from 1) the exercise of semantic agency, albeit in new ways and with new strategies and forms of assistance that outwit impairment; and 2) being re-membered or recognized as a self who is a subject rather than an object and as a self who is (once more and still) a member of an ongoing social web of meaningful communicative relationship. (Jennings, 2009, p 430)

Semantic agency, in this case, describes one's 'capacity to communicate, to engage in meaning-sending and meaning-receiving relationships ... with others, and to evince understanding and evaluation of such communication' (Jennings, 2009, p 430). This agency goes beyond verbal communication and includes other forms of communication such as through gestures, eye contact, facial expressions or even sitting closely together (Jennings, 2009). To 'flourish', then, is to participate fully and voluntarily in social connectedness with another in a way that gives and provides personal meaning.

Play

We have explored the notion of 'play' in the context of the creative arts and dementia in detail elsewhere (Swinnen and de Medeiros, 2018). We define play as 'a voluntary act whereby the player enters into a purposeful yet spontaneous imagination-based encounter, one which may have mutually agreed upon rules (e.g., what constitutes appropriate behaviour) but lacks competition or an end-goal (e.g., winning, producing a piece of art)' (Swinnen and de Medeiros, 2018, pp 262–3). We draw from Dutch historian Johan Huizinga's (1949) concept of the *homo ludens* or 'man the player', which he argues is a more fitting description than *homo sapiens* or 'man the thinker' or 'knower'. For Huizinga, play has no other end than play itself. This does not imply that play is meaningless. On the contrary, according to Huizinga, play is what gives meaning to life and what makes us human. In reference to dementia care, play allows a person to 'transcend the immediate needs of life' (Huizinga, 1949, p 1). Through play, one can experience a temporary reprieve from the confines of reality and thereby create an active and imaginative space with limitless possibilities. The perspective of 'man the player' makes us better understand what people with and without dementia have in common and how participatory arts are capable of capitalising on these similarities.

Selfhood and personhood

We note that selfhood and personhood have slightly different meanings, although the two are often used interchangeably. 'Selfhood' is sometimes described as an internal state, as compared to personhood, which implies a 'status bestowed' (Kitwood, 1997, p 9) on an individual by others, although this distinction is not absolute. For both concepts, the idea of social verification or acknowledgement is integral and perhaps more important than any fine differences in definitions. For example, George Herbert Mead (1934), Irving Goffman (1959) and Sharon Kaufman (1986) described the self not as an independent element but, rather, as something arising from the social experience in which it is made known and influenced by the behaviour of other individuals. The feedback received from these individuals, typically in the form of communication, becomes a validation of the self.

Kitwood (1997, p 9) defined personhood as 'a standing or status that is bestowed upon one human being, by others, in the context of relationship and social being'. Sabat (2006) has described personhood through a Zulu saying, 'A person is a person through others'. In both descriptions, personhood is understood in the context of social relations. One need only be recognised as a person to be so. This standing as person, by description, stresses the social nature of personhood rather than specific qualities. Again, a similar claim can be made for selfhood. As Mead (1934, p 64) wrote, 'it is impossible to conceive of a self arising outside of social experience'. The self, in this respect, does not exist merely as an internal structure but, rather, as something that is actively tested, questioned, performed and maintained through the actions and reflections of the individual.

Overall, limited views of what is socially possible may interfere with expressions of selfhood and opportunities to confirm personhood status for people living with dementia if 'outsiders' do not think that participation in the social world is possible. As philosopher Bruce Jennings (2009, p 431) writes, 'the work of imagination by others rather than the exercise of memory by others may be more crucial to the fabric of moral personhood which must be recognized and to which attention must be paid'. In other words, a key part of being human is being able to imagine what it means to live meaningful lives with people who may be different from us. Social recognition is an important consequence of this imaginative act.

Methods

Case study and participants

To further explore the larger idea of social connection through the creative arts, we focus on an illustrative case study of a poetry intervention for people with dementia. The original purpose of this small (n=5) ethnographic study was to: (1) understand the daily lives of the people living with dementia in a secure dementia care facility in the week prior and after our intervention; (2) determine what types of behaviour were observable through close observation and thorough note taking; (3) introduce a 7-week poetry intervention; and (4) record the behaviours of the study participants before, during and after a poetry session, for all nine weeks. Participants were recruited from a 12-bed secure dementia care unit located within a larger nursing home. All of the residents had a moderate to advanced-stage dementia. The research team was composed of a faculty member (the lead author), a doctoral student (the lead facilitator), a master's student (the second facilitator), three undergraduate students and an international collaborator. The student observers were trained by the lead author. Permission was obtained from the Institutional Review Board at the first author's university. Written informed consent was provided by the legally authorised representatives of the participants. We also obtained verbal assent from the participants at the start of each session. Since our focus was on what we observed rather than what had been recorded by staff or medical personnel, we did not obtain access to medical records at any time during the study.

Alzheimer's Poetry Project

We conducted seven interactive poetry sessions using guidelines from the Alzheimer's Poetry Project (Glazner, 2005) developed by poet Gary Glazner. This 30-minute poetry programme[3] has three components. First, people with dementia participate in a 'call-and-response' performance of classic or less-familiar poems on a certain topic. The group facilitator says a line (for example, 'Once upon a midnight dreary'), then asks the group to repeat after him or her (10–15 minutes). Next, the facilitator asks participants to interact with objects related to the topic of the recited poems (for example, touching bird feathers) and talk about something related (for example, 'What is your favourite bird?') (10 minutes). Finally, the group participates in writing and reciting a group poem, whereby the facilitator asks each person to contribute a line (5–10 minutes). This intervention introduces at least three different ways for people to engage and connect with each other through language: (1) repetition of atypical words and phrases, (2) opportunity to share their views with others on a novel topic and (3) contribution to and performance of a group poem. The two graduate students were trained in person by Glazner prior to the start of the intervention. The lead facilitator connected with him via the internet periodically during the course of the seven weeks. All poetry sessions were audio recorded and transcribed.

Direct observations and field notes

In addition to the audio recordings, three members of the research team engaged in close observation of the participants. Each researcher had a maximum of two people to observe, to ensure accuracy of notes. During the pre-study phase, the research team piloted several ways to gather information on the range of verbal and non-verbal responses of people living with dementia in the setting under study. One was a checklist used in a study of observed well-being in people with dementia by Kinney and Rentz (2005). Their scale focuses on seven domains of well-being: interest, sustained attention, pleasure, negative affect, sadness, self-esteem and normalcy. They included detailed operational definitions for each domain. After pilot-testing the instrument in our population, we found that it was difficult to determine domains such as 'sadness' or 'pleasure' since there were many occasions in which the affect of the residents was situated somewhere in between these two poles (for example, sometimes participants had a flat affect or were unresponsive to questions). We also used a checklist from a study on television by the lead author and colleagues (de Medeiros et al, 2009), which has five domains: smile/laugh, frown, wander, kick, talking and dozing. This checklist did not seem to accurately reflect the variety of actions of the residents in our group, which were often difficult to distinguish. For example, although some residents in our study had their eyes closed, they did not appear to be asleep, since they would sometimes open their eyes to respond before closing them again afterward. The final checklist developed for the study consisted of the following five categories: laughing/smiling, communication, sleep/sleep-like, attention/participation and bored/lack of attention (Table 3.1). Observers checked the appropriate

Table 3.1: Response categories and definitions

Laughing/smiling	Any time a participant laughs or smiles. Provide details in the notes to describe the nature of laughing/smiling.
Communication	Any attempt, verbally or through gestures, that a participant appears to be making to convey something to another. Communication can be between residents, members of the research team, staff or visitors. Provide details in the notes regarding the circumstances of when the communication occurred. If verbal, write down what was said (if possible).
Sleep/sleep like	Any time a resident closes his or her eyes for more than 5 seconds. Add additional details on the notes regarding the nature of sleep to include length of time, anything related to 'waking up' or opening eyes, or other relevant details.
Attention/participation	Any time the participant contributes to the intervention (e.g., answers the facilitator) and/or is making eye contact with the facilitator or others to suggest that he/she is engaged and participating. Note any relevant details.
Bored/lack of attention	Any time the participant appears to be unaware or uninterested in the intervention. This can include looking around, focusing on other events (e.g., staff cleaning) that are not part of the intervention. Provide a description in the notes. Also note if the participant leaves the poetry session.

behaviour(s), actions and affects in five-minute increments. In addition, observers also took detailed notes about what participants were saying or doing so that these notes could then be used to help make sense of the transcripts. The frequencies of the observed patterns in the checklist were recorded. In addition, transcripts were analysed for examples of connection, creativity, play and 'flourishing'.

Quantitative results

The average frequencies for the observed categories are shown in Figure 3.1.

In addition, we noted the following. From Week 2 until the end of the programme the amount of smiling/laughing was consistently higher than during the pre-intervention week, Week 1, or the post-intervention week. Attention/participation frequency was higher and boredom/lack of attention lower on days when a poetry session was offered. Communication frequency was higher on four days with poetry sessions than in the pre- and post-intervention weeks, but was not higher on all of the poetry days. Sleep/sleep-like behaviour frequencies were lower on four days with poetry sessions. There was great intra-individual variation in the separate categories.

Figure 3.1: Average frequencies by week for five observation categories

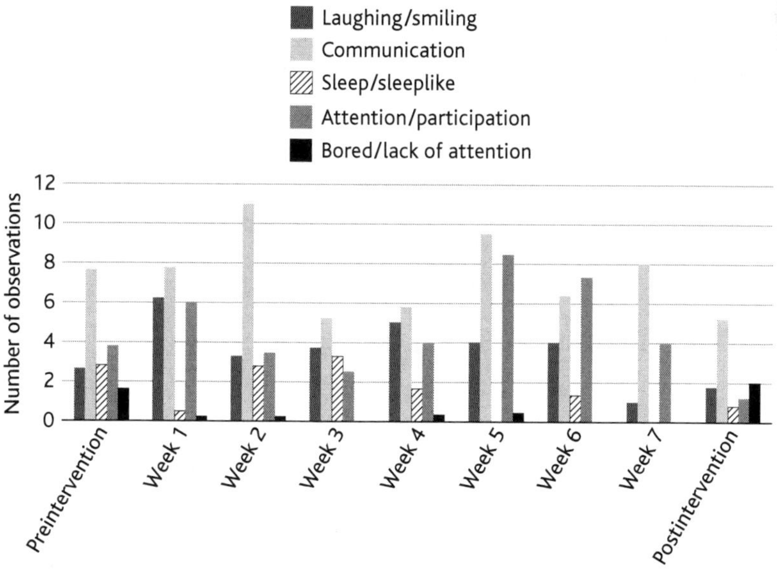

Transcripts and notes

As mentioned, we also analysed transcripts and observer notes for each poetry session. What follows is a summary organised by week. All names have been replaced with pseudonyms.

Pre-intervention observations

During the time allotted for the poetry intervention (10am–11am), the typical activity was having a staff member read from the newspaper to the residents. Following is an example of researcher notes for one resident, Marlene.

10:41am: eyes open, biting upper lip
10:46am: moves and looks at finger nails
10:50am: drinks juice
10:52am: talks to Alice (another resident). (Voice is too soft to hear.)
10:54am: coughs. Bites upper lip

Although there are periodic comments between residents during the hour, much of what was observed for the residents present that day included drinking juice and sleeping/eyes closed.

Intervention Week 1

During the first intervention week, the lead facilitator (LF) read a poem about snow falling. The second facilitator (SF) distributed paper snowflakes that she had made before the session. Following is an excerpt of conversations between the facilitators and participants.

> LF: The great thing about snowflakes is that every snowflake is unique. Marlene [the resident noted in the previous section], what does your snowflake look like? What does your snowflake remind you of?
> Marlene: Being there when you're being taken care of by them. And they went there to do that and my mother was there.

Although Marlene's speech has features of 'empty speech' in that the referents for the pronouns and prepositions (for example, them, they, there, that) are not clear, she does specifically mention "being taken care of" and "mother", which could suggest a feeling of familiarity or closeness, although we can't be certain. Marlene, who was fond of singing 'Jesus Loves Me', sang it at two separate times during the observation period. The first time, she sang a verse by herself, and when she had finished the group proceeded with the poetry session. The second time, SF sang along with her, which then prompted others in the group to sing as well.

After Marlene's initial exchange with SF, Betty was asked what she thought of the paper snowflake:

> Betty: It looks like something you might put on the table to put the glasses on.
> SF: Like a doily. [The group starts laughing.]
> Betty: We're a little crazy.
> LF: A little crazy is the best type.

One interpretation of this exchange is that Betty might have been making a sort of apology of sorts to not identifying the paper as a snowflake. Another is that she used humour ("We're a little crazy") and specifically introduced the pronoun "we" to signal group belonging.

Later, LF read the poem about snow again, but changed the tempo. She then asked different people in the group what they liked best about winter.

> Betty: It's crisp and every day is new. And you can do all kinds of winter things.
> LF: Absolutely.
> Betty: Like ski.
> LF: I tried skiing but it was a disaster.
> Betty: It's still skiing even if you fall. [Laughing]

Betty also used humour again, as she did earlier with the snowflake, to respond to LF's comment about skiing.

Week 2

The second intervention week coincided with Valentine's Day, so love poems were selected by LF. Although LF and SF brought Valentine's Day cards with them as well as red hearts they had cut from paper, they had a difficult time engaging the group. LF asked several participants if they would be her valentine, to which they answered "No". Marlene sang 'Jesus Loves Me' three different times during the intervention.

Week 3

The notes reflect a positive shift in the group during week 3. It began with Marlene starting a conversation with one of the student observers.

> Marlene: (to student) Hey lady, how old are you?
> Student: I'm 20.
> Marlene: I'm 19.
> Student: Oh, so I'm a year older than you.

Marlene then sang a verse of 'Jesus Loves Me' but refrained from doing so once the programme started. Instead, she was very talkative throughout the programme. After reading a poem about a food fight, LF asked Marlene if she had ever participated in throwing food.

> Marlene: Well I had four older brothers. And two or three older sisters. And they were all doing it. And they'd have someone come over and grab me. And tell me what to say and do. They'd give me all of that and then I could do it. And then my mother would come in and she would help me out.

As noted earlier, Marlene's speech often was difficult to follow but she clearly told a story about her family. This story seemed to be about others helping her, not unlike her comment from week 1 about feeling a sense of belonging.

Another interesting turn was that Dorothy, a new resident who had not spoken yet during a session, engaged in a dialogue with LF. After reading a poem about being a picky eater, LF asked the group if anyone was a good cook, mentioning that she 'burns everything' when she tries to cook.

> Dorothy: You got to stay with them and you got to keep the burner low. You can't have it too high or else you'll burn it.
> LF: This is good advice.
> Dorothy: And you have to be careful stirring it or else you'll get it all over the stove and into the burner.
> LF: This is all really good advice. [laughs] Everything boils over.

Dorothy:	You have it up too high.
LF:	I thought that having it up high would mean it was done faster.
Dorothy:	Well you have to stay with it. 'Til you see where it's at and it's not going up. [laughs]
LF:	Dorothy, where were you a week ago when I was trying to make something?
Dorothy:	I don't know.
LF:	I was trying to make pasta.
Dorothy:	I've been around here the whole time. I don't go too far. [She then mentions two nearby local towns.]

Dorothy responds to LF with some practical advice on how to avoid burning things when she cooks.

Weeks 4 through 7

The subsequent weeks followed a similar pattern to Week 3. Marlene did not sing. More residents began to participate and contribute with more substantial dialogue in the group sessions. One of the most striking examples occurred during week 5. At this occasion, LF had selected poems about smiling and happiness. She was asking group members, "What makes you smile?" to which they responded with various things such as "playing the clarinet" or "going camping". When Sarah was asked, she responded:

> "I like camping. I like waking up in the middle of the night when nobody else in the camp is awake. And just listening. And you hear sometimes, like wild cats. Something like that. And one time I heard a crack. And I look up, my eyes looked. And there was a bob cat. Just sitting there. So I sat up real slowly and nodded at him. He nodded. I put my hand out and he licked it. My husband said, 'Where's the bite marks?' I said, 'I didn't get bitten.' [laughs]. He says, 'Just keep your hands in your pockets.' I said, 'My pyjamas don't have pockets.' But he was as interested in me as I was in him."

This story marked the longest time that Sarah had spoken.

Post-intervention week

In the week after the poetry intervention concluded, the observations were similar to the week before the intervention started. One observer noted that Marlene had attempted to talk to several other residents and a staff member. The notes said the following:

10:42am: Marlene stares at staff member.
10:43am: Marlene stares at staff and makes a comment about baseball.
10:47am: Staff reads out the horoscope for Dorothy but Marlene says "that's me."
10:49am: Staff asks Marlene about her birthday. Says date. Then says "Other kids knocked me down." Staff member stops Marlene from talking about her childhood and makes her listen to the horoscope.
10:53am: Marlene talks about her siblings but no one seems to listen. Staff member ignores her.

Later, Marlene began singing 'Jesus Loves Me'.

Discussion

The case study of the poetry intervention was meant to illustrate some key components of a participatory arts-based intervention, rather than to provide guidelines for future sessions, evaluate its effectiveness or examine resident change over time. Although we did note in the frequency counts that the actions of the residents changed in the group during the poetry programme, with more laughter and conversation and less boredom being noted than in the non-intervention weeks, a more robust and larger study would be needed to test this claim. This is not to say that we cannot learn from the detailed descriptions sketched out earlier, especially with an eye to future research.

Since we are interested in resilience, creativity, play and 'flourishing' and their potential links to selfhood/personhood and connectivity, we look into the examples from our case study to further consider and explore these concepts. When approaching resilience as a way to 'bounce back, to overcome negative influences that block achievement' (Harris, 2008, p 45), we can see several instances of performances of resilience in the examples cited. Outside of the poetry intervention, most interactions between staff and residents typically consist of simple questions (for example, Would you like some juice? How are you feeling today?). In the case of Marlene, the staff member reading the horoscope not only controlled the subject of the talk (that is, horoscopes) but directly asked Marlene to stop talking about her childhood, creating a clear communication barrier. In contrast, the poetry intervention invited and welcomed new conversational opportunities for and with residents.

Also, as noted earlier, Marlene's speech was often missing clear referents, which meant that many times her speech was ignored, as in the post-intervention observation. Marlene's creative response to having no conversational partners seemed to be singing, specifically 'Jesus Loves Me'. When opportunities to talk and be heard were presented during the poetry workshop, Marlene stopped singing and shared her thoughts and stories (albeit still with missing referents.) When the poetry workshop stopped, the singing returned. It seems that Marlene's preference for the song 'Jesus Loves Me' is meaningful. As a popular hymn, the repetition of its words and melody may have become ritualised to the extent that the words no longer matter on a cognitive level (Swinnen, 2016). Still, 'Jesus Loves Me' is an act of self-affirmation in that it acknowledges that the 'me' in the song is worthy of being loved and part of a community of people who share this belief. As such, the song is a creative solution to the consequences of institutionalisation sketched out earlier.

Sarah's story about the bob cat is also an example of someone breaking away from the conversational limits within care environments, and one of the narratives that may not have been told, had a unique opportunity not arisen. The story itself, whether true or imagined, speaks to meaningful interaction and connectivity on a few levels. In the story, Sarah is able to make a connection with a wild and potentially dangerous animal. It is through careful listening at night, when no one else is awake, that she is able to hear the crack that eventually allows her to open her eyes and see the bob cat, who in turn is fascinated with her. Her story is also an object of great interest for the group members, who listen very attentively as she tells her story. In another sense, Sarah is a 'camper' of sorts in the facility, surrounded by noise throughout the day, potential conflicts with other residents and other dangers. Yet, she is curious and pays attention to the small details around her. It's as if the story is a metaphor or maybe even a cautionary tale for arts facilitators about how not to approach people living with dementia as fearful others – although it is very unlikely that Sarah intended it to be so. This story also appears to be personally meaningful to Sarah on multiple levels and allows her to share a part of her experiences with others. In the narrative, Sarah positions herself as a woman with curiosity and courage. This positioning is transposed to the setting of the closed unit where she now appears as a different, more able woman. It is a tale of adventure, now accessible through the collaborative imaginative play of poetry improvisation.

Another important component of the sessions was play including playful use of language. Dorothy, for example, responds to LF's playfulness about her cooking skills by laughing as she explains the importance of 'staying with it'. Although LF was then trying to be light-hearted by using a colloquialism, "Where were you a week ago?", Dorothy responds with a more literal answer, explaining that she didn't know but must have been close by. This doesn't meant that 'play' has stopped. Instead, Dorothy is given a space where she can connect with LF through conversation. Dorothy is not simply responding to a question by LF but provides her with guidance. When LF invites Dorothy to contribute more, Dorothy does. In this way, the exchange becomes more than just an interaction but instead starts to create meaningful dialogue.

We note that Week 2, which focused on love and Valentine's Day, was not successful in engaging the participants. We suggest that asking, "Would you be my valentine?" is too intimate a question if a connection with the facilitator is not yet established. Also, it is not playful in a way that borrowing a line from a verse to use as a question would be in imaginative play. Instead, the questions in Week 2 border on not being sincere and, as such, did not leave opportunity for connectivity.

An important component worth noting is how the poetry programme notably differed from the usual activities organised for the people living in this ward (that is, having the newspaper read aloud). During the newspaper readings, residents were passive listeners who were neither asked nor encouraged to respond or contribute. Poetry recitation and improvisation, on the other hand, offered a new set of opportunities for residents to react to such diverse topics as thinking about snow or what makes them happy. The types of topics and questions introduced by the facilitators fell outside of the realm of the daily routine and interactions of the participants. The sessions appealed to the ability of people living with dementia to imagine a fictional world that departs from their direct surrounding. In this world, they are able to touch a bob cat or cook pasta without any problem and they can be 19 and loved and cared for by family or Jesus. In this way, they are both creative and resilient. They use their imagination to connect with others and, in doing so, seem to 'bounce back' in an observable way that Harris (2008) described in her work on resilience.

Providing residents of care homes with opportunities to socially connect in new ways, we argue, can potentially result in 'flourishing', or the ability to participate fully and voluntarily in social connectedness with another in a way that gives and provides personal meaning. Flourishing, in this way, becomes the result of creativity and resilience. Dorothy could share her thoughts on cooking to help LF stop burning her food. Betty could make jokes about skiing. Marlene could talk about feeling like she was being taken care of. In addition, 'play' – both using playful words and being playful in the group, seemed central to opportunities to 'flourish'. This requires facilitators who are capable of developing the antennae needed to enter into language play on 'equal' ground, that is, the sensitivity to understand which subjects are appropriate to bring up as well as to take the limited verbal repertoire of residents into account. Gentle teasing and joking added to a 'light' atmosphere within the care environment, which also contributed to resident enjoyment. However, humour could sometimes fall flat, as in the case of the Valentine's Day session or in the interaction with Dorothy about cooking.

Conclusion

Overall, the programme provided opportunities for people to confirm their selfhood/personhood in a way that Jennings (2009) calls 'reminding'. He writes:

> Reminding is changing the environment and the external support system that surrounds a person so that different abilities do not become *the* absence of abilities. Reminding … is remembering who one is, most fundamentally – as a relational human subject, person, agent – a maker and interpreter of meaning. (Jennings, 2009, p 427)

He also adds:

> The tragedy of dementia is not so much that it alters brain function and changes what people can think and do; the real tragedy occurs when and if we allow those changes to objectify persons, reducing them to their impaired body and altered behaviour, rather than working with them to re-mind themselves and to be re-membered among us. (Jennings, 2009, p 427)

As we've argued, participatory arts programmes can provide opportunities for people to be re-minded of their humanness and re-membered as valuable human beings (which is not entirely the same as the people they once were in the past). Opportunities to be creative and engage with others contribute to resilience or the ability to transcend many dementia-associated losses (for example, declining social networks, communicative challenges). Through imaginative play, regardless of cognitive ability, people can express and/or enact important aspects of meaning and selfhood/personhood that might otherwise go unacknowledged in the care environment. While arts interventions may not be able to reverse cognitive decline, the case study points to ways that the poetry intervention creates a time-space in which people can 'flourish', express affinity with others and foster social bonds, and how, in turn, these contribute to meaningful moments in people's lives.

Notes

[1] The *Diagnostic and Statistical Manual of Mental Disorders* (5th edn) (DSM-5), published in 2013 by the American Psychiatric Association, is considered the definitive classification and diagnostic source in the United States.

[2] We use 'flourishing' within quotation marks because of its reference to 18th-century science and philosophy (for example, Goethe's famous comparison between the progression of plants and the development of an ideal human relationship). As we discuss later in the chapter, 'flourishing' here specifically relates to the word's use in positive psychology and current ageing and dementia research.

[3] The programme is designed to last for 60 minutes. However, given the small size of our group, we reduced the time to 30 minutes.

References

Basting, A.D. (2009) *Forget memory: Creating better lives for people with dementia*, Cambridge: Cambridge University Press.

Blair, M., Marczinski, C.A., Davis-Faroque, N. and Kertesz, A. (2007) 'A longitudinal study of language decline in Alzheimer's disease and frontotemporal dementia', *Journal of the International Neuropsychological Society*, 13(2): 237–45.

Blazer, D. (2013) 'Neurocognitive disorders in DSM-5', *American Journal of Psychiatry*, 170(6): 585–7.

Campo, M. and Chaudhury, H. (2012) 'Informal social interaction among residents with dementia in special care units: Exploring the role of the physical and social environments', *Dementia*, 11(3): 401–23.

Clarke, C., Wolverson, E., Stoner, C. and Spector, A. (2016) 'Overview and ways forward for a positive psychology approach to dementia', in C. Clarke and E. Wolverson (eds) *Positive Psychology Approaches to Dementia*, Philadelphia, PA and London: Jessica Kingsley Publishers, pp 253–79

Cohen, G.D. (2001) *The creative age: Awakening human potential in the second half of life*, New York, NY: Harper Collins.

Cornwell, E.Y. and Waite, L.J. (2009) 'Social disconnectedness, perceived isolation, and health among older adults', *Journal of Health and Social Behaviour*, 50(1): 31–48.

de Medeiros, K. and Basting, A. (2013) '"Shall I compare thee to a dose of donepezil?": Cultural arts interventions in dementia care research', *Gerontologist*, 54(3): 344–53.

de Medeiros, K. and Sabat, S.R. (2013) 'Friendships for people living with dementia in long-term care', in F. Moghaddam and R.C. Harre (eds) *The psychology of friendship and enmity: Relationships in love, work, politics, and war (Vol. 1)*, New York, NY: Praeger, pp 215–38

de Medeiros, K., Beall, E., Vozzella, S. and Brandt, J. (2009) 'Television viewing and people with dementia living in long-term care: A pilot study', *Journal of Applied Gerontology*, 28(5): 638–48.

Doyle, P.J., de Medeiros, K. and Saunders, P.A. (2011) 'Nested social groups within the social environment of a dementia care assisted living setting', *Dementia*, 11(3): 383–99.

Foundation, M.H. (2011) *An evidence review of the impact of participatory arts on older people*. Available at: https://baringfoundation.org.uk/wp-content/uploads/2011/04/EvidenceReview.pdf.

Glass, T.A., De Leon, C.F.M., Bassuk, S.S. and Berkman, L.F. (2006) 'Social engagement and depressive symptoms in late life', *Journal of Ageing and Health*, 18(4): 604–28.

Glazner, G.M. (2005) *Sparking memories: The Alzheimer's poetry project anthology*, Santa Fe, NM: Poem Factory.

Goffman, E. (1959) *The presentation of self in everyday life*, Garden City, NY: Doubleday

Harris, P. (2008) 'Another wrinkle in the debate about successful ageing: The undervalued concept of resilience and the lived experience of dementia', *The International Journal of Ageing and Human Development*, 67(1): 43–61.

Huizinga, J. (1949) *Homo ludens. A study of the play-element in culture*, translated by R.F.C. Hull, London: Routledge & Kegan Paul.

Jang, Y., Mortimer, J.A., Haley, W.E. and Graves, A.R.B. (2004) 'The role of social engagement in life satisfaction: Its significance among older individuals with disease and disability', *Journal of Applied Gerontology*, 23(3): 266–78.

Jennings, B. (2009) 'Agency and moral relationship in dementia', *Metaphilosophy*, 40(3–4): 425–37.

Kaufman, S. (1986) *The ageless self: Sources of meaning in late life*, Madison, WI: The University of Wisconsin Press.

Keyes, C.L.M. (2002) 'The mental health continuum: From languishing to flourishing in life', *Journal of Health and Social Behaviour*, 43(2): 207–22.

Keyes, S.E., Clarke, C.L., Wilkinson, H., Alexjuk, E.J., Wilcockson, J., Robinson, L., ... Cattan, M. (2016) '"We're all thrown in the same boat ...": A qualitative analysis of peer support in dementia care', *Dementia*, 15(4): 560–77.

Kinney, J.M. and Rentz, C.A. (2005) 'Observed well-being among individuals with dementia: Memories in the Making©, an art program, versus other structured activity', *American Journal of Alzheimer's Disease and Other Dementias*, 20(4): 220–7.

Kitwood, T. (1997) *Dementia reconsidered: The person comes first*, Buckingham: Open University Press.

Machielse, A. (2015) 'The heterogeneity of socially isolated older adults: A social isolation typology', *Journal of Gerontological Social Work*, 58(4): 338–56.

Mead, G.H. (1934) *Mind, self and society* (Vol. 111), Chicago: University of Chicago Press.

Moore, K.D. (1999) 'Dissonance in the dining room: A study of social interaction in a special care unit', *Qualitative Health Research*, 9(1): 133–55.

Post, S. (2002) *The moral challenge of Alzheimer disease: Ethical issues from diagnosis to dying*, Baltimore, MD: Johns Hopkins University Press.

Sabat, S.R. (2006) 'Mind, meaning, and personhood in dementia: The effects of positioning', in J.C. Hughes, S.J. Louw and S.R. Sabat (eds) *Dementia: Mind, meaning, and the person*, Oxford: Oxford University Press, pp 287–302.

Saunders, P.A., de Medeiros, K., Doyle, P. and Mosby, A. (2011) 'The discourse of friendship: Mediators of communication among dementia residents in long-term care', *Dementia*, 11(3): 347–61.

Swinnen, A. (2016) 'Healing words: Critical inquiry of poetry interventions in dementia care', *Dementia*, 15(6): 1377–404.

Swinnen, A. and de Medeiros, K. (2018) '"Play" and people living with dementia: A humanities-based inquiry of TimeSlips and the Alzheimer's Poetry Project', *The Gerontologist*, 58(2): 261–9.

FOUR

Narrative identity and resilience for people in later life with dementia living in care homes: the role of visual arts enrichment activities

Andrew Newman, Bruce Davenport and Teri Howson-Griffiths

Editorial introduction

This chapter is based on data from a large-scale, mixed methods project wherein groups of people with dementia were invited to take part in visual arts activities. The project generated a wide range of data, but this chapter takes a fine-grained approach to analysing the qualitative data from the project. Through this the authors explore the narrative processes and identity work that were evoked through the activities. These are considered from the perspective of resilience to explore how such activities might contribute to the resilience of people with dementia.

Introduction

This chapter explores how visual arts enrichment activities might play a role in the resilience of people in later life living with dementia in care homes, through the development or preservation of narrative identities. This complements previous work on the role of arts enrichment activities in the resilience of older people with dementia (Newman et al, 2018) that originated from the results of the same research project, entitled Dementia and Imagination.[1] That paper concluded that arts enrichment activities support resilience in the domains of creative expression, communication and self-esteem and through their effects on carers and family members. This chapter differs in that it explores the role that the arts enrichment activities might have in supporting narrative agency and expression, and how that might facilitate resilience in older people living with dementia (Randall, 2013). This is viewed as a way through which the personhood of a person living with dementia might be supported or enhanced (Kitwood and Bredin, 1992; Kitwood, 1997). The wider contribution is that the work provides an understanding of the potential of narrative care, where 'people make sense of their experiences, and indeed their identity, through the creation and sharing of stories' (Villar and Serrat, 2017, p 44) to improve the lives of people in later life with dementia.

The Dementia and Imagination project examined how arts enrichment activities[2] might improve the lives of people in later life living with dementia in different settings. The research was funded by the UK Arts and Humanities Research Council's Connected Communities Programme[3] and the UK Economic and Social Research Council[4] (reference AH/J011029/1) and was undertaken between 2013 and 2017.

This chapter begins with the proposition that 'the biographical side of human life is as intricate and dynamic and as critical to consider as, say, the biological side. [...] We are continually constructing stories about our lives, stories that reflect a combination of genetic predisposition, past experience and personal choice' (Kenyon and Randall, 2015, p 143). However, it might be expected that the nature of dementia, with its associated memory problems and sometimes language difficulties, would mean that constructing a narrative using textual language would be challenging. In response to this, visual arts enrichment activities have the potential to encourage the use of embodied forms of communication, such as those that involve 'primordial and sociocultural characteristics of the body that reside below the threshold of cognition' (Kontos, 2005, p 559). While not explicitly concerned with 'illness narratives' (Bolaki, 2017), the examples discussed in this chapter do, at times, suggest a 'changing sense of self and identity' (Woods, 2011, p 73) that may or may not be recognised by the individual (in particular see the discussion of participant ND34, later in the chapter). Nevertheless, the approach 'valu[es] the individual as the empowered author-narrator of her own story' (Woods, 2011, p 73), despite some of the difficulties that, by the nature of their dementia, exist.

This chapter aims to examine how, and the extent to which, resilience in older people with dementia may be facilitated through narrative identities, and the extent to which visual arts enrichment activities may support this. We present the theoretical framework used to support the analysis, followed by a description of the methodology, analysis, results, discussion and conclusion.

Theoretical framework

Narrative and narrative inquiry

The lack of precision about how the terms narrative and narrative inquiry are used means that it is difficult to produce a categorical definition. As is noted by Phoenix et al (2010, p 2), 'it is difficult to give a single definition of narrative, or draw a precise boundary around its meaning. In part, this is because it means different things to different people and is used in a variety of ways by different disciplines'. Riessman (2008, p 11) defines it as 'a family of methods for interpreting texts that have in common a storied form' and these texts can be oral, written or visual. None the less, Mishler (1995) suggests that narrative inquiry can be divided into a number of areas for consideration. Those relevant for this study are:

- representation – temporal sequence of events;
- linguistic and narrative strategies;
- cultural, social and psychological contexts and functions of stories; and
- narrative and culture, myths, rituals and performance.

Narrative and resilience

The approach to resilience adopted in this chapter follows Windle (2011, p 152), who defines it as 'the process of effectively negotiating, adapting to, or managing significant sources of stress or trauma. Assets and resources within the individual, their life and environment facilitate this capacity for adaptation and "bouncing back" in the face of adversity. Across the life course, the experience of resilience will vary'. Links between narrative and resilience are traced through the narrative construction of identity. '[Identity] is a life story. A life story is a personal myth that an individual begins working on in late adolescence and young adulthood in order to provide his or her life with a purpose' (McAdams, 1993, p 5). This is supported by Singer (2004, p 445), who states that 'individuals' ongoing sense of self in contemporary Western society coheres around a narrative structure, which casts the individual as a protagonist in a lifelong journey'. Randall (2013, p 9) then makes links with resilience, stating, 'resilience itself has a narrative dimension. It's a function of narrative openness, I propose. It's a function of a good strong story, a story of oneself and one's world.' A strong story might be described as one that has complexity and the resources that allow the person to respond to the narrative challenges they encounter. In a similar vein, Staudinger, Marsiske and Baltes (1995, p 818) suggested that 'having access to a larger set of well-developed possible selves may be a protective factor as we confront and manage growing old', acting as a resource for resilience. These authors also emphasise the importance of hobbies and activities, described as identity projects, as important in the construction of self and, so, resilience. Also of importance is autobiographical reasoning, which is described by Pasupathi and Mansour (2006, p 798) as how people construct a 'sense of unity across their lives by creating connections between their experiences and self-views'; they also report that the tendency to undertake this increases with age.

The suggestion that resilient older adults will story their lives in particular ways, being 'more detailed and complex in nature – so to speak stronger overall', is explored by Randall et al (2015, p 155). These authors used the Connor Davidson Resilience Scale (Connor and Davidson, 2003) to score resilience in 116 community-dwelling older adults. The results showed that the highest scorers had interests and hobbies or 'identity projects', a 'sense of narrative agency' and a degree of 'narrative openness' (Connor and Davidson, 2003, p 157). The lowest scorers demonstrated 'negative or unresolved memories of their childhood' and were 'generally less optimistic' and they appeared to have 'low self-esteem' (Connor and Davidson, 2003, p 159). Randall et al (2015, p 156) suggested that 'narrative identity continues all life long, ageing being no exception' and that the challenges that older people face can 'constitute challenges to our very sense of self'.

A possible threat to the resilience of people in later life is 'narrative foreclosure', where narrative identity development may falter (Freeman, 2011), implying 'that one already knows the ending of one's life. No other alternative endings are considered as realistic' (Bohlmeijer et al, 2011, p 365). This situation also shapes the ways that a life narrative is constructed as it becomes static, with a future predestined (Bohlmeijer et al, 2011).

Dubovska et al (2016, p 10) identified a number of thematic lines used by a group of older people in their narrative construction of resilience. These were:

- interest in life;
- ability to take pleasure from life;
- enjoyment of small pleasures;

- liking to learn new things;
- liking contact with young people;
- emphasis on importance of movement;
- love of life, and;
- good social relations.

These are used later in the chapter as a way of understanding the autobiographical narrative that resident respondents provided during the interviews.

Narrative identity and dementia

Caddell and Claire (2010, p 121) found that 'most people in the moderate and severe stages of dementia were able, at least to some degree, to construct a narrative which consisted of autobiographical memories' and that this process enabled them to preserve aspects of their self, and so identity. However, Hyden and Orulv (2009, p 206) 'found that persons with this diagnosis have problems telling stories on the topics suggested, and that they needed much interactional support in order to produce a narrative which was less chronologically organised'. These authors also identify that there has been little analysis of spontaneously produced narratives around a self-selected topic, and this is viewed as problematic, as stories are produced in direct relation to their audience. People do not tell their stories in isolation, and 'if a dementia sufferer is to sustain his or her part in the social world other people, with their corresponding expectations and performances are required' (Kitwood, 1993, p 53). The role of others in the co-production of life stories might be seen as a potentially important contributory factor in the preservation of personhood of persons with dementia (Baldwin, 2008).

This study utilises Baldwin's (2008, p 225) approach to the form and content of stories, which states that 'stories can be articulated, for example, as much through dance, movement and artistic expression as they can though language – if we as readers are sensitive enough to the narrative features of such media'. In focusing on arts enrichment activities for those with dementia, this study assumes that narratives can be constructed through activities which are both individual and collaborative and which may involve non-verbal forms of expression.

Methodology, data and visual arts enrichment activity

Study design

The approach adopted used mixed methods and analysed the processes that were observed within the context of the arts activity as well as the art pieces that were produced. For a description of the research protocol, see Windle et al (2016) and for a discussion of the epistemological challenges that were faced when deciding upon the research methods, see Newman et al (2016). This was of particular significance, as the project used approaches that were derived from both the social sciences and the arts and humanities. It was viewed as important to use perspectives derived from creative practice, as this added new perspectives to traditional research approaches (Hope, 2016).

The study took place in three locations across the UK. This chapter focuses on the data gathered in North East England, where the art activities took place in four care homes where participants were residents.

Sample size

Forty-eight people with dementia and 37 carers/family members were recruited. The activities were led by two participatory artists, both of whom were present at each session and who were also part of the sample.

Setting and participants

Three carers/family members and three people in later life living with dementia were interviewed in each of the four care homes, which resulted in 72 transcripts. Resident participants were included if they had a diagnosis of dementia or evidence of age-related memory impairment. They were excluded if they had a recent or current episode of major mental illness, were at the end of life or terminally ill, had a debilitating illness that would preclude regular attendance, had a severe uncorrected sensory or communication difficulty or were completely unable to communicate verbally (although a number of the resident participants became non-verbal over the time of the project). The settings for the arts enrichment activities were four privately owned care homes in North East England, UK.

Procedure

The study received UK National Health Service ethical approval from the North Wales Research Ethics Committee – West. The recruitment protocol (Windle et al, 2016) followed the provisions of the UK Mental Capacity Act 2005. If the potential participant was unable to make an informed choice, which was the case for all but three of the resident participants, an authorised family member or carer provided consent on their behalf. Those involved in the project, including the participatory artists, received training by the lead investigators, covering the Mental Capacity Act 2005, informed consent, dementia awareness and the study protocol procedures, including data collection methods and data management. The participatory artists and those carrying out data collection had worked with people in later life in previous research projects, but not all had worked with people with dementia.

In order to facilitate the data collection it was important to build a strong relationship with those working in the care homes concerned. The timing of visits needed to be negotiated and planned to fit in with other activities, such as when lunch and dinner was served to residents. The participatory artists were introduced to the participants, who were informed about the purposes of the study during recruitment (Windle et al, 2016).

The visual arts enrichment activities

Within the care homes, the visual arts enrichment activities were undertaken for two hours a week for three months. Two artists were present at each session, and the activities were organised to give participants as much control as possible. The activity could be individual or co-created and the artists would attempt to engage as many of the senses as possible, which was important for those who lacked verbal language to varying degrees or/and had more advanced dementia. Participants were divided into groups depending on their language proficiency, ensuring that the activities were as person-centred as possible.

Guidelines for the arts enrichment activities were produced that ensured that they were of high quality and had comparable elements (Parkinson, Windle and Taylor, 2017). The participatory artists mainly used an approach that has been developed by Basting (2001, 2009) that uses creativity and attempting to look forward to generate new stories rather than focusing on memory and that is common in reminiscence sessions undertaken in cultural institutions for people in later life with dementia in the UK.

An excerpt from one of the artists' notes serves to illustrate the sort of activity that was undertaken:

> The starting point for the session was a David Hockney[5] tree scene.[6] It was aimed to engage the senses through smell, touch, sound and taste. Both sessions started with a general discussion using sensory prompts such as smelling cedar wood, lavender, rose water, wood shavings, tasting crystallised flower petals and Turkish Delight. This set the scene to go into the art work.

Dementia was not mentioned by the participatory artists. Those with severe dementia needed one-to-one support from carers/family members and it was important to ensure that the artwork was created by the resident and not by the carer/family member.

A visit for each of the four groups was organised to the Baltic Centre for Contemporary Art[7] in Gateshead, UK and a celebratory event was held at the end of the three months of activities to which family members and carers were invited.

Sources of data

This chapter draws on data collected from the care homes. These were:

- qualitative semi-structured interviews undertaken at baseline (T1), at the end of the activity (T2) and three months after (T3) with a sub-set of participants and separate interviews with their associated carers/family members. This was done in each of four waves;
- structured notes made by the participatory artists of their experiences of each of the sessions immediately after each was completed;
- socio-demographic and clinical data (for example age, occupational status, education, gender and medication use);
- the level of dementia, measured by the Clinical Dementia Rating Scale (CDR) (Hughes et al, 1982), which is used as a context for qualitative judgements. This consists of scoring the categories of memory, orientation, judgement and problem solving, community affairs, home and hobbies and personal care (healthy CDR 0, questionable dementia CDR 0.5, mild dementia CDR 1, moderate dementia CDR 2, severe dementia CDR 3); and

- images of respondents created as an artwork and a poem created by the respondents and artists.

The interviews ranged from a few minutes' (when respondents had become non-verbal after they had been recruited) to 120 minutes' duration. They were digitally recorded and the recordings were professionally transcribed and then anonymised for analysis. Participant names were replaced by alpha-numerical codes assigned in this study. Participants were recorded as NDXX and carers/family members NSYY. Individual respondents are distinguished by 'XX' and 'YY' and N represents the North East England data collection site.

Analysis

The transcripts were coded using QSR NVivo 10, with nodes being identified through close multiple readings of the transcripts. It was not possible for all participants to comment on the findings, although carers and family members attended a one-day seminar at Newcastle University, Newcastle upon Tyne, UK, where they were discussed. While the interview schedule did not ask directly for an autobiographical narrative, some questions could be said to have autobiographical overtones and a number of the care home-resident respondents responded by talking about their past lives. However, what was said did have the advantage of being a self-selected topic rather than one that was chosen by the researcher (Hyden and Orulv, 2009), and by implication was expressing sentiments that were of importance.

Categories (Morse, 2008) were identified that originated from the data. These were:

- autobiographical narratives;
- narratives created through the visual art enrichment activities:
  - textual narrative created as a response to an artwork; and
  - visual embodied narratives constructed through asking resident respondents to create a theatrical pose that was subsequently photographed.

Results

As well as having a diagnosis of dementia or evidence of age-related memory impairment, care home residents often had other medical problems that, for example, could result in a lack of mobility and/or poor eyesight (for example, age-related macular degeneration). For some, the symptoms of dementia appeared stable, while for others they got worse over the period of the data collection. The characteristics of the sample are given in Table 4.1.

Table 4.1: Baseline characteristics of the study sample from care homes in North East England

	Care home sample (n=48)	
Age, mean (SD)	84.9	7.4
Female gender, n (%)	35	72.9
Marital status, n (%)		
Married/cohabiting	10	21.3
Single	3	6.4
Widowed	30	63.8
Divorced/separated	4	8.5
Ethnicity, n (%)		
White	44	95.7
Asian/Asian British	–	–
Other	2	4.2
Age leaving full-time education, mean (SD)	15.8	2.7
Educational level, n (%)		
Low	23	47.9
Middle	4	8.3
High	8	16.7
Level of main activity/occupation ('SES'), n (%)		
Unskilled	3	6.3
Partly skilled	3	6.3
Skilled (manual)	16	33.3
Skilled (non-manual)	9	18.8
Managerial/technical		
Professional	9	18.8
Level of main activity/ occupation ('SES', 0-5), mean (SD)	2.7	1.5
CDR rating, n (%)		
0.5 Questionable	6	12.5
1 Mild	18	37.5
2 Moderate	8	16.7
3 Severe	16	33.3
Use of dementia- or mood-related medication, n (%)		
None	31	67.4
Only dementia related	11	23.9
Only mood related	4	8.7
Both	0	

Note: SD = standard deviation; SES = socio-economic group.

Autobiographical narratives created by respondents

While all of those care home-resident respondents who were still verbal were capable, to some degree, of providing an autobiographical narrative, there were differences in the richness of stories that were told. Following Randall et al (2015), this provides an indication of how resilient the respondents were. The following presents two examples of narrative identities and explores how they might be viewed as representing different levels of resilience.

The first example was ND2 (an 86-year-old female with a CDR of 3, severe dementia), who was unable to answer the questions that were asked and was unable to remember the art activity at the T2 and T3 interviews. She mainly spoke about her family members and domestic situation when she was younger. The interviewer encouraged her to speak during the interviews, providing an audience and facilitating conversation.

She states at T1:

> "So I've come down because at the moment there's not much on at me house. So I thought I'll come here.
> "Well me mother brought me up, you know? And me father. Me dad's still alive.
> "Me mother, she's just, you know, having to take her time.
> "And me mother died, you know. Me mother's, er, down. And it was terrible. Five daughters."

At T2 she states:

> "Me sisters. I've got sisters. And, and quite a few.
> "Me mother died. Me father is still alive.
> "He's a good man."

The first sentence provides an explanation to herself for her presence in the care home, yet maintaining a sense of still living in her own home. She is able to justify to herself her current circumstances while maintaining continuity with a prior life narrative. Her belief that her father was still alive was contradicted by her brother-in-law, who was present at the T3 interview and who said he had died some 20 years before, which she did not believe, saying she had seen him recently. The loss of her mother was strongly felt, as well as the positive aspects of the relationships with her sisters and father, memories of which remained (Mills, 1997). According to Hyden and Orulv (2009, p 206) 'the repetition of smaller "frozen" segments although seemingly misplaced, may capture something important in the way the person makes sense of his or her life'. It is also possible that she wished to communicate moral values associated with family relationships.

Despite the advanced nature of her dementia and the limited number of topics that were addressed, this respondent was able to express a narrative identity. This is demonstrated by the correct use of the first person indexicals (me, I've, and so on), which suggests an 'intact self' (Sabat and Harre, 1992). She was also able to demonstrate a narrative identity through the social context of the interview: because she was unable to answer the questions, the interview became a conversation on the topics that she chose, which were mainly about her family. She also asked questions of the researchers, demonstrating an understanding of the normal social expectations and rules of conversation.

The second example is ND15 (a 94-year-old male with a CDR of 2, moderate dementia) who, according to his carers, was very sociable and joined in all the available activities in the care home. He had a very limited memory of the arts activities at T2 and none at T3. He was able to answer questions but mainly wanted to talk about his early life as a marine engineer. Once he started talking about this he needed to continue (at both T2 and T3) until it was completed, and only then responded to interview questions.

He states at T2:

> "But I, I went to sea and I, naturally the war was on, might seem silly to you, the wife went with us.
>
> "I'm saying that roughly, you know, and, er, brought up, I was [one of] five sons.
>
> "Two daughters.
>
> "Yes, and, er, that was just before the war, so canny[8] years ago.
>
> "We went to the, you know, the, near Australia.
>
> "So I loved the, I'd already been to Australia and, erm, with the port, and, er, I was an engineer so ... But ... I thoroughly enjoyed it.
>
> "The life was good."

At T3 he said:

> "On the er, we were, ships, you see, but I was the one that made life a bit, I say made me life a bit, I was late start – oh I wasn't, I just thought, what am I talking about? The war

started in 1920 – in, no, I was born then. Er, 1920 I was born. And then we had a go after that. And, er, family were, two girls, they were first, and, and five lads in succession."

While he demonstrates difficulties in word finding and memory, he was able to present a reasonably coherent autobiographical narrative even though the temporal aspects were sometimes confused and he spoke only about his early life. He was using first person indexicals correctly (Sabat and Harre, 1992) and was able to present a social identity constructed in the interview of someone who had had an enjoyable life, was adventurous, was prepared to study hard to achieve his ambitions and had very good relationships with friends and family. Both of these resident respondents used the opportunity of the interview for narrative expression (Baldwin, 2008), which can be limited for those with dementia, particularly those whose condition has advanced.

In order to talk of resilience, we need to show that these respondents were overcoming adversity and that they were 'doing alright' (Braudy Harris, 2008, p 45) in the opinion of the carers or family members. Their life situation represented a range of chronic stressors that they needed to be able to respond to (both had dementia and were living in care homes). In this respect, ND2 was doing less well than ND15. Her dementia was more advanced (with a CDR of 3 as opposed to 2) and she became distressed if she did not have company, which was not possible to have all of the time because of resource constraints in the home. In ND2's autobiographical narrative, the only example of Dubovska et al's (2016) categories (representing the narrative construction of resilience) is in the importance she placed on relations with family members. In contrast, ND15 demonstrated many more, for example, interest in life, liking to learn new things (that is, the art activities), good social relations, more or less coherent storytelling and not taking things too seriously. ND15 focused upon the more positive aspects of his life and downplayed the negative ones, such as the loss of his wife and the onset of dementia (Cain, 1991). For these two respondents the richness of their narrative identities corresponded to the resilience that they exhibited (Randall et al, 2015). ND2's narrative was simpler than ND15's and, in the context of the interview, she had access to a less complex narrative self. ND15's greater narrative complexity and intelligence gives him a wider range of options when responding narratively to the chronic stressors of his condition and environment. Both of these respondents could be said to be exhibiting resilience, although there were major differences between them.

The following section builds on the ideas that narratives can be textual/visual or collective/individual by examining two of the arts enrichment activities undertaken by care home-resident respondents.

The creation of narrative identities through visual art enrichment activities

Textual narrative created as a response to an artwork

The following is an example of a poem constructed in one of the care homes as a response to *The Fall of Icarus* by Matisse (1869–1954).

The words were crafted by those participants who still had language, which were then put into poetic form by the participatory artists. Those who took part in the exercise, including the artists, were both the creators of and the audience for the narrative.

The poem created by the resident respondents is as follows:

> **Icarus**
> 'This is me', says Nancy
> Blue is the colour of new
> Blue is colour or you
> Yellow is the colour of stars
> He could be a man flying, weighty or light
> The spot on his chest glows red
> He could be a man floating through the sea –
> Or a ghost.

The poem is constructed from the respondents' interpretation of the narratives encoded into the artwork while adding aspects of their own feelings about the piece (Newman, Goulding and Whitehead, 2014). One respondent linked the image, of a disembodied person, to how she feels herself, enabling her to explore and to communicate to the others in the group her experience of dementia and its impact upon her personhood. This becomes a culturally shared story (Mishler, 1995), which is a frame for exploring feelings and can be seen as an adaptive response rather than a narrative of personhood that is often more overtly and consciously autobiographical. Its construction must depend on a shared habitus among respondents, where symbolic expression and exchange is understood. This enables a form of collective creative expression, and so narrative agency that is often difficult for those with dementia.

The role of visual arts enrichment activities

Visual embodied narrative constructed through a theatrical pose

While creating and sharing the poem was open to those who still had verbal language, those who had lost it over the period of the research could not get involved. However, they were able to contribute to other types of arts enrichment activities that did not require verbal language.

The images[9] in Figures 4.1 and 4.2 were taken of two of the participant residents after they were asked to take up theatrical poses, which were then photographed. Figure 4.1 shows participant ND36 (aged 91 with a CDR of 1, mild dementia) and Figure 4.2 shows participant ND34 (aged 85 with a CDR of 1, mild dementia). Both

Figure 4.1: Pose by respondent ND34

101

Figure 4.2: Pose by respondent ND36

of these individuals had difficulties with language and memory. A qualitative interview was attempted with ND34, although she struggled to understand the questions and was unable to answer them. The artist described the activity as follows: 'this allowed the residents to be something that they aren't normally ... they really let go! Everyone took part in one way or another – watching and applauding or posing – it was a pleasure to be part of and you can see their individual characteristics coming out.'

Through this activity the resident respondents were able to communicate a self to others that was different to that normally presented. This involved the use of creativity and the ability to express that self physically. As with all narratives, these poses were created in a dialogue with those who were viewing and who were actively involved as an audience. In order to do this they needed the ability to understand symbols and behaviours as communicating particular points. The generation of the newly presented self involves imagination, dramatic presentation and narration – skills that the participants retained.

Such behaviour can also represent the ability of the respondents to communicate using embodied approaches that do not rely on verbal language (Kontos, 2005; Kontos and Naglie, 2009; Kontos and Martin, 2013). However, it is difficult to determine the form of embodiment involved. For example, a distinction can be made between that which is associated with previous socialisation within particular contexts, captured in the concept of habitus (Bourdieu, 1977), and that which is never learned[10] (Merleau-Ponty, 1962), both of which function below the level of consciousness. Resident ND36 had a theatrical background, so for her, the more embodied forms of learned habitus might have been important in this context.

In the session the following week the resident respondents were shown the images and the response was described in the artists' notes in the following way:

> We started the session by presenting the life size prints of each resident – these were hung on the walls of the dining room. That was a huge part of the session and what was really interesting was that everyone in the room recognised themselves ... apart from ND34, who said 'That's not me – I am not frightened'.

This suggests that ND34 *did* actually recognise herself. However, the image had unfortunately disrupted her sense of self to the extent that she became upset.

Discussion

Both of the arts enrichment activities described earlier demonstrate narrative characteristics, as identified by Randall (1999). The narratives constructed were not straightforwardly autobiographical, in that they did not attempt to construct a timeline of events, but they both include aspects of the self which are communicated to an audience. There is a possibility in both instances that the selves presented in the artworks are created rather than aspects of existing identities, although it is likely that both might be happening. Again in both instances the choices made demonstrate emplotment[11] and summarising aspects of identity through the process of imagining and then, in the case of the theatrical poses, physically articulating the imagined self. Both also demonstrate characterisation, where respondents imagined the identities that they wished to communicate to the group. This involved imagining their 'thoughts and feelings, and their possible actions and reactions in particular situations' (Randall, 1999, p 17). The poses required the mastery of a visual social grammar, and the poem a mastery of textual grammar, to communicate what they wished to in the context of the group. Both exercises were successful and demonstrate that those with dementia can exhibit narrative intelligence in different ways. The impacts of arts activities have been described as being 'in the moment' in the literature. However, what is meant by 'in the moment' differs between authors. MacPherson et al were unable to identify any long-term therapeutic effect of an art gallery access programme for people with dementia but concluded that 'this does not obviate the value of the programme', stating, 'you do it for the moment' (MacPherson et al, 2009, p 751). Burnside et al (2017) take a different approach, where being 'in the moment' is associated with the idea of flow (Csikszentmihalyi, 2014) and what they describe as 'mindfulness' is a pleasurable concentration on the task in hand. Burnside et al (2017) quote one of their respondents as saying 'the realities of the world kind of fade away'. However, it can argued that whatever the subjective feeling of the participant, it is not possible for respondents to be unencumbered by habitus (the realities of the world) in the creation of artworks, as even those with advanced dementia, in this study, used remaining memory to support the activity.

Such narrative construction supports resilience through the ways that it facilitates the development and expression of new possible selves and the thickening of existing stories through embodied (Kontos, 2004) and textual narrative. The possible selves that are expressed through creative practice are different to those discussed in the literature, in that they are only partially anchored in respondents' past lives and have the potential to represent change as much as stability. The creative activity in this context can be viewed as underpinning growth, rather than decline, as a response to the stressors experienced that are associated with having dementia and sometimes frailty (Polk, 1997).

Within this dataset, those with more complex narratives tended to be happier and more resilient, in the views of carers (Braudy Harris, 2008), than those with more restricted stories. However, even those with simpler narratives were able to communicate a narrative identity and be resilient at times and in certain contexts. According to carers, resident respondents often did better, in terms of social interaction, in the arts enrichment activity than they did outside of it. An example was ND36 (aged 91 with a CDR of 1, mild dementia), who appeared more socially fluent within the activity group, knowing the words to songs (despite having lost everyday language) and giving other group members and care staff hugs, communicating in more embodied ways. These forms of communication were used successfully in the photographed theatrical pose that she undertook.

As might be expected, the participants' responses prior to the arts activities were mixed. The activities encouraged narrative openness and this, in turn, encouraged increased narrative richness, which is associated with resilience (Randall, 2013). The act of creating the art works and the narratives that they express requires participants to be open to the possible selves that they represent, which appeared normal for those who took part. The possible selves created were not practical in the sense that they would express a series of actions, motivations or be an attempt to re-story events. Instead, they are an emotional response occurring in relation to the stimulus provided in the session, as shown in both the examples given earlier. The interview process itself may provide an opportunity to perform/construct a narrative that fosters a more resilient response to their lives.

While for the purposes of analysis a distinction is made between narratives produced visually and textually it may be useful to view them collectively as resources that participants make use of in interactions (Iwasaki, 2011). Bach (2008), writing about visual narrative inquiry, notes that it 'adds the layer of meaning so that photographs and visuals become ways of living and telling one's stories of experience' (Bach, 2008, p 938). In most instances verbal and non-verbal resources are used in a fluid and complementary fashion (Clark and Henetz, 2014), although in the examples given earlier one form dominates others. This may help people with dementia by offering multiple forms of communication and expression and allowing for their personhood to be seen by carers.

This multifaceted approach to narrative also makes a contribution to discussions on narrative care (Kenyon and Randall, 2015; Villar and Serrat, 2017) that can respond to the narrative dispossession or narrative loss often associated with institutional care. In this situation residents are unable to narratively express themselves because of cognitive decline (Baldwin, 2008) and/or lack of opportunity. The arts enrichment activities discussed earlier go beyond life review, focusing upon the present (Basting, 2009) rather than the past. The theatrical poses enabled all to contribute, including those with more advanced dementia, and were not dependent on autobiographical memory and the ability to verbally articulate a life narrative. The roles played by the artists in this process were critical: they were able to facilitate the enrichment activity in a way that scaffolded the narrative that was being produced while enabling the respondents to control the content and creative expression involved. The arts enrichment activities produced cannot be directly viewed as a response to negative societal meta-narratives (Hammack, 2011) of dementia or age because the majority of the respondents lacked the awareness required to do this. However, they did have an effect upon some of the care staff and family members who had internalised the view that those with dementia were less able than they actually were.

Conclusion

The resident respondents were able to express a narrative identity despite their dementia. However, the richness of their autobiographical narratives varied considerably (expressed at T1, T2 and T3) and corresponded to how well they were doing, in terms of Dubovska et al's (2016) categories representing the narrative construction of resilience. The arts enrichment activities can be understood as an identity project and a form of narrative expression. The respondents demonstrated narrative intelligence that was expressed through the poem and the theatrical poses. Both of the activities supported the resilience of those who took part through facilitating narrative expression, for which those living in care homes often have few opportunities. The forms of narrative involved focused on the present and demonstrated that those with dementia were capable of creativity. This work contributes to thinking about the nature of narrative care (Kenyon and Randall, 2015; Villar and Serrat, 2017), suggesting new approaches that help those in care institutions to retain their existing and develop new identities, facilitating narrative openness and, ultimately, resilience.

Notes

[1] http://dementiaandimagination.org.uk/.
[2] 'Intervention' is not used; it is considered inappropriate in work that uses the arts because of the positivist assumptions that underpin the term (Newman et al, 2016).
[3] www.ahrc.ac.uk/research/fundedthemesandprogrammes/crosscouncilprogrammes/connectedcommunities/.
[4] www.esrc.ac.uk/.
[5] https://www.royalacademy.org.uk/artist/david-hockney-ra.

6 For example www.theartsdesk.com/visual-arts/david-hockney-bigger-picture-royal-academy.
7 www.balticmill.com/.
8 'Canny' is local dialect for 'many'.
9 Permission was received to use the images for research purposes.
10 It is open to question how much of this pre-reflexive behaviour is innate and how much is learned.
11 To weave a series of events into a narrative or plot.

References

Bach, H. (2008) 'Visual narrative inquiry', in L.M. Given (ed), *The Sage encyclopaedia of qualitative research methods*, London: Sage, pp 938–40.

Baldwin, C. and Bradford Dementia Group (2008) 'Narrative(,) citizenship and dementia: The personal and the political', *Journal of Aging Studies*, 22(3): 222–8.

Basting, A. (2001) '"God is a talking horse", dementia and the performance of the self', *The Drama Review*, 45(3): 78–94.

Basting, A. (2009) *Forget memory: Creating a better life for people with dementia*, Baltimore, MD: Johns Hopkins University Press.

Bohlmeijer, E., Westerhof, G., Randall, W., Tromp, T. and Kenyon, G. (2011) 'Narrative foreclosure in later life: Preliminary considerations for a new sensitizing concept', *Journal of Aging Studies*, 25: 364–70.

Bolaki, S. (2017) *Illness as many narratives: Arts, medicine and culture*, Edinburgh: Edinburgh University Press.

Bourdieu, P. (1977) *Outline of a theory of practice*, Cambridge: Cambridge University Press.

Braudy Harris, P. (2008) 'Another wrinkle in the debate about successful aging: The undervalued concept of resilience and the lived experience of dementia', *International Journal of Ageing and Human Development*, 67(1): 43–61.

Burnside, L., Knecht, M., Hopley, E. and Logsdon, R. (2017) 'Here: now – Conceptual model of the impact of an experiential arts program on persons with dementia and their care partners', *Dementia*, 16(1): 29–45.

Caddell, L. and Claire, L. (2010) 'The impact of dementia on self and identity: A systematic review', *Clinical Psychology Review*, 30: 113–26.

Cain, C. (1991) 'Personal stories: Identity acquisition and self-understanding in Alcoholics Anonymous', *Journal of the Society of Psychological Anthropology*, 19(2): 210–53.

Clark, H. and Henetz, T. (2014) 'Working together', in T. Holtgraves (ed) *The Oxford handbook of language and social psychology*, Oxford: Oxford University Press, pp 85–97.

Connor, K. and Davidson, J. (2003) 'Development of a new resilience scale: The Connor-Davidson Resilience Scale (CD-RISC)', *Depression and Anxiety*, 18(2): 76–82.

Csikszentmihalyi, M. (2014) *Flow and the foundations of positive psychology: The collected works of Mihaly Csikszentmihalyi*, New York and London: Springer

Dubovska, E., Chrz, V., Tavel, P. and Solcova, I. (2016) 'Narrative construction of resilience: Stories of older Czech adults', *Ageing and Society*, 1–25.

Freeman, M. (2011) 'Narrative foreclosure in later life: Possibilities and limits', in G. Kenyon, E. Bohlmeijer and W. Randall (eds) *Storying later life: Issues, investigations, and interventions in narrative gerontology*, Oxford: Oxford University Press, pp 3–19.

Hammack, P. (2011) 'Narrative and the politics of meaning', *Narrative Inquiry*, 21(2): 311–18.

Hope, S. (2016) 'Bursting paradigms: A colour wheel of practice-research', *Cultural Trends*, 25(2): 74–86.

Hughes, C., Berg, L., Danziger, W., Coben, L. and Martin, R. (1982) 'A new clinical scale for the staging of dementia', *British Journal of Psychiatry*, 140 (June): 566–72.

Hyden, L-C. and Orulv, L. (2009) 'Narrative and identity in Alzheimer's disease: A case study', *Journal of Ageing Studies*, 23: 205–14.

Iwasaki, S. (2011) 'The multimodal mechanics of collaborative unit construction in Japanese conversation', in C. Goodwin, C. LeBaron and J. Streeck (eds) *Embodied interaction: Language and the body in the material world*, Cambridge: Cambridge University Press, pp 106–20.

Kenyon, G. and Randall, W. (2015) 'Introduction', *Journal of Aging Studies*, 34: 143–5.

Kitwood, T. (1993) 'Person and process in dementia', *International Journal of Geriatric Psychiatry*, 8(7): 541–5.

Kitwood, T. (1997) 'The experience of dementia', *Ageing and Mental Health*, 1(1): 13–22.

Kitwood, T. and Bredin, K. (1992) 'Towards a theory of dementia care: Personhood and well-being', *Ageing and Society*, 12(3): 269–87.

Kontos, P. (2004) 'Ethnographic reflections on selfhood, embodiment and Alzheimer's disease', *Ageing and Society*, 24: 829–49.

Kontos, P. (2005) 'Embodied selfhood in Alzheimer's disease: Rethinking person-centred care', *Dementia*, 4(4): 553–70.

Kontos, P. and Martin, W. (2013) 'Embodiment and dementia: Exploring critical narratives of selfhood, surveillance, and dementia care', *Dementia*, 12(3): 288–302.

Kontos, P. and Naglie, G. (2009) 'Tacit knowledge of caring and embodied selfhood', *Sociology of Health and Illness*, 5: 688–704.

McAdams, D. (1993) *The stories we live by: Personal myths and the making of the self*, New York: William Morrow and Company.

MacPherson, S., Bird, M., Anderson, K., Davis, T. and Blair, A. (2009) 'An art gallery access programme for people with dementia: "You do it for the moment"', *Aging and Mental Health*, 13(5): 744–52.

Mental Capacity Act (2005) London: The Stationery Office

Merleau-Ponty, M. (1962) *Phenomenology of perception [Phénoménologie de la perception]*, London: Routledge and Kegan Paul.

Mills, M. (1997) 'Narrative identity and dementia: A study of emotion and narrative in older people with dementia', *Ageing and Society*, 17(6): 673–98.

Mishler, E. (1995) 'Models of narrative analysis: A typology', *Journal of Narrative and Life History*, 5(2): 87–123.

Morse, J. (2008) 'Confusing categories and themes', *Qualitative Health Research*, 18: 727–28.

Newman, A., Goulding, A. and Whitehead, C. (2014) 'Contemporary visual art and the construction of identity: Maintenance and revision processes in older adults', *International Journal of Heritage Studies*, 20(4): 432–53.

Newman, A., Goulding, A., Davenport, B., and Windle, G. (2018) 'The role of the visual arts in the resilience of people living with dementia in care homes', *Ageing and Society*, 45(11): 5609–16.

Newman, A., Baber, M., O'Brien, D., Goulding, A., Hedd Jones, C., Howson, T., Jones, C., Parkinson, C., Taylor, K., Tischler, V. and Windle, G. (2016) 'Carrying out research across the arts and humanities and social sciences: Developing the methodology for dementia and imagination', *Cultural Trends*, 25(4): 218–32.

Parkinson, C., Windle, G. and Taylor, C. (2017) *Dementia and imagination: Research informed approaches to visual arts programmes*, Manchester: Manchester School of Art.

Pasupathi, M. and Mansour, E. (2006) 'Adult age differences in autobiographical reasoning in narratives', *Developmental Psychology*, 42: 798–808.

Phoenix, C., Smith, B. and Sparkes, A. (2010) 'Narrative analysis in ageing studies: A typology for consideration', *Journal of Ageing Studies*, 24: 1–11.

Polk, L. (1997) 'Toward a middle range theory of resilience', *Advances in Nursing Science*, 19(3): 1–13.

Randall, W. (1999) 'Narrative intelligence and the novelty of our lives', *Journal of Ageing Studies*, 13(1): 11–28.

Randall, W. (2013) 'The importance of being ironic: Narrative openness and personal resilience in later life', *The Gerontologist*, 53(1): 9–16.

Randall, W., Baldwin, C., McKenzie-Mohr, S., McKimd, E. and Furlong, D. (2015) 'Narrative and resilience: A comparative analysis of how older adults story their lives', *Journal of Aging Studies*, 34: 155–61.

Riessman, C. (2008) *Narrative methods for the human sciences*, London: Sage.

Sabat, S. and Harre, R. (1992) 'The construction and deconstruction of self in Alzheimer's disease', *Ageing and Society*, 12(4): 443–61.

Singer, J. (2004) 'Narrative identity and meaning making across the adult lifespan: An introduction', *Journal of Personality*, 72(3): 437–60.

Staudinger, U., Marsiske, M. and Baltes, P. (1995) 'Resilience and reserve capacity in later adulthood: Potentials and limits of development across the life span', in D. Cicchetti and D. Cohen (eds) *Developmental psychopathology*, 2: *Risk, disorder, and adaptation*, New York: Wiley, pp 801–47.

Villar, F. and Serrat, R. (2017) 'Changing the culture of long-term care through narrative care: Individual, interpersonal, and institutional dimensions', *Journal of Aging Studies*, 40: 44–8.

Windle, G. (2011) 'What is resilience? A review and concept analysis', *Reviews in Clinical Gerontology*, 21(2): 152–69.

Windle, G., Newman, A., Burholt, V., Woods, B., O'Brien, D., Baber, M., Hounsome, B., Parkinson, C. and Tischler, V. (2016) 'Dementia and imagination: A mixed-methods protocol for arts and science research', *BMJ Open*, doi:10.1136/bmjopen-2016-011634.

Woods, A. (2011) 'The limits of narrative: Provocations for the medical humanities', *Medical Humanities*, 37: 73–8.

FIVE

After the earthquake: narratives of resilience, re-signification of fear and revitalisation of local identities in rural communities of Paredones, Chile

Cynthia Meersohn Schmidt, Paulina Osorio-Parraguez, Adriana Espinoza and Pamela Reyes

Editorial introduction

Many of the chapters in this book focus on resilience as a response to the chronic (that is, long-term and on-going) challenges of later life. This chapter focuses on a distinctly acute (that is, traumatic and time-limited) challenge – rebuilding life after an earthquake in rural Chile. The project explores the impact of creative interventions in the resilient responses at the individual and communal level. The creative interventions mix visual arts with storytelling. The chapter touches on the issues of creativity, resilience, social relationships and place-based identities.

Introduction

In this chapter, we examine the development of a psychosocial intervention (Forsman et al, 2011) specifically designed to support rural-living elders in Chile to overcome the trauma of an earthquake. We explain how we approached creativity during the intervention, and how it proved to be effective in dealing with multiple dimensions of individual and community resilience. We first explain our methodological approach and some of the key activities that were helpful for dealing with trauma, as well as gaining insights about ageing rural communities in post-disaster contexts. We then lay out how creative expression and imagination were fundamental in the re-conceptualisation of local community identity, in accepting ambiguous emotions towards past events and in finding safe outlets for trauma, and thus allowing the reconstruction of individual and collective well-being. We end the chapter with a discussion of the advantages and challenges of the psychosocial intervention in Paredones, and we argue for the importance of considering community resilience in response to natural disasters.

Chile is a country characterised by being constantly hit by natural disasters. One summer night in 2010, the rural district of Paredones was awoken by the shaking and roaring of the earth in an earthquake that reached 9.1 points on the Richter Scale at its epicentre. For nearly three minutes, the residents of the valleys at the foot of the Andes range saw their adobe houses crumbling around them. They tried to take shelter under any solid structure they could find, they ran out into the dark, attempting to avoid collapsing structures, and some, too frail to move, or refusing to leave their frail loved ones behind, prayed and waited for death. By the coast, seasoned fishermen, women and children ran towards the higher land. From there, they saw the sea first recede, and then return to knock down cottages 'like they were matchboxes'. The aftershocks continued for days, weeks and even months following the most destructive natural disaster in Paredones' memory, the second worst nationwide and in the top 10 most violent earthquakes in recorded history. Considering that over 80% of the population of the district are over 65 years old and that they have endured many natural disasters in their lifetimes, the impact of this particular quake was severe. To compound the effects of the quake, the older people of Paredones have experienced material and historical devastation, and are acutely vulnerable due to social conditions such as poverty, isolation, difficulties in accessing health services, low literacy levels and unemployment.

This chapter does not trace material reconstruction in the wake of the earthquake but, rather, the process of retrieving resistance to fear and anxiety from memory and identity, through the reconstruction of individual and collective narratives of resilience. Resilience is here understood as 'a process linking a set of adaptive capacities to a positive trajectory of functioning and adaptation after a disturbance' (Norris et al, 2008, p 130). Following the earthquake and the tsunami of 2010, we conducted interdisciplinary action in Paredones. In response to a request from older adults' organisations in Paredones, we conducted a series of psychosocial interventions to support coping with social instability, fear and anxiety. The interventions were based on principles derived from arts therapy (Kaplan, 2007; Kapitan, 2011), community psychology (Montero, 2000, 2005) and social anthropology (Geertz,

2005; del Valle, 2008). The use of creative tools allowed us to tease out the creative personal and community resources of the older people of Paredones.

Methods

The project was carried out over two years of fieldwork in which we developed an interdisciplinary action-research methodology. The choice of this design strategy came through conversations with leaders and members of older people's organisations of Paredones, in addition to on-going interdisciplinary reflections that developed organically throughout the duration of the project. The advantage of action-research was that the method facilitated the co-construction of knowledge with the community through art-based interventions and memory workshops. In this regard, we adopted a qualitative and participatory approach, which is based on the premise that the social world is built from meanings and symbols. From this perspective, the researcher/facilitator works in a natural context, attempting to know, make sense and interpret the event in relation to the meaning that the participants make of it (Denzin and Lincoln, 1998). When introducing participatory perspectives we included some of the premises of Fals-Borda (1985), who proposes that in every community research project there is an exchange of knowledge between participants and researchers/facilitators, which is constructed through the use and validation of popular culture. Consequently, collective memory is a key element in accessing people's history and traditions through testimonies, archives and popular stories. In addition, the return and dissemination of the knowledge co-constructed with the community was achieved through material objects (for example, books, pamphlets), artistic pieces such as poetry, painting and other forms of expression (Fals-Borda, 1985). The participatory method was complemented with an interdisciplinary approach that emerged from the specialisms of the principal investigators: social anthropology, community psychology and art therapy. We integrated conceptual and theoretical elements from each discipline in order to create a synergy that would benefit the design of fieldwork activities. For instance, we concurred that collective knowledge is a co-construction that is then presented to and validated by the older-people participants. We argue here that creative techniques allow people to engage in much deeper processes of individual and collective understanding.

We conducted five workshops in different locations, reaching approximately 150 older men and women between the ages of 60 and

80. Our participants were members of multiple seniors' organisations of the region. Most participants were in receipt of a small government pension and still worked the land to meet their basic needs, so were considered as socio-economically disadvantaged.

Our methodological strategy comprised of psychosocial workshops to diagnose the effects of disasters on mental health and help people to deal with the fear of aftershocks. Given that the participants all came from different places, the workshops included body exercises to help them to relax and get to know each other. Then they worked in small groups to discuss their experiences of the earthquake and how they had confronted other major natural disasters. The resulting reflection led them to identify their responsive actions and thus their strengths as a community. Another aspect of these workshops was to identify what would they do differently in another similar situation. This reflection stressed the importance of being prepared to face further aftershocks by preparing an emergency kit comprised of medications, clothes and significant objects for them. Each workshop finished with a community activity where participants shared biscuits and tea and sang traditional local folk songs.

The diagnosis stage revealed the need to explore collective memory regarding natural disasters, coping strategies and the vulnerabilities of rural older people. Therefore, we designed 'collective memory' workshops. These workshops consisted of group conversations among the participants where they were asked to talk about their experiences when coping with natural disasters and other stressful events in their lives, both individually and as a community. During the workshops, we were able to identify that most resilience-building memories of the older people of Paredones were connected to the land and their sense of identity as a rural community. In their narratives they spoke about their arrival at the place, their years in the local rural school, how the met their partners, their weddings, the birth of their children and later their grandchildren, as well as the hardships they had endured in this territory.

Closely connected with the memories that surfaced in the memory workshops, we observed the cultural strengths of this community, such as folk music and cultural traditions, which are rooted in the territory. We used this connection to the land to design culturally relevant group interventions for this particular population (Harris, 2009). Thus, we used their stories about the earthquake to create folk songs, poems and traditional dance music. Likewise, we attempted to make visible their affective relationship with the land through the construction of a collective collage that represented their local identity.

We identified the potential of art therapies to externalise experiences, creating symbolic representations of the participants' inner world, thus promoting metaphoric interpersonal forms of communication in a supportive environment (Schaverien, 1999; Marxen, 2009; Reyes, 2014).

Restoring community resilience

An interdisciplinary outlook was fundamental to understanding how multiple dimensions of creativity come into play in psychosocial interventions. At the heart of our project aim was the desire to help individuals to recover from trauma and develop well-being. We also strove to retrieve elements of the local culture and social organisation that could strengthen the resilience of the community not just to these particular natural disasters, but future ones as well. Developing community resilience has been argued to be fundamental to fostering collective positive feelings about the social environment, improving quality of life and helping people to find the energy to rebuild their lives (Norris et al, 2008). In this regard, creativity was not limited to exposure to the arts, but included the use of creative expression and imagination to re-articulate memories of the past, images of the future and perceptions of local identity.

Dealing with trauma through artistic and cultural expression

In our study, following the epistemological framework of art therapies, creativity is understood as a health-promoting resource in its own right (Harris, 2009; American Art Therapy Association, 2017). Evidence indicates that after adverse experiences such as natural disasters survivors can demonstrate resilience in their mental and physical health and avoid developing chronic pathological symptoms (Abeldaño and Fernández, 2016). In this study we understand resilience as the capacity of a person or a group to recover from adverse environments and to continue imagining the future.

Theories of resilience developed by Boris Cyrulnik (2009) highlight art as an approach to support mental health in potentially traumatogenic scenarios, such as disasters. The therapeutic value of using such approaches comes from using the voice of artists or writers. Literary works, films, plays, philosophical essays allow people to avoid speaking about themselves. Cyrulnik calls these narrations 'autobiographies in third person'. Art as a medium for expression is argued by Cyrulnik to be liberating because it eases the effort of sharing with others what has happened, but by tempering the emotions, and it opens the possibility of being accepted as heard by others.

We argue that art therapies support the relevance of the interaction of resilience and creativity during recovery from disaster, and that there are therapeutic advantages from using art as a medium for expressing emotions. Additionally, art therapies sustain the experience of engaging with artistic materials (for example, painting, modelling and collage) and can induce situations where individuals increasingly develop a sense of control and security. Such experiences also allow the restoration of a sense of stability (Shore, 2007).

During our work with older adults, these materials were progressively introduced in a bundle of ludic (playful) and expressive-creative activities that promoted a sense of personal control within a social environment. The workshops were designed to offer safe and pleasant experiences. These comprised a series of physical exercises that promoted body awareness and increased relaxation. Then, ludic-creative activities gradually helped participants to narrate their personal and collective experiences.

In addition, the sharing of popular culture that was relevant to participants was felt to be an important aspect of resilience building. Popular folk music emerged as a strong interest of some of the older people. The knowledge of diverse forms of local expression in

Figure 5.1: Body awareness workshop

popular folk songs helped to identify creative resources held within the community of Paredones. During the initial group workshops we fostered this interest in folk music, and encouraged the creation of sung tales within a playful and reassuring environment. We felt that this artistic medium was particularly effective in facilitating the retrieval of collective memories of previous natural disasters. Performing the songs brought a sense of well-being and bonded group members, providing a sense of security, and therefore marked a step in participants recognising their resilience.

We gradually introduced other expressive techniques into group dynamics, especially visual techniques and plastic artwork, a form of visual art involving the hand-made creation and transformation of pictorial and graphic material. Enabling plastic-visual activities with personal images promoted an accepting environment, a sense of protection and facilitated the flow of emotions. Given the strong attachment to the natural environment and the landscape shown by the older adults, collective creative work was steered towards group discussions about visual representations of the natural environment. Each participant created freestyle plastic artwork in response to the briefing 'describe visually an element of the landscape that is significant to you', and in a second stage they assembled a group image using the collage technique on a wooden structure. Thus, each piece was individual, but using a common theme, and then processed as a group. The creation of collective pieces was intended to encourage mutual support and trust as well as to stimulate creativity.

Each of these activities aimed to fulfil our goals of promoting the collective processing of disaster, offering an alternative to externalise participants' experiences. Creating collective pieces of artwork or song incorporated individual subjective experiences as part of a community response, thereby promoting both personal and community post-disaster recovery.

The land as the foundation of narratives of local identity

Ties with both the land and nature were pivotal to the lifestyles and life experiences of the older people of Paredones. Nature bound together narratives of past and present because, as Ponzetti (2003) has pointed out, older people in rural communities are, first and foremost, attached to the land, and their social environment develops in connection with the natural environment. In Paredones the natural environment was fundamentally important and formed the basis for many narratives created during the workshops; stories about natural disasters were part of a larger narrative revealing shared conceptions of people's local identity (Ricoeur, 1980; Rankin, 2002). Individuals were familiar with nature as a provider of their livelihood, but also as the source of personal and community hardship. The ability of individuals to articulate narratives that mirrored, synthesised and created close analogies between natural events and personal stories was pivotal to individual and collective identities. It was in overcoming hardship – droughts, geographical isolation and material destruction – that these communities built narratives of resistance to natural disasters. Through the creation of these stories, skills were retrieved and resilience was developed. Within the stories, individuals and communities as a whole could be cast as suffering heroes braving the blows of life and nature. Allusions to personal suffering were a common form of validation of the self and proved the moral worth of individuals – life achievements were measured by the number and magnitude of the tragedies participants had endured. Suffering was a marker of legitimacy within a community that the older people of Paredones were proud of belonging to (Derxx, 2013).

> "In this sense, it may be that disasters ... they are almost natural to us, we have even seen tornados, whirlwind, things like such, tsunamis as well, but none like this last one. Everything else is bearable because ... we have all been born in rigour [hardship], so we have become used to suffering like that, others don't." (82-year-old male)

At the same time, the people in Paredones expressed an implicit perception of loneliness and isolation within their own communities. Such perceptions undermined their sense of social cohesion and presented a major hindrance to post-earthquake and tsunami reconstruction:

> "When I was affected [by the earthquake], myself and my youngest son were left homeless, and the eldest almost died in Santiago, I just wanted to die, and I didn't get out during the earthquake, I stayed inside waiting for the house to fall over me. My youngest son took all his family out, and then he remembered me, he came back in the house and carried me outside, but I didn't want to go outside, I didn't want to keep on living [...] Despite all of these things, I try to go around and see to the neighbours' needs, but not just stay there [...] That is why God said, 'help thyself and

> I shall help thee'. That's why one has to help oneself, and not just wait for the Lord's doing. Faith in God and the Virgin strengthen us." (Female speaker, group discussion, age range 63–72 years)

This quote articulates the conflicted perceptions of community cohesion. The woman narrates a story in which she appears on the one hand to be isolated and helpless, but on the other hand as someone compelled to lend a hand to her neighbours. These types of stories, in which the older people of Paredones perceived that their concerns for others were not necessarily reciprocated, were quite common among participants from different locations.

Both themes – bountiful nature and broken communities – were frequently referenced in relation to God. God was viewed by participants as being embedded in nature, and is thus a part of the territory that is central to their past, to their ancestry and to their families. However, in these communities with traditionally tight kinship ties, the dissolution of social capital, lack of trust and personal rivalries was sometimes interpreted as an affront to God himself. He is seen to make his displeasure known in the form of an earthquake:

> "This [the earthquake] must have been something God sent us so we straighten up. God sent us this tremor so we come to agree with him, so we become better believers in God's existence, that's why God sent us this tremor." (69-year-old male)

The use of the word "tremor", in a context where a tremor is known to be far less severe than an earthquake, represents the mimesis between nature, community and the divine. A tremor in Paredones is considered as God's equivalent to a slap on the wrist.

During our intervention in Paredones, we aimed to tease out community strengths. We felt that collage-based techniques were effective in articulating personal narratives of suffering and resilience (Gauntlett and Holzwarth, 2006) in relation to the natural landscape. By using magazine cut-outs and common art supplies such as crayons, pencils and paint in collage making, we also averted possible dis-identification associated with written language-based activities (Cole and Knowles, 2008) among a population where regional illiteracy reached 22.6% at the time of the study (MINSAL, 2009). Each individual was encouraged to portray their personal stories on a sheet of paper. Trained activity monitors interacted with participants

Figure 5.2: Collage workshop

individually in order help with story elicitation, and assisted with composition or actions that required fine motor skills (for example, cutting with scissors) when required.

Afterwards, the landscape was outlined on a large canvas and individuals placed their personal visual stories in the spot on the canvas that felt right to them. Most participants shared an oral account of their stories, giving way to conversations that were felt to be cathartic. As the stories unfolded, monitors and participants also included landscape and weather elements that emphasised or connected aspects of the stories, such as rivers, shadows, trees, clouds and sunshine. The completed picture resulted in a tangible landscape of the communal identity and challenged the initial perceptions of social isolation brought up during the discussion.

The roots of the individual and community narratives of resilience

The methodology developed through the project allowed us to identify the role of memory in creating and maintaining individual and collective identity. Individual identity is constructed in the intersection of familial, social, cultural, ethnic, religious and professional contexts (Kordon and Edelman, 2002). In this sense, acts of remembering and memory are an essential part of our personal lives. Our individual memories are repeatedly re-enacted and collectivised through sharing our memories. Through the construction of collective images, Connerton (1989) argues that perceptions of the community are shaped. As social and cultural beings, we share memories to confirm our experiences and perceptions of the past and to establish and maintain a sense of continuity and social identity (Lowenthal, 1985; Halbwachs, 1992). Among the older people of Paredones, continuity was rooted in history and knowledge passed across generations. This idea is reflected in the following quote:

> "I was born here, my mother was from here. And we have fought, we have worked and we have had children. The first job we had here when we were young was making straw hats. I said that almost all of us made them because our moms taught us … that our work was making hats. I still work making hats." (65-year-old female)

It is through this interplay with the past and with others that we construct a sense of continuity or discontinuity, like in the case of mass trauma. Memories have the power to trigger mechanisms and processes of recognition that allow the individual and the collective to give meaning and purpose to their lives and affirm their identities (Lowenthal, 1985; Rüsen, 1989; Lira, 1997). In this regard, Pierre Nora (1989) asserts that the need for identity is also a driving force for the individual. The 'law of remembrance' has great coercive force for the individual; the discovery of roots of 'belonging' to some groups becomes a source of identity and therefore belonging becomes a true commitment (Nora, 1989, p 11). The earthquake experience led to reinforcement of the sense of belonging and community commitment among the older people of Paredones, as shown in the following quotation:

> "The neighbours are very important; that is why it was so terrible when I went to my daughter's house. She would tell me don't cry mom, go for a walk. And I would tell her what I am going to go out for. If you are lucky people say hello to you. … Instead, here if you go out you talk to everybody, because everybody knows you, everybody talks to you, and everybody asks how you are doing." (75-year-old female)

The process that unfolded for the participants throughout the intervention process also included a creative component that reinforced their sense of belonging and commitment to their territory. In this way, artistic activity brought about a combination of conscious and unconscious desires and affect in workshop participants, which were often accompanied by conflicting feelings about themselves, their community, their families and the recent and distant past. Creating the artwork appeared to provide the stimulus to merge these different desires. The final artwork not only reflected individuals' inner conflicts but also communicated these to the professional and community group members. Therefore, we argue that, by understanding the therapeutic potential of artistic creation, both artist and spectator could potentially identify, work through and resolve their unconscious conflicts. Moreover, Vygotsky (1990) proposes that, given that art is an expression of human feelings and passions, these are embodied in the content of the artistic work. Hence in transforming materials, colours and textures to express feelings, these feelings and passions are transformed as well.

Discussion and conclusions

The results revealed that the construction of individual and collective narratives of resilience (Epston, White and Murray, 1996) increased older people's awareness of the strengths they have as a community. The memory workshops allowed participants to reflect on, and share, their previous experiences when confronting past disasters or community crises. Thus, these interventions were a tool that helped them to identify their strength as a community. This is particularly important, considering that they are a vulnerable group experiencing economic hardship in a rural context.

Likewise, symbolising their emotions through creating music and collages allowed participants to collectively resignify their fear of the earthquake. In this way participants transformed the meanings given to the disaster and simultaneously validated their own spontaneous responses to natural disasters or community crises (Johnson and Sullivan-Marx, 2006; Marxen, 2011). In addition, the intervention process mobilised older people's sense of local identity (Ponzetti, 2003) by providing the opportunity to communicate shared conceptions of the landscape. Both types of interventions, the memory- and arts-based workshops, allowed these communities of older people to search their own individual and community narratives of resilience, which seemed to have a positive impact on how they intended to confront future uncertainty. A key element in the success of the project was that its scope expanded beyond the recent earthquake and tsunami and adopted a biographical and cultural outlook that delved into individual and collective images of present, past and future in search of resilience-reinforcing capacities. From our perspective as researchers/facilitators, the challenge was to adapt strategies that were consistent with the community work we were engaged in. This explains the decision to align our work with the principles of participatory action-research. Likewise, we were able to apply our disciplinary knowledge in the context of the fieldwork we were conducting, away from the more theoretical academic environment.

There were several lessons learned from our experience, which could contribute to designing similar interventions in future disaster contexts for older adult populations. This research revealed the challenges of dealing with the expectations of the leaders of organisations, who acted as informants about the needs of the group. Although the presence of strong leadership within the community initially facilitated access to participants, the interactions between the leaders, their organisations and what was expected of our team were not always clear. These interactions demanded that we use conflict resolution skills in order to resolve these impasses. The geographical isolation of some of the participating villages impeded smooth communication with the communities in the early stages. The communicational hiccups at times affected logistics in terms of conducting the workshops.

During the two-year duration of the project relationships with the community were strengthened through regular and consistent communication strategies. These strategies included maintaining regular visits, phone calls, message relaying and coordination with the community leaders, as well regular meetings with these leaders. In time, communications became smoother and expectations on both sides were more clearly defined. The project finished with a community activity that included all the participants involved, the research team, and also the local authorities and the wider community. Ending our presence in Paredones with a festive and inclusive tone was important, as it represented the transition of the community from one disrupted by disaster to one that was more recovered and energised. We also took the opportunity to return the outputs produced during the intervention, such as presentations, evaluations and a video of the entire process, to the group.

We argue that reconstructing people's own sense of resilience through such interventions is fundamental in facilitating psychosocial reconstruction strategies in post-disaster situations. Consequently, community resilience-strengthening strategies must be included early in emergency response planning. This interdisciplinary action-research project using creative interventions promoted a dialogical relationship where the local knowledge of older people was used to design strategies of resistance to natural disasters (Mileti, 1999; Geis, 2000; McEntire, Gilmore Crocker and Peters, 2010), while also taking advantage of the disciplinary knowledge of the researchers (Fals-Borda, 1985). In this sense, the collective creative process that unfolded has proved to be effective in preparing people for the psychosocial reconstruction of their homes, communities and territories.

Funding

This work was conducted in the context of the 2010 Project, SOC 10/24–2 VID, Natural Disasters, Resistance and Vulnerability from Local Identity and Collective Memory in Older Adults in the Commune of Paredones, funded by the Vice Rectorate of Research and Development of the University of Chile. It was also supported by the Valentin Letelier Outreach Fund 2010, Post Earthquake and Tsunami Support for the Reconstruction in the Commune of Paredones: Organizational, Psychosocial and Health Intervention in Children and Older People, funded by the Vice Rectorate of University Extension of the University of Chile.

References

Abeldaño, R.A. and Fernández, R. (2016) 'Community mental health in disaster situations. A review of community-based models of approach review', *Ciência & Saúde Coletiva*, 21(2): 431–42.

American Art Therapy Association (2017) *About Art Therapy*. Available at: https://arttherapy.org/about-art-therapy/.

Cole, A.L. and Knowles, J.G. (2008) 'Arts-Informed Research', in J.G. Knowles and A.L. Cole (eds) *Handbook of the arts in qualitative research : perspectives, methodologies, examples, and issues*, Los Angeles: SAGE Publications, pp 55–70.

Connerton, P. (1989) *How societies remember*, New York: Cambridge University Press.

Cyrulnik, B. (2009) 'Vencer el trauma por el arte [Defeating trauma through art]', *Cuadernos de Pedagogía*, pp 42–7.

del Valle, T. (2008) 'Los intersticios en el eje de una mirada etnográfica al espacio', in E. Imaz (ed) *La materialidad de la identidad*, San Sebastián: Hariadna Editoriala, pp 21–40.

Denzin, N. and Lincoln, Y.S. (1998) 'Introduction: Entering the field of qualitative research', in N. Denzin and Y.S. Lincoln (eds) *The landscape of qualitative research. Theories and issues*, Thousand Oaks, CA: Sage, pp 1–33.

Derxx, P. (2013) 'Humanism as a meaning frame', in A.B. Pinn (ed) *What is humanism and why does it matter?* Durham, UK: Acumen, pp 194ff.

Epston, D., White, M. and Murray, K. (1996) 'Una propuesta para re-escribir la terapia. Rose: La revisión de su vida y un comentario. [A proposal to re-write therapy. Rose: The review of her life and a commentary].', in S. McNamee and K. Gergen (eds) *La terapia como construcción social [Therapy as social construction]*, Barcelona: Paidos, pp 121–41.

Fals-Borda, O. (1985) *Conocimiento y poder popular: Lecciones con campesinos en Nicaragua, México y Colombia* [Knowledge and popular power: lessons with peasants in Nicaragua, Mexico y Colombia], Bogotá: Siglo XXI.

Forsman, A.K., Schierenbeck, I. and Wahlbeck, K. (2011) 'Psychosocial interventions for the prevention of depression in older adults: Systematic review and meta-analysis', *Journal of Aging and Health*, 23(3): 387–416.

Gauntlett, D. and Holzwarth, P. (2006) 'Creative and visual methods for exploring identities', *Visual Studies*, 21(1): 82–91.

Geertz, C. (2005) *La interpretación de las culturas [The interpretation of cultures]*, Barcelona: Gedisa.

Geis, D.E. (2000) 'By Design: The Disaster Resistant and Quality-of-Life Community', *Natural Hazards Review*, 1(3): 151–60.

Halbwachs, M. (1992) *On collective memory*, Chicago: University of Chicago Press.

Harris, D.A. (2009) 'The paradox of expressing speechless terror: Ritual liminality in the creative arts therapies' treatment of posttraumatic distress', *Arts in Psychotherapy*, 36(2): 94–104.

Johnson, C.M. and Sullivan-Marx, E.M. (2006) 'Process for Healing and Hope', *Geriatic Nursing*, 27(5): 309–16.

Kapitan, L. (2011) 'Testimonio Creativo de nuestro tiempo: Arteterapia y acción social comunitaria [Creative testimony of our time: Art-therapies and community action]', in M. Marincovic and P. Reyes (eds) *Arteterapia, reflexiones y experiencias para un campo profesional*, Santiago de Chile: Editorial TEHA. Facultad de Artes. Universidad de Chile., pp 61–71.

Kaplan, F. (ed) (2007) *Art Therapy and social action*, London, UK: Jessica Kingsley Publishers.

Kordon, D. and Edelman, L. (2002) 'Impacto psíquico y transmisión inter y transgeneracional en situaciones traumáticas de origen social [Psychic impact and inter and transgenerational transmission on traumatic situations of social origin]', in L. Edelman, D. Kordon, D. Lagos and D. Kernsner (eds) *Paisajes del dolor, denderos de esperanza. Salud mental y derechos humanos en el cono sur*, Buenos Aires: CINTRAS, EATIP, GTNM/RJ, SERSOC Editores.

Lira, E. (ed) (1997) *Reparación, derechos humanos y salud mental [Reparation, human rights and mental health]*, Santiago: Ediciones CESOC.

Lowenthal, D. (1985) *The past is foreign country*, Cambridge: Cambridge University Press.

Marxen, E. (2009) 'La etnografía desde el arte. Definiciones, bases teóricas y nuevos escenarios [Ethnography from art. Definitions, theories and new sceneries]', *Alteridades*, 19(37): 7–22.

Marxen, E. (2011) 'Pain and knowledge: Artistic expression and the transformation of pain', *Arts in Psychotherapy*, Elsevier Ltd, 38(4): 239–46.

McEntire, D., Gilmore Crocker, C. and Peters, E. (2010) 'Addressing vulnerability through an integrated approach', *International Journal of Disaster Resilience in the Built Environment*, 1(1): 50–64.

Mileti, D.S. (1999) 'Disasters by design', in N.R. Britton (ed) *The changing risk landscape: Implications for insurance risk management*, Sydney, Australia: Aon Group Australia Limited.

MINSAL (2009) *Contribuyendo a mejorar nuestra calidad de vida. Plan Comunas Vulnerables Región de O'Higgins [Contributing to improve our quality of life. Plan for vulnerable districts O'Higgins Region]*.

Montero, M. (2000) 'Participation in participatory action research', *Annual Review of Critical Psychology*, 2: 131–43.

Montero, M. (2005) *Teoría y práctica de la psicología comunitaria. La tensión entre comunidad y sociedad [Theory and practice of community psychology. The tension between community and society]*, Buenos Aires: Editorial Paidós.

Nora, P. (1989) *Between memory and history: Rethinking the French past, Vol. 1*, New York: Columbia University Press.

Norris, F.H., Stevens, S.P., Pfefferbaum, B., Wyche, K.F. and Pfefferbaum, R.L. (2008) 'Community resilience as a metaphor, theory, set of capacities, and strategy for disaster readiness', *American Journal of Community Psychology*, 41(1–2): 127–50.

Ponzetti, J.J.J. (2003) 'Growing old in rural communities: A visual methodology for studying place attachment', *Journal of Rural Community Psychology*, 6(1): 1–11.

Rankin, J. (2002) 'What is narrative? Ricoeur, Bakhtin, and process approaches', *Concrescence: The Australasian Journal of Process Thought*, 3: 1–12.

Reyes, P. (2014) 'Arte, salud y comunidad: 1992–2012. Una perspectiva autoetnográfica [Art, health and community: 1992–2012. An autoethnographic perspective]', *ATOL Arte therapy online*, 5(1). Available at: http://journals.gold.ac.uk/index.php/atol/article/view/351/381.

Ricoeur, P. (1980) 'Narrative time', *Critical Inquiry*, 7(1): 169–90.

Rüsen, J. (1989) 'The development of narrative competence in historical learning – as ontogenetic hypothesis concerning moral consciousness', *History and Memory: Studies in Representations of the Past*, 1(2): 35–59.

Schaverien, J. (1999) *The revealing image: Analytical art psychotherapy*, London: Jessica Kingsley.

Shore, A. (2007) 'Some personal and clinical thoughts about trauma, art, and world events', in F. Kaplan (ed) *Art therapy and social action*, London: Jessica Kingsley, pp 272ff.

Vygotsky, L. (1990) *Psicología del arte [Psychology of art]*, edited by B. Editores, Barcelona.

SIX

Integrating sense of place within new housing developments: a community-based participatory research approach

Mei Lan Fang, Judith Sixsmith, Ryan Woolrych,
Sarah L. Canham, Lupin Battersby, Tori Hui Ren
and Andrew Sixsmith

Editorial introduction

This chapter presents work from a Canadian project exploring the potential of community-based participatory research for drawing out how communities play a role in resilient ageing. The project used creative approaches as part of the research method rather than as the subject of the study. The chapter focuses on the importance of place and the authors helpfully explore the nuances of 'place'. This common interest in community resilience, ageing and place is one of the features that draw Chapters Five, Six and Seven together. Another is the action-oriented nature of the research. The research discussed here, much like Chapter Seven, was intended both to explore the views of older people in the community and, through that, to give those people a voice in local processes of housing development.

Introduction

This chapter critically explores the potential of an action-oriented, community-based participatory research (CBPR) approach to reveal ways in which communities can be resilient to the opportunities and challenges of ageing-in-place. In particular, the chapter considers the potential for using qualitative and creative methods to bring distinct viewpoints of local community stakeholders to the fore in terms of embedding aspects of place into the development of affordable housing for older adults. Community resilience refers here to the 'existence, development and engagement of community resources by community members to thrive in an environment characterized by change, uncertainty, unpredictability and surprise' (Magis, 2010, p 401). This is particularly important in the context of supporting ageing-in-place, where living in resilient communities can provide opportunities for civic participation, remaining active and sustaining community identity (Woolrych, 2017). Within the field of urban studies, there has been a shift towards a more transdisciplinary appreciation for community resilience, which combines the physical and psychosocial aspects of urban resilience (Coaffee, 2008). As such, the affordances of physical space play a role in supporting or constraining community resilience, particularly for older adults who may rely on the immediate neighbourhood for service supports and maintaining social roles (Hildon et al, 2009). This is important both in terms of the everyday life of the community and in responding to the challenges and opportunities of old age. As Dainty and Bosher (2008, p 357) have suggested, 'a resilient built environment should be designed, located, built, operated and maintained in a way that maximises the ability of built assets, associated support systems (physical and institutional) and the people that reside or work within the built assets' to withstand, recover from and mitigate societal challenges.

The affordable housing redevelopment project, based in the City of Richmond, British Columbia, Canada, centred on the demolition of an existing low-rise block of housing units, which were replaced with the construction of a new housing development for older adults. For the redevelopment process, the research team were invited by the City of Richmond in British Columbia as community partners to:

1. capture sense of place as experienced by older people transitioning into an affordable housing development;
2. understand the lived experiences of older adults to inform the provision and programming of effective formal and informal supports within the development; and
3. develop practical guidelines and recommendations for supporting the place-based needs of older adults.

Research conducted alongside the project presented a unique opportunity, through the application of a CBPR approach (described later), to inquire into, understand and document nuanced meanings of place, identity, attachment to and detachment from place from the perspective of a sample of low-income, older adults comprising a unique cultural mix (70% Chinese and 30% European). The research spanned a three-year period and involved collaboration between academics, older adults, city government and community organisations. Community resilience, which enabled and enhanced shared solutions between multiple stakeholder groups, was found to help older adults transition and age well in their new homes.

Older people and 'a sense of place'

Research has explored the often complex and multifaceted relationship between individuals and their immediate environment and revealed a person–place dynamic where place acts as a strong determinant of individual, social and community well-being (Relph, 1976; Tuan, 1977; Proshansky, Fabian and Kaminoff, 1983; Sixsmith, 1986; Twigger-Ross and Uzzell, 1996; Devine-Wright and Lyons, 1997; Dixon and Durrheim, 2000). According to Relph (1976, p 61), formulation of 'place is comprised of three inter-related components, each irreducible to the other – physical features or appearances, observable activities and functions and meanings or symbols'. Such components are directed by our visual senses and cognitive processes. They have been argued to capture our emotions and generate meaningful linkages to place (Relph, 1976). Canter (1977) builds on Relph's phenomenological conceptualisation of place by focusing more clearly on the linkage between the three features, emphasising, from a psychology perspective, the built features and individual conceptualisations of place as well as the activities that occur there.

Alongside this understanding of place, and of particular relevance from a gerontological perspective, is the notion that as people age, the number of place experiences accumulate and, as such, various memories of home and community become important (Oswald and Wahl, 2003). Environmental studies of older adults place particular importance on sense of place, as older people depend upon close social and community ties to place and are sensitive to immediate changes to their home and community environment (Phillips et al, 2012). Establishing home and community belonging are key factors in creating the most favourable environmental conditions for older adults to live out their lives (Sixsmith and Sixsmith, 1991). However, a substantial number of older adults experience dislocation of place (Sixsmith et al, in press). Dislocation of place can occur through both voluntary and forced relocations in old age (for example, to more institutional forms of living or moving to alternative neighbourhoods), which can be driven by urban changes, including gentrification and urban renewal (Walks and Maaranen, 2008; Woolrych and Sixsmith, in press). The process of displacement can negatively impact on older adults with limited financial means, casting a shadow on dominant over-positive notions of 'ageing in place' (Sixsmith and Sixsmith, 2008; Golant, 2015; Sixsmith et al, 2017). This problematises the simple assumption that ageing in place is an inherently good thing and draws attention to Golant's (2015) notion of ageing in *the right* place by ensuring that the necessary supports and resources are in place. Yet, through community resilience, individuals who are displaced can regain their agency through the process of negotiating, managing and adapting to change.

Evoking 'a sense of place' in research and service provision

To understand sense of place for older adults, it is important to acknowledge that sense of place is not necessarily a stable experiential state and that it can change depending on the different experiences people have in places (Williams, 2014). Accordingly, it is necessary to explore how older adults' place experiences can shift and change, giving rise to new and different perspectives and different experiences of place. The research team took the position that an over-reliance on traditional research techniques conducted in isolation (for example, surveys, face-to-face interviews and focus groups) can create limitations in understanding the social and relational aspects of place, since they each limit the data in specific ways. Both focus groups and face-to-face interviews are strongly dependent on older people's confidence, comfort with being interviewed and verbal communication skills. In addition, they can overly prioritise researcher preconceptions in the pre-design of the data-collection schedule as well as the way the research is conducted (Anyan, 2013). Nevertheless, interviews and focus groups can generate rich, contextual information about the topic area. Often undertaken face-to-face in a single location (for example, home, office, community centre), these methods alone may not always generate the necessary insights from older marginalised people, such as important memories of place and/or objects of importance. Such memories may be accessible through more creative, participant-led methods, such as storytelling, photovoice and community 'walk-alongs' (Carpiano, 2009). Application of multiple research methods also enables triangulation, a process that can strengthen the depth of information gathered (Guion, Diehl and McDonald, 2011). Triangulation prioritises in-depth understanding of a problem area by acquiring knowledge from different standpoints, which in turn enables the development of solutions that are holistic and multifaceted (Farmer et al, 2006).

Meanwhile, local community stakeholders, such as older adults and non-profit service providers, who are often invited to vocalise their knowledge during redevelopment phases, are absent from the decision-making process (Woolrych and Sixsmith, 2013). As such, a CBPR approach was selected as a guiding framework to ensure equity among partners. In this chapter, we first outline the principles of CBPR and its importance as a guiding framework for the research and redevelopment process, particularly when determining the most effective and engaging research methods; and second, we demonstrate the purpose, applicability and combined use of five qualitative methods carefully selected for generating nuanced information about older adults' specific needs, desires and expectations when transitioning into new housing.

CBPR: a guiding framework for collaborative research

Community-based participatory research (CBPR) has become a popular approach across academic disciplines, government and non-government sectors and other philanthropic domains (Minkler and Wallerstein, 2008; Jagosh et al, 2015). This collaborative approach promotes the reciprocal transfer of knowledge and expertise; inclusive participation; power sharing and equity; and data ownership across all partners (Jones and Wells, 2007).

To prioritise the perspectives of older adults, CBPR was selected for our research, principally, to provide older adults with the space and platform to share their experiences. Achieving genuine involvement of local older adults as active decision makers and knowledge experts required a conscious shift from the notion of developing urban places *for* older people to building meaningful environments *with* and *by* older people (Buffel, Phillipson and Scharf, 2012). This approach enabled effective, collaborative dialogue between resident, professional and academic communities (Fang et al, 2016; Sixsmith et al, 2017; Canham et al, 2017). Together, local researchers, community stakeholders (for example, older adults and service providers) and professionals with a vested interest in an affordable housing redevelopment project (for example, housing providers, service providers, developers and the municipal government) asserted community resilience through the formulation of equitable partnerships to co-create action-oriented research (Sixsmith et al, 2017) with the shared goal of improving community health and social outcomes and knowledge production and exchange (Minkler and Wallerstein, 2008; Jagosh et al, 2015).

It is important to establish, at the outset of a CBPR project, a set of priorities that emphasise the presence of older adults during the research and development process. Older people's viewpoints need to be taken into account during the research planning, development and implementation phases in order to empower them to voice their desires, needs and expectations for determining place initiatives in their community (Davitt et al, 2015). As such, a conceptual model integrating principles of CBPR (Figure 6.1) evolved during the research to:

1. establish a process for equitable decision making among multiple stakeholders with shared and, at times, varied aims, objectives and goals;
2. direct the selection of interactive methods that prioritised community engagement and local knowledge; and
3. generate creative and sustainable solutions that were relevant to the needs of older adults utilising resources available from the local community.

The conceptual model described in Figure 6.1 depicts, at a fundamental level, the shared vision of this action research: to create a healthy, sustainable living environment for low-income older adults who are transitioning into a newly developed 16-storey affordable housing development. This underlying vision is associated with Golant's (2015) idea of positive ageing in the right place, which argues that positive ageing experiences are not solely determined by *a place* for older adults, but are dependent upon the appropriate environmental and social conditions for creating the *right place* for older adults to age well (for example, necessary financial supports, opportunities for social participation, accessible health and social services, age-specific built features in the home, green spaces, and policies to ensure safety and security).

Accordingly, several key elements were identified in the conceptual model to ensure that research outcomes coincided with the needs of older adults. First, to facilitate collaborative working and equitable partnerships it was important that we established collective thought with the shared intent of achieving 'real-world' impact (Boger et al, 2016). This required collective team decision making at the outset to establish the aims and objectives of the project, which were based on identified shared interests and goals (for example, creating spaces

Figure 6.1: Conceptual framework for an inclusive, participatory redevelopment strategy for seniors transitioning into new housing

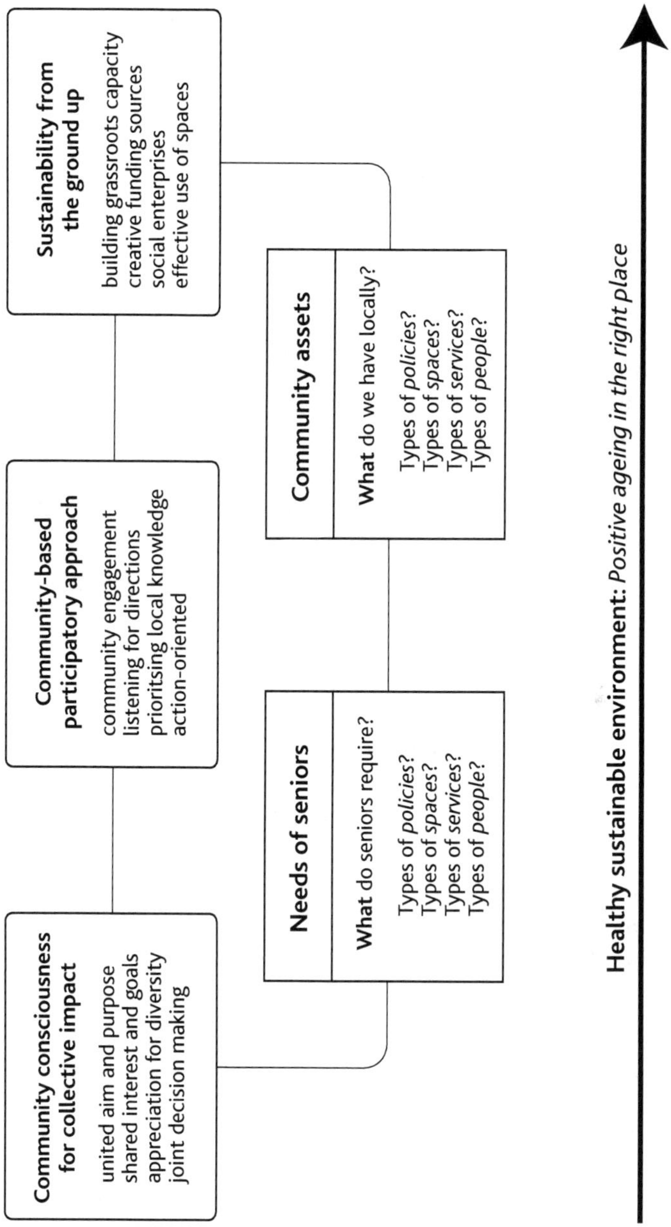

Community consciousness for collective impact
- united aim and purpose
- shared interest and goals
- appreciation for diversity
- joint decision making

Community-based participatory approach
- community engagement
- listening for directions
- prioritsing local knowledge
- action-oriented

Sustainability from the ground up
- building grassroots capacity
- creative funding sources
- social enterprises
- effective use of spaces

Needs of seniors

What do seniors require?

Types of *policies*?
Types of *spaces*?
Types of *services*?
Types of *people*?

Community assets

What do we have locally?

Types of *policies*?
Types of *spaces*?
Types of *services*?
Types of *people*?

Healthy sustainable environment: *Positive ageing in the right place*

for brainstorming, discussion and debate), appreciation for diverse expertise and knowledge bases (for example, ensuring multiple stakeholders are given a voice), and having systems in place for joint decision making (for example, mechanisms for eliciting input from hard-to-reach older adults; protocols for sharing research findings; and generating input to and from local leaders and experts). Second, the methods had to be grounded in participatory concepts such as community engagement, prioritisation of local knowledge and action-oriented solutions. These methods needed to be carefully selected and implemented by project investigators with sufficient training in and experience of conducting CBPR, with combined expertise in urban studies and gerontology. Third, this model is based on the recognition that long-term resilience can often be achieved through building community capacity and implementing creative solutions to address complex problems. As a result, team members worked together with community partners (for example, developer, building management, non-profit housing association and municipal government) to develop creative ideas for acquiring funding sources for activities for older tenants (for example, hosting learning tours in the new building for international scholars and professionals) and to develop engaging community environments for older tenants (for example, establishing a tenant-led social events committee).

In terms of analysis, all narrative (for example, in-depth interview, storytelling) and discussion (for example, deliberative dialogue) data was transcribed and analysed thematically via HyperResearch 3.7.2 or QSR NVivo 10 and coded and categorised using a structured framework approach (Gale et al, 2013). Where possible, visual data was co-analysed with participants through discussion generated by jointly reflecting on the captured images (Pink, 2013).

Ethical approval was obtained from the Office of Research Ethics at Simon Fraser University, Canada, for which informed consent was obtained from all participants whose privacy and confidentiality were protected.

Applying multiple qualitative methods to prioritise marginalised place perspectives

To embed CBPR principles in the research process, specific creative and qualitative methods (highlighted in Table 6.1) were selected and applied in combination, including: narrative inquiry techniques (including storytelling), photovoice, and participatory mapping.

Table 6.1: Purpose and use implications of the five qualitative methods selected for the study

Method	Population(s)	Key characteristics	Purpose	Use implication(s)
In-depth interviews	Older adults transitioning into affordable housing	Narrative method; open-ended questions; semi-structured; led by researcher to seek understanding and interpretation; often audio-recorded or video-recorded	Applied as a 'discovery-oriented' approach to obtain rich background stories of tenants	Elicited depth of contextual information from relatively few participants
Storytelling	Older adults transitioning into affordable housing	Narrative method; unstructured; led by participant to reveal and inspire understandings about a particular topic or phenomenon in relation to self while simultaneously providing important, in-depth information to the researcher; often audio-recorded or video-recorded	To acquire richer and more complex understandings, triggering memories that reveal people's emotional ties to place	Generated richer contextual information from relatively fewer participants than in-depth interviews, while simultaneously enabling the participant to reveal understandings of self
Deliberative dialogue	Stakeholders with vested interest in the redevelopment project	Involves multiple stakeholder participants; shared platform; informal; encourages ideas exchange; requires generation of actionable tasks at the end of the dialogue session	To facilitate co-creation of solutions through the exchange of diverse perspectives from multiple stakeholders	Enabled multiple stakeholders to work together with researchers to generate ideas and future directions for developing supportive home environments for older adults
Photovoice	Older adults transitioning into affordable housing	Visual method; participant led; informal; uses photography to explore personal experiences of a particular phenomenon	To empower older adults to share stories of place though a creative outlet	Enabled older adults to capture, or direct the taking of, photographic images to illustrate their everyday experiences
Participatory mapping	Older adults transitioning into affordable housing and stakeholders with vested interest in the redevelopment project	Visual method; multiple stakeholders; participant led; map making; community 'walk-alongs'; informal	To identify locally available services and resources and pinpoint service and resource gaps through community 'walk-alongs' and mapping exercises	Enabled the researchers to access older people's attitudes and their expert knowledge, to understand the types of relationships participants had with their community and created networking space for engagement and generating shared solutions

Because the participants were of Chinese or European heritage, two researchers who were fluent in Mandarin, Cantonese and English led the data collection process. This comprised 25 in-depth interviews with older adults; 16 photovoice sessions with older adults; 15 storytelling sessions with older adults; four deliberative dialogue workshops with building management, local service providers, members of the municipal government and members of the building development team and four participatory mapping workshops with older adults, local service providers, building management and members of the municipal government. In the following section, we demonstrate how the combined application of these innovative methods enabled older adults to share their lived experiences.

Narrative inquiry: storytelling and in-depth interviews

Storytelling and in-depth interviews are methods of narrative inquiry that can be used to acquire deep understandings of self and the relationships of individuals to their immediate environment (Polkinghorne, 1988; Bruner, 1990). Place scholars (Relph, 1976; Tuan, 1991) have explored the holistic nature of 'being-in-place' by collecting narratives on how people construct their sense of self through attributing and attaching meanings to place. The storytelling method is unstructured and often led by the participant (as opposed to the researcher). It has been argued that this method can enable participants to link together multiple meanings and identities associated with a particular place (Taylor, 2003). As such, in-depth interviews were applied as a 'discovery-oriented' approach (Guion et al, 2011) in order to elucidate the tenants' experiences throughout the phases of redevelopment. Concentrating on different places where residents had lived throughout the redevelopment process helped to shape the structure of storytelling sessions.

For instance, prior to the move, many of the older adults agreed with the sentiment of one participant who described having "been shuffled around here, there and everywhere". One of the main difficulties revealed by older-adult participants was the relocation process. Finding a new home and all the associated tasks is challenging for most people, but can be particularly so for older adults with limited financial resources. This can lead to heightened stress, anxiety and poor mental and physical health outcomes. Due to the nature of the redevelopment process, older-adult participants were required to find temporary accommodation for three years while the new building was under development. According to some older-adult participants, this had an impact on their ability to establish new social networks and relationships. One individual stressed that it can be challenging to "get out into the community" and that "it takes a lot of work to make friends" so they did not "want to have to do it twice". Transient dwellings impinged on some older-adult participants' ability to firmly adjust and re-establish themselves in the community where they lived during the transition period. Through interview data it was established that the notion of home is much more than just a physical space and shelter; that home is also about community faces and places. Making new friends, finding useful service locations (for example, grocery stores, pharmacies, family doctor) and establishing social support takes time and effort, which can be rewarding, yet also daunting and stressful. Temporary living spaces were considered by many participants to not be homes, but rather as transient dwellings.

Accordingly, in place research, narratives can provide participants and researchers with the opportunity to share and acquire rich and more complex understandings of participants' experiences, creating new perspectives and knowledge (Keats, 2009). Of importance to this study was the acknowledgement that an individuals' place experiences are complicated by the interlocking or intersection of the social positions they hold and the social factors that shape their everyday lives; that is, an interweaving of multiple systems of oppression (Collins, 2000) and opportunity. How such systems are organised through interrelated domains of power and what this means for the ways in which their lives can be lived is of critical importance in understanding how and why particular places are experienced in the way they are. As such, an intersectional analysis (Hankivsky and Christoffersen, 2008) was included as part of the study design so as to provide a better understanding of how experiences of oppression and opportunity across place and time are influenced by a person's position and social identity. Storytelling, a method that uses a reflexive approach, facilitates inquiry into a person's life story without having to use language that is difficult for a participant to comprehend. For instance, instead of 'Tell me about your social position(s) in society', we asked the participant to 'Take us to a time and place when you were the most happy, or felt the most challenged'. This technique enabled a conversation that naturally drew out the information that we aimed to acquire. Simultaneously, it offered older adults a means of sharing their stories and triggered experiences that highlighted participants' emotional ties to place and observations of their physical surroundings. Also, further ideas were generated through a two-way process of storytelling that involved mutual recognition of experiences and situations. In this way, the researchers exchanged stories that touched on their own lives, creating a sense of reciprocity and inspiring new ideas to emerge.

Table 6.2 presents a summary of data analysis from a storytelling session with one older-adult participant, outlining at three different significant 'place time points' the individual's social identity, position in society, opportunities, oppressive experiences and local place environments.

The study of narrative information in Table 6.2 revealed important aspects of combined social identities (for example, Chinese, widower,

Table 6.2: Data analysis matrix of information captured through a storytelling session with an older-adult participant

Identity	Positionality	Opportunities
Time point 1: Mainland China		
• Chinese • Student	• Having work • Married • Living with partner • Wealthy in-laws	• Education
Time point 2: Hong Kong		
• Widower • Chinese • Housewife • Mother	• Married	• None identified
Time point 3: Canada		
• Hospitable • Consumer • Unwasteful • Prudent • Indonesian • Immigrant • Older person • Carer • Grandparent • Chinese • Canadian citizen • Dual national identities • Ordinary or common • Not a gossip • Quiet • Reader • Mother	• Living alone • Has a social support network • Poor • Middle class • Debilitated	• Establishing ownership • Place affordance • Higher powers • Self-care • Convenience • Social welfare system • Place freedom • Having more space • Engaging with cultures different than your own • Appreciating other cultural norms • Living in a democratic society

grandparent) and positionalities (for example, wealthy in-laws, married, poor) reflecting oppressions (for example, Cultural Revolution, living in small spaces, lack of mobility) and opportunities (for example, education, place freedom) experienced at three key time points in different places and national homes (Mainland China, Hong Kong, Canada).

In line with previous research (Caine, 2010), the application of combined narrative methods enabled – as compared to single data collection methods – more comprehensive understandings of the place experiences of older adults through a three-dimensional inquiry

Oppression	Places
• Place restrictions • Cultural revolution	• School
• Overcrowded • Uncomfortable weather • Oppressive political culture • Living in small spaces	• Apartment • City
• Being unwell • Reliance on others • Getting old • Lack of or restricted place agency • Fear and shame of being burdensome • Moving homes • Transient places • Lack of mobility • Stolen or wasted time • Self-care • Experiencing urban development • Social and cultural shift • Carer responsibilities • Limited employment opportunities • Agentic limitations by circumstance • Place restrictions • Ageism • Language barrier • Negative experiences with different cultural groups • Inappropriate window blinds let in too much light • Enduring cigarette smoke • Lack of knowledge and understanding of technology	• New building • Long-term care home • Hospital • Supermarket • Chinatown (area of the city) • Church

that included time, space and relationality. Narratives consisting of rich descriptions facilitated the discovery of participants' relocation experiences. The stories of older adults helped to depict the physical attributes of place and the intimacies of place over time by revealing the socio-spatial (for example, identities, positionalities) and relational aspects, as well as oppressions and opportunities experienced in the different communities.

Visualising place through photovoice

Narrative data was complemented by visual imagery in order to identify the ambiguities and complexities of the intersecting social factors that impacted on the everyday lives of the older adults. As our research required in-depth understandings of key place moments, photovoice was used. Photovoice is a visual method (Wang and Burris, 1997) grounded in qualitative participatory research principles used to explore personal experiences of a particular phenomenon (Nowell et al, 2006), in this case personal experiences of place. It has been used to facilitate community engagement while simultaneously producing powerful images that have the potential to influence policy agendas in the areas of public health, education and social work (Catalani and Minkler, 2010). This visual technique not only provided participants with a creative activity to engage with, but also helped to generate important conversation pieces.

During the photovoice sessions conducted in this research, older adults took or directed the taking of photographs to illustrate their everyday experiences. The images were used to stimulate conversations with researchers where themes and potential actions were identified. For older-adult participants, photovoice provided an avenue to visually portray experiences and share and discuss personal knowledge about issues that may be difficult to express through words alone. For example, through visual imagery and personal narrative, one participant was able to describe the importance of Christianity not only as a religion, but as part of her everyday spiritual and social life. Figure 6.2 shows the participant's Bible, translated into Chinese characters.

During data analysis, this photograph, paired with the participant's narrative, enabled a deeper understanding of her sense of place. As she showed us her Bible, this participant revealed how religion and religious activities were central to her daily routine:

> "Everyday I get up and cook breakfast for myself. After eating, I read Bible and pray. In the afternoon I watch the

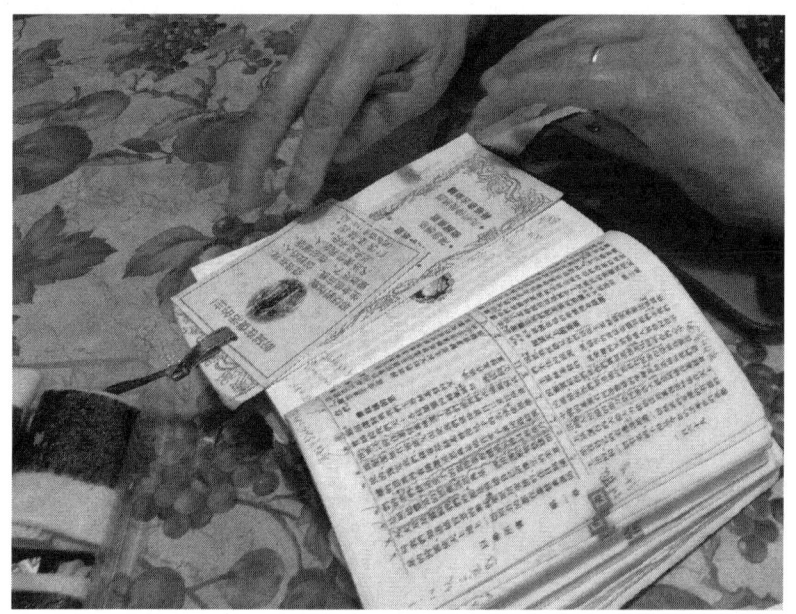

Figure 6.2: An older-adult participant shows her Bible

Hong Kong news and then I read Bible again and go to bed at 9:00pm. Tuesdays every week, I go to church for a group activity and Saturdays I attend another group activity for older adults at church."

Through this creative process, participants were able to direct and communicate understandings of their everyday realities and the specific meanings and significance they attached to place.

Photovoice was a particularly useful tool for this study as it empowered older people to share stories of place though creative and collaborative photo-taking, self-reflection and joint analysis. When supplementing the narratives of older adults, the photographs provided 'additional stimulus to the participant(s)' (Nowell et al, 2006, p 31) to bring up and navigate difficult conversations. The visual stimulus often presented opportunities to discuss issues that can be difficult to conceptualise. The recalling of place memories also enabled participants to become self-aware of their personal resilience through the disclosure of the challenges they had overcome. This was especially so for some Chinese migrant participants who described overcoming socio-cultural and political challenges experienced during the Cultural Revolution.

According to Baker and Wang (2006), photography is a creative outlet that enables some people to better identify and present important aspects in their lives, since it acts as a conduit for individuals to both define a phenomenon of interest and link it with the meaning it has for them. One older woman participant photographed where she had her meals every day. As we reflected on the image, she expressed, "Yes. I usually eat here. I have no fancy furniture, nor other pretty items." On a superficial level, she was identifying the place where she had her meals. However, the underlying message conveyed was that she was poor. For this participant, it was easier to capture her social position through the image, which ultimately helped to facilitate later discussions on how she had lived a humble life, and her previous struggles living in China during the Cultural Revolution.

Methodologically, photo images facilitated the storytelling process and improved the rapport between researcher and participant, which subsequently enabled a shared analytical process. The active agency involved in choosing to photograph or choosing existing photographs often involves a process of personal in-depth thinking about why such an image represents the topic area. This process serves the dual purpose of both self-realisation and the creation of new insights. Data co-creation in this context involves a rich personal analytical process that is then further transformed into a more social analytical framework in the development and the sharing of stories. Such depth of personal and shared analytics is often difficult to achieve in more traditional data collection methods. For example, survey methods are typically formulaic, providing a selection of answers to questions rather than allowing the participant to self-describe, self-identify and self-prioritise important and complex historical aspects of their past. While in-depth interviews can provide the opportunity to reveal nuances of participants' day-to-day experiences, they often do not require preparation and an intense level of personal analysis prior to the co-creation of data. An unexpected benefit of the photovoice technique was the extent to which the storied use of photographs encouraged participants to identify new issues to discuss and to foreground aspects of their lives of which they were proud, further generating an awareness of their personal agency. However, the difficulties of using this method were also evident when people were less comfortable with taking photographs or felt inhibited or anxious about photographing their surroundings. In these instances, the researchers offered to accompany participants and take the actual photographs under the participants' instructions. Careful attention to ethical issues was also necessary, and participants were informed about the problematics of taking photographs of people when this might constitute an invasion of privacy, and about ways to gain verbal consent. When existing photographs were used showing people or family scenes, ensuring that participants had gained the permission of others in the photograph was emphasised. Knowing how the photographs would be used in the context of the research was also an important part of the photovoice negotiation process. These issues, encountered while using photovoice method, paralleled those encountered by Mountian et al (2011) in their use of the experience sampling method to investigate well-being in the workplace.

Facilitating knowledge co-creation, ideas exchange and actions for change

Deliberative dialogue

Deliberative dialogue is a method aimed at generating thoughtful discussion, which is distinct from other forms of public discourse technique such as debating, negotiating, ideas mapping and generating consensus (Kingston, 2005). This method provided an opportunity for concurrently generating and analysing data, engaging participants and synthesising evidence, with the end goal of establishing a set of actionable items (Plamondon, Bottorff, and Cole, 2015). Deliberative dialogue workshops enabled a shared platform for building management, developers, local service providers and representatives from the municipal government to exchange diverse perspectives toward potential solutions for creating socially engaging spaces in the new building (Canham et al, 2017). While the process of deliberative dialogue was immensely helpful in focusing different stakeholders on the key issues at hand and potential solutions, difficulties were experienced in terms of supporting them to transcend the boundaries of their different knowledge bases and levels and types of expertise. Initially, some stakeholders were perceived as being more knowledgeable or powerful than others, which meant that some deferred to others or expected direction from them in terms of what to think. With careful facilitation, active listening, reiteration of what expertise participants held and reinforcement that all perspectives were equally valued, a more trusting and open attitude developed where constructive challenges were welcomed and important agreements were made. In this way, discussions generated directions for the effective use of design to enhance social connectedness between tenants. The discussions also helped stakeholders to design features, shared community spaces, and social programming to enhance independent living for older adults in the new building. Key discussion topics and quotes exemplifying deliberative dialogue data are highlighted in Table 6.3.

The use of deliberative dialogue promoted community resilience, as several community groups came together to co-create ideas and actionable solutions using community assets to help residents to overcome the disruptive change of relocation. We argue that deliberative dialogue sessions, unlike traditional focus groups, provided the opportunity for local stakeholders to view themselves as contributors and decision makers in the community. They were able to develop shared visions at the outset and to confirm appropriate actions and changes at the individual, group and community levels. For instance, participants worked with researchers to generate ideas and future directions for developing supportive home environments. They

Table 6.3: Key discussion topics and associated quotes from the deliberative dialogue sessions

Discussion topics	Quotes
Design features to enhance social connectedness with neighbours	"They're all connected, the two towers are connected with this hallway with centralised hobby room, et cetera, the games room. The idea was, is that we don't want the tenants of one tower to feel that that is their tower and Tower 2 is not part of us, or vice versa. We wanted them to feel like they can flow easily between one tower and the other. That is basically the concept of the amenities that we have."
Design features to enhance independent living	"And we have dedicated space in both buildings for power scooters. There's plug-ins in them, and also room in them for bicycle parking. So we're trying to encourage these other alternative means of moving around the community."
Community spaces	"We made every attempt we could to promote a more healthy social atmosphere. So we started right with the lobby area. It's going to be a busy place ... what we did was, we have the main entrance and then we have a little seating, reading area, waiting area off the side, that kind of allows [tenants] to sit down there comfortably. It's got a little electric fireplace in it. It has a little ambience."
Social programming in the new building	"That is one of the things ... is to find people that want to come in and put on these programmes for our tenants. And there is the key: it is limited to our tenants. We are not trying to service an outside community. And if our tenants want something that we haven't provided, there is the seniors' centre just down the street ... or availability all within a close proximity. So, what we are trying to do is to find those programmes that our tenants want, that we can attract somebody to come and put those programmes on, whether it's dancing, yoga, bingo, or whatever."

focused on the effective use of shared amenity spaces; identified and mobilised local resources and partnerships; brought in tenant-specific programming; and informed tenants of local resources (Canham et al, 2017). Participants who attended the deliberative dialogue sessions were also invited to attend subsequent participatory mapping workshops with tenants.

Participatory mapping

Participatory mapping is a research process that provides the opportunity to create a visible display of people, places and experiences that make up a community through map making (Corbett, 2009). Stemming from Participatory Rural Appraisal (developed in the 1980s to further understanding of rural life), it is part of 'a growing family of approaches and methods to enable local people to share, enhance and analyse their knowledge of life and conditions to plan and act' (Chambers, 1994, p 953). Established as a collaborative approach for generating understandings of locations and sense of place (Fang et al, 2016), participatory mapping is grounded in local knowledge, with the resulting spatial solutions co-created with stakeholders. The resultant maps are subsequently owned by local people (Chambers, 1994). As such, the method begins with the knowledge held by community members, enabling them to take charge of the narration of the places that are meaningful to them.

To further understand older adults' sense of place (generated via storytelling and photovoice methods), and the necessary actions and changes required to rebuild the community for older adults (acquired through deliberative dialogue), we conducted a series of co-created mapping exercises. Older adults and service providers were invited to four participatory mapping workshops. During the workshops participants identified locally available services and resources and pinpointed service and resource gaps on a large aerial map depicting the housing development and surrounding area. Other materials were made available to annotate the map and identify opportunities and barriers within the local community to ageing in place.

The use of maps is both reflective and productive of power, and mapping practices can reinforce those dynamics (Wood, 2010). Once again, mediating the established power hierarchies was necessary between the groups to ensure that older adults were able to situate and position their own knowledge in relation to the map. Even among the community there were diverse perspectives and experiences, and common agreement was sometimes difficult to achieve. In this respect the maps were neither neutral nor unproblematic with respect to positionality and the partiality of knowledge in different sections of the community. The map itself can exert a form of power, for example in assuming that space is fixed and invariable rather than fluid and contested. This showed that it might be wise to begin with the premise that maps are rooted in and essential to power and knowledge (Harley, 1989).

Those people who were much more comfortable with maps were initially more involved than those who self-identified as not being able to navigate the community using maps. Community mapping was anathema to many, and top-down aerial maps were not necessarily commensurate with how older adults constructed their understandings of community at a street level. As a new type of exercise for many, the dynamics of mapping took much facilitation to ensure that collective understandings of place emerged. Sitting at tables restricted people from reaching the parts of the map that they were concerned about. Once the decision was made to stand and to walk around the room, more people got involved in pointing out aspects of their community to share and discuss. This resulted in small groups that talked together and then collectively joined the mapping process.

Community 'walk-alongs'

A key methodological variation from traditional participatory rural appraisals was the integration of community 'walk-alongs' into the research process. Established as the 'go-along' method (Carpiano, 2009; Garcia et al, 2012), it is a form of qualitative interviewing that is often conducted while walking with the research participant (Kusenbach, 2003). Community 'walk-alongs' were used to further explore neighbourhood contexts, enabling older-adult participants to adopt the role of the expert, highlighting in real time meaningful places, spaces and activities in their local environment (Fang et al, 2016). These were a crucial component in this study (Fang et al, 2016). The ability to visualise existing community assets helped older-adult tenants to identify additional types of programmes and activities (Table 6.4) that could take place in the new building, alongside those already in existence in the neighbourhood. The process of walking and talking tends to reproduce friendship relationships, tending to minimise to some extent the researcher–participant power dynamics by placing participants in control of the walk. The movement of walking also tended to provide a natural rhythm to the data collection process, whereby silences (sometimes experienced as uncomfortable

Table 6.4: Activities, services and other social and physical design features identified by participants to enhance ageing in place

Activities	Services/classes	Other
• Tai Chi • Barbeques (twice per year) • Dancing • Mah Jong • Knitting • Bible study • Book club • Life-history learning lessons about residents • Ladies' coffee hour • Glee Club singing • Holidays/birthday parties/ potlucks • Sculpturing • Scrabble • Theatre	• Language classes (for example, English, Mandarin, Spanish) • Assistance with tax returns • Family practitioner • Grocery store/help with groceries • Health and well-being seminars • Fire safety seminars • Health checks and monitoring • Balance classes • Art classes • Music classes • Manicures • Pedicures • Yoga classes • Learn to paint • Calligraphy • Making frames	• Culturally sensitive emergency evacuation plan • Pedestrian crosswalk needed on the main street outside the building • Age-friendly exercise equipment • Reduced membership fee at the seniors' centre • Air conditioning in games/hobbies room • Replacing blinds • More ping-pong tables • Peer-to-peer training on 'living in the condo'

in focus groups or interviews) were no longer problematic but were experienced as more companionable. The 'walk-along' process revealed participants' desires, hopes and expectations for their new community by facing them with the difficulties or deficiencies in their current surroundings. However, the process was difficult to track, as some people walked more quickly than others, splitting the group, with the result that some conversations were lost to the data collection process. Additionally, at times it was difficult to establish a walking route, with different residents wanting to show different aspects of their community. Care was also needed to address the needs of less mobile participants and to ensure that adequate resting places were available. In retrospect, the research team needed to scout out the area, finding resting places and understanding the topographical features of the environment so as to enable the walk-along to progress more smoothly.

Earlier research suggested participatory mapping as a useful tool to encourage collaboration as well as dialogue and relationship building among participants (Amsden and VanWynsberghe, 2005). Participatory mapping in terms both of workshops with actual maps and 'walk-alongs' enabled the researchers to access older adults' attitudes and knowledge. This provided further understandings of the types of relationships that participants have with their community and surrounding environment, and the types of programmes and activities they wanted (Carpiano, 2009). Community 'walk-alongs' also facilitated older adults' social participation by creating a networking space for engaging with service providers and other older adults. Participant evaluations identified the strengths of this method. Evaluation feedback emphasised the value of having opportunities to network with others whom they could engage with after the workshop to establish 'in-house' activities, programmes and services. However, the difficulties of 'walk-alongs' were also identified by participants, as well as by the researchers, who were frustrated by knowing that some potentially important information had been lost.

In summary, the multiple methods applied in this study provided older adults, community partners and local stakeholders with various opportunities to contribute to decision making and enabled them to articulate their views on the redevelopment process. This helped to redirect the focus away from the purely physical aspects of the built environment and to include non-physical, psychosocial support for residents.

Conclusions: outcomes and limitations

As part of the 'Place-making with Seniors' housing redevelopment project, a CBPR approach was applied in order to understand the sense of place of older adults through multiple vantage points. A variety of qualitative methods were used (see Table 6.1), some of which are inherently creative in nature (for example, storytelling, photovoice and mapping exercises). Knowledge and solutions (Fang et al, 2015; Fang et al, 2017) were co-created with local stakeholders who had a vested interest in the health and well-being of older adults. This resulted in a number of positive outcomes that revealed how community resilience and empowerment, articulated through participants' voices within the action research project, transformed the redevelopment in ways that were beneficial for older adults. As such, and in recognition of community requirements and aspirations, a number of changes were implemented so as to create a better living environment for older tenants. These included the establishment of a social committee that was led and organised by tenants living in the building; several annual cultural and social events, which were funded by building management; also, a number of on-going, in-house, age-friendly activities and strategies were established to generate income to fund equipment and events (for example, hosting international tours for architects and designers from Mainland China, bake sales and grant submissions).

In terms of study limitations, participatory methods are resource intensive and time consuming, particularly since the research is embedded within the community. Gaining access to community members requires dedicated time to build partnerships, demonstrate accountability and develop trust. This drawback can lead to small recruitment numbers and lack of perspectives from harder-to-reach people. Also, if participants are not involved in all stages of the project, involvement can seem tokenistic. An important step towards gaining access to the community and establishing trust was through employing researchers fluent in Mandarin, Cantonese and English who could communicate with participants in their first language.

As participatory methods are firmly grounded in principles of empowerment, this methodological strength transcended the limitations. As such, we highly recommend CBPR for future place research, especially for its ability to capitalise on and enhance community resilience through joint approaches to decision making by drawing on knowledge and expertise from a full range of professional and community groups. In order to avoid some of the challenges described throughout the chapter we suggest establishing partnership building and developing relationships with stakeholders before the start of the project (ideally, during the proposal development phase). Frequent meetings with partners are needed to enable active and open communication. In order to access harder-to-reach participants it is recommended that researchers meet participants in their homes. When recruiting participants, information sheets with photos of people involved in the project help participants to know what to expect and make them feel less intimidated. Importantly, all stakeholders need to be included in all aspects of the research so as to avoid tokenistic engagement. Finally, as researchers, we need to be aware of and reflect upon the power dynamics that are inherent in participatory research and the need to document how methods reinforce and reproduce power, not only through the different stakeholders involved in the research, but in how we use research materials such as maps and ask people to document their experiences in relation to place.

References

Amsden, J. and VanWynsberghe, R. (2005) 'Community mapping as a research tool with youth', *Action Research*, 3(4): 357–81.

Anyan, F. (2013) 'The influence of power shifts in data collection and analysis stages: A focus on qualitative research interview', *The Qualitative Report*, 18(18), 1.

Baker, T.A. and Wang, C.C. (2006) 'Photovoice: Use of a participatory action research method to explore the chronic pain experience in older adults', *Qualitative Health Research*, 16(10): 1405–13.

Boger, J., Jackson, P., Mulvenna, M., Sixsmith, J., Sixsmith, A., Mihailidis, A., ... Martin, S. (2016) 'Principles for fostering the transdisciplinary development of assistive technologies', *Disability and Rehabilitation: Assistive Technology*, 12(5): 480–90.

Bruner, J. (1990) *Acts of meaning*, Cambridge, MA: Harvard University Press.

Buffel, T., Phillipson, C. and Scharf, T. (2012) 'Ageing in urban environments: Developing "age-friendly" cities', *Critical Social Policy*, 32(4): 597–617.

Caine, V. (2010) 'Visualizing community: Understanding narrative inquiry as action research', *Educational Action Research*, 18(4): 481–96.

Canham, S.L., Fang, M.L., Battersby, L., Woolrych, R., Sixsmith, J., Ren, T.H. and Sixsmith, A. (2017) 'Contextual factors for aging well: Creating socially engaging spaces through the use of deliberative dialogues', *The Gerontologist*, 58(1): 140–8.

Canter, D. (1977) *The psychology of place*, London: Architectural Press.

Carpiano, R.M. (2009) 'Come take a walk with me: The "go-along" interview as a novel method for studying the implications of place for health and well-being', *Health Place*, 15(1): 263–72.

Catalani, C. and Minkler, M. (2010) 'Photovoice: A review of the literature in health and public health', *Health Education & Behavior*, 37(3): 424–51.

Chambers, R. (1994) 'The origins and practice of participatory rural appraisal', *World Development*, 22(7): 953–69.

Coaffee, J. (2008) 'Risk, resilience, and environmentally sustainable cities', *Energy Policy*, 36(12): 4633–8.

Collins, P. (2000) 'Gender, black feminism, and black political economy', *The ANNALS of the American Academy of Political and Social Science*, 568(1): 41–53, doi: 10.1177/000271620056800105.

Corbett, J. (2009) *Good practices in participatory mapping: A review prepared for the International Fund for Agricultural Development (IFAD)*, Rome, Italy: International Fund for Agricultural Development.

Dainty, A. and Bosher, L. (2008) 'Afterword: Integrating resilience into construction practice', in L. Bosher (ed) *Hazards and the built environment: Attaining built-in resilience*, London: Taylor and Francis, pp 357–72.

Davitt, J.K., Lehning, A.J., Scharlach, A. and Greenfield, E.A. (2015) 'Sociopolitical and cultural contexts of community-based models in aging: The village initiative', *Public Policy & Aging Report*, 25(1): 15–19.

Devine-Wright, P. and Lyons, E. (1997) 'Remembering pasts and representing places: The construction of national identities in Ireland', *Journal of Environmental Psychology*, 17: 33–45.

Dixon, J. and Durrheim, K. (2000) 'Displacing place-identity: A discursive approach to locating self and other', *British Journal of Social Psychology*, 39: 27–44.

Fang, M.L., Woolrych, R., Sixsmith, J., Canham, S., Battersby, L. and Sixsmith, A. (2015) 'Our place, our space: Resident stories and place priorities'. Available at: www.sfu.ca/content/dam/sfu/starinstitute/Reports/English Sense of Place.pdf.

Fang, M.L., Woolrych, R., Sixsmith, J., Canham, S., Battersby, L. and Sixsmith, A. (2016) 'Place-making with older persons: Establishing sense-of-place through participatory community mapping workshops', *Social Science & Medicine*, 168: 223–9.

Fang, M.L., Battersby, L., Canham, S., Ren, T.H., Woolrych, R., Sixsmith, J. and Sixsmith, A. (2017) 'Aging well at home: An implementation and sustainability plan'. Available at: https://bcnpha.ca/wp_bcnpha/wp-content/uploads/2017/05/Implementation-Sustainability-Guidelines_28April2017_Final.pdf.

Farmer, T., Robinson, K., Elliott, S.J. and Eyles, J. (2006) 'Developing and implementing a triangulation protocol for qualitative health research', *Qualitative Health Research*, 16(3): 377–94.

Gale, N.K., Heath, G., Cameron, E., Rashid, S. and Redwood, S. (2013) 'Using the framework method for the analysis of qualitative data in multi-disciplinary health research', *BMC Medical Research Methodologies*, 13: 117.

Garcia, C.M., Eisenberg, M.E., Frerich, E.A., Lechner, K.E. and Lust, K. (2012) 'Conducting go-along interviews to understand context and promote health', *Qualitative Health Research*, 22(10): 1395–403.

Golant, S.M. (2015) *Ageing in the right place*, Baltimore, MD: Health Professions Press.

Guion, L.A., Diehl, D.C. and McDonald, D. (2011) 'Conducting an in-depth interview', https://www.betterevaluation.org/en/resources/guide/conducting_an_in-depth_interview.

Hankivsky, O. and Christoffersen, A. (2008) 'Intersectionality and the determinants of health: A Canadian perspective', *Critical Public Health*, 18(3): 271–83.

Harley, J. (1989) 'Deconstructing the map', *Cartographica*, 26: 1–20.

Hildon, Z., Montgomery, S.M., Blane, D., Wiggins, R.D. and Netuveli, G. (2009) 'Examining resilience of quality of life in the face of health-related and psychosocial adversity at older ages: What is "right" about the way we age?' *The Gerontologist*, 50(1): 36–47.

Jagosh, J., Bush, P.L., Salsberg, J., Macaulay, A.C., Greenhalgh, T., Wong, G., ... Pluye, P. (2015) 'A realist evaluation of community-based participatory research: Partnership synergy, trust building and related ripple effects', *BMC Public Health*, 15:725.

Jones, L. and Wells, K. (2007) 'Strategies for academic and clinician engagement in community-participatory partnered research', *JAMA*, 297(4): 407–10.

Keats, P.A. (2009) 'Multiple text analysis in narrative research: Visual, written, and spoken stories of experience', *Qualitative Research*, 9(2): 181–95.

Kingston, R.J. (2005) *Public thought and foreign policy: Essays on public deliberations about americans' role in the world* (1st edn), Washington, DC: Kettering Foundation Press.

Kusenbach, M. (2003) 'Street phenomenology: The go-along as ethnographic research tool', *Ethnography*, 4(3): 455–85.

Magis, K. (2010) 'Community resilience: An indicator of social sustainability', *Society & Natural Resources*, 23: 401–16.

Minkler, M. and Wallerstein, N. (eds) (2008) *Community-based participatory research for health* (2nd edn), San Francisco: Jossey-Bass.

Mountian, I., Lawthom, R., Kellock, A., Duggan, K., Sixsmith, J., Kagan, C. and Purcell, C. (2011) 'On utilising a visual methodology: Shared reflections and tensions', in P. Reavey (ed) *Visual methods in psychology: Using and interpreting images in qualitative research*, 346–60.

Nowell, B.L., Berkowitz, S.L., Deacon, Z. and Foster-Fishman, P. (2006) 'Revealing the cues within community places: Stories of identity, history, and possibility', *American Journal of Community Psychology*, 37(1–2): 29–46.

Oswald, F. and Wahl, H.W. (2003) 'Place attachment across the life span', in J.R. Miller, R.M. Lerner, L.B. Schiamberg and P.M. Anderson (eds) *The encyclopedia of human ecology*, Santa Barbara: ABC-CLIO Inc., pp 568–72.

Phillips, J., Walford, N. and Hockey, A. (2012) 'How do unfamiliar environments convey meaning to older people? Urban dimensions of placelessness and attachment', *International Journal of Ageing and Later Life*, 6(2): 73-102.

Pink, S. (2013) *Doing visual ethnography*, London, UK: SAGE.

Plamondon, K.M., Bottorff, J.L. and Cole, D.C. (2015) 'Analyzing data generated through deliberative dialogue: Bringing knowledge translation into qualitative analysis', *Qualitative Health Research*, 25(11): 1529–39.

Polkinghorne, D.E. (1988) *Narrative knowing and the human sciences*, New York: State University of New York Press.

Proshansky, H.M., Fabian, A.K. and Kaminoff, R. (1983) 'Place-identity: Physical world socialization of the self', *Journal of Environmental Psychology*, 3(1): 57–83.

Relph, E. (1976) *Place and placelessness*, London: Pion.

Sixsmith, A.J. and Sixsmith, J.A. (1991) 'Transitions in home experience in later life', *Journal of Architectural and Planning Research*, 8: 181–91.

Sixsmith, A. and Sixsmith, J. (2008) 'Ageing in place in the United Kingdom', *Ageing International*, 32(3): 219–35.

Sixsmith, J. (1986) 'The meaning of home: An exploratory study of environmental experience', *Journal of Environmental Psychology*, 6: 281–98.

Sixsmith, J., Fang, M.L., Woolrych, R., Canham, S., Battersby, L. and Sixsmith, A. (2017) 'Ageing well in the right place: Partnership working with older people', *Working with Older People*, 21(1): 40–8.

Sixsmith, J., Fang, M., Woolrych, R., Canham, S., Battersby, L. and Sixsmith, A. (in press) 'Understanding sense-of-place for low-income seniors: Living at the intersections of multiple oppressions, positionalities and identities', in O. Hankivsky and J. Jordan-Zachery (eds) *Bringing intersectionality to public policy*.

Taylor, S. (2003) 'A place for the future? Residence and continuity in women's narratives of their lives', *Narrative Inquiry*, 13(1): 193–215.

Tuan, Y.F. (1977) *Space and place: The perspective of experience*, Minneapolis: University of Minnesota Press.

Tuan, Y.F. (1991) 'Language and the making of place: A narrative-descriptive approach', *Annals of the Association of American Geographers*, 81(4): 684–96.

Twigger-Ross, C.L. and Uzzell, D.L. (1996) 'Place and identity processes', *Journal of Environmental Psychology*, 16: 205–20.

Walks, R.A. and Maaranen, R. (2008) 'Gentrification, social mix, and social polarization: Testing the linkages in large Canadian cities', *Urban Geography*, 29(4): 293–326.

Wang, C. and Burris, M.A. (1997) 'Photovoice: Concept, methodology, and use for participatory needs assessment', *Health Education and Behavior*, 24(3): 369–87.

Williams, D.R. (2014) 'Making sense of "place": Reflections on pluralism and positionality in place research', *Landscape and Urban Planning*, 131: 74–82.

Wood, D. (2010) *Rethinking the power of maps*, New York: Guilford Press.

Woolrych, R. (2017) 'Delivering age-friendly environments: Social justice and rights to the city', *The Planner*, 169: 10–11, London: Royal Town Planning Institute.

Woolrych, R. and Sixsmith, J. (2013) 'Mobilising community participation and engagement: The perspective of regeneration professionals', *Journal of Urban Regeneration and Renewal*, 6(3): 309–21.

Woolrych, R. and Sixsmith, J. (in press) '"Place, space and displacement": Gentrification and urban regeneration in the UK', in A. Portella and G. Pereira (eds) *Insights on favelas*, London: Sage Press, pp 137–50.

SEVEN

Ageing in place: creativity and resilience in neighbourhoods

Cathy Bailey, Rose Gilroy, Joanna Reynolds, Barbara Douglas, Claire Webster Saaremets, Mary Nicholls, Laura Warwick and Martin Gollan

Editorial introduction

In common with the first two chapters of this book, this chapter takes a creative, participatory approach to exploring older people's experiences of resilience in their neighbourhoods. In this case, the authors used a 'World Café' approach to eliciting responses and generating consensus and, at the same time, used creative methods both to support participation and to communicate the findings to a wider audience. As such, this chapter has much in common with Chapters Five and Six, in so far as the researchers are explicitly concerned with helping participants to become aware of the resources they have to support resilience (which is seen as social) and to become engaged in wider social and political processes that impact on their resilience.

Introduction

How do we age in place? How, in the UK, do we grow older in our communities and find support in these times of austerity? The UK central government presents the hollowing out of the state as an inevitable consequence of globally created and nationally experienced austerity (Phillipson, 2012). The impact, however, is that the risk of exclusion arising from public sector withdrawal is disproportionately weighted towards groups who are vulnerable through individual or social and community factors. As we detail in the next section, support for adult care is now severely reduced, while neighbourhood institutions of community centres and libraries providing structured activity have also been thinned. Between 2010 and spring 2016 an estimated 343 libraries have been closed, including 132 mobile services targeted at housebound readers (Woodhouse and Dempsey, 2016). Two thousand bus routes were altered or withdrawn between 2010 and 2015 (Campaign for Better Transport, 2015); while 2,500 bank branch closures are expected by 2018 (Edwards, 2015). These lead to a loss of local services and, importantly, a loss of meeting places for social interaction.

This chapter reports on the findings of an arts-based participatory consultation with older people living in the English north-east city of Newcastle upon Tyne. In 2014–15 and over a period of eight months we shared conversations about what people do to support themselves and others and what else they need to enjoy a 'good later life', living at home, being part of a place and neighbourhood. Conversations were managed through the World Café approach (Brown, Isaacs and Wheatley, 2005) and further developed through a week-long arts residency, directed by a multi-media arts organisation, Skimstone Arts. Drama, dance, mime, music and writing techniques were used to fictionalise the key issues raised, into a 40-minute public performance. The co-created production was intended to capture and celebrate everyday lives, but also to provoke the thinking of the service funders, commissioners and providers among the audience.

We argue that the use of participatory creative tools can foster honest and messy public conversations. Such conversations have the potential to shift social care policy and practice, and neighbourhood budgets, away from a narrow focus on older persons' needs. Instead, participatory tools can encourage policy makers to listen to personal and collective stories and consider a more creative use of local resources. Our stance is not to see resilience as a matter of individual psychology but, in common with Windle (2011) and Windle and Bennett (2012), to see people as situated in a landscape of potential resources that recognises the concept of social resilience. Our work suggests the need to closely monitor the strain that informal networks and neighbourhood mechanisms are placed under and to find appropriate ways to strengthen these to promote longer-term sustainability.

Before detailing the consultation and our findings, we briefly reflect on 'ageing in place' and consider the current discourse on creative and resilient alternative ways of living in later life.

Ageing in place: measuring the gap

Fange, Oswald and Clemson (2012, p 1) state that 'Ageing in place is about being able to continue living in one's own home or neighbourhood and to adapt to changing needs and conditions', and that it is 'an important concern throughout the world'. The drivers for the focus on ageing in place are diverse. Global demographic trends suggest that few countries are exempt from the phenomena of decreasing fertility and longer lives (UNFPA, 2017). In the UK, the number of people over 60 years of age outnumbers those under 16 and the fastest-growing group are the 'oldest old', aged 85 or more (ONS, 2017). Decades of research suggest that many older people want to stay within familiar communities where they are known through a network of strong and weak ties (Gilroy, 2008). In this chapter we focus on this definition. Counter narratives from the Royal Institute of British Architects (Parkinson, Hunter and Barac, 2013) suggest future 'active third agers' may prefer time-share global travel with their possessions and identity markers of photographs, music and books stored on an iPad in their pocket. These possible scenarios remind us not to make assumptions about the needs, much less the aspirations, of older people.

In England, local authorities have tightened their eligibility criteria for publicly funded care. People with low dependency are unlikely to qualify, while those no family members or none nearby to provide unpaid care or sufficient income to purchase support may be left with unmet needs, exacerbating inequalities (Humphries et al, 2016). In 2017 there were nearly 1.2 million people aged 65+ who didn't receive the help they needed with essential daily living activities. It is argued that an additional £4.8 billion a year would ensure that every older person who currently has one or more unmet need, would have access to social care (Age UK, 2017a), while the Commission on the Future of Health and Social Care in England (2014) recommended that public spending on health and social care should increase to between 11 and 12% of GDP by 2025. The impact of the shortfall is that informal support deals with increasingly complex needs, with the cost falling on the carer and the economy. An estimated £5.3 billion has been wiped from the economy in lost earnings due to people who have left the workforce to take on caring responsibilities for older or disabled family members, including £1 billion in forgone taxes (Pickard, 2012). Increasingly, elder support may be non-familial for reasons such as geographically scattered families or ageing without children (AWOC, 2017).

There are also housing challenges. Seventy-six per cent of older UK households (aged over 55) are owner-occupiers (Age UK, 2017b). Of these, more than three-quarters of a million people aged 65 and over have a medical condition or disability that would benefit from specially adapted accommodation, while 145,000 of these people report living in homes that do not meet their needs (Age UK, 2017b). The situation is not improving as rapidly as required and developing new-build accessible and adaptable housing has been downgraded as a planning priority (Shanks, 2016, p 2).

Older people looking to remain in their current accommodation may find it unadaptable or too costly to adapt. For example, within our case study city of Newcastle upon Tyne, 51.6% of the housing stock was built before 1945 (Newcastle City Council, 2012), as compared with 41.6% nationally. Older homes can be more challenging to adapt – for example, in the case of remodelling for the needs of a wheelchair user (Newcastle City Council, 2017). Although the increase in funds available to local authorities for Disabled Facilities Grants that support adaptations (announced in the 2015 Government Spending Review) was welcomed, the need continues to outstrip the available resources (Mackintosh and Leather, 2016). The lack of public resource allocation to realise older citizens' housing and welfare needs is not unique to the UK (Beard et al, 2011). The World Health Organisation (WHO) warns that a current global financial crisis is likely to become a global social and health crisis for older people (WHO, 2017).

WHO (2017) and the World Economic Forum (Beard et al, 2011) also promote global ageing as a unique opportunity. Rather than a focus on 'dependency ratio' economic models, we can move to working with older people's largely untapped social capital. Social contracts can provide financial security with intergenerational solidarity, providing flexible workforce participation and investing in preventative and enabling health and social care services. Under such a model, longevity in itself becomes an asset, not a deficit.

Newcastle upon Tyne, along with many UK and European cities, has been taking steps to comprehensively review the city's structure and services to determine the extent to which they offer opportunities for human flourishing (see WHO, 2017; Centre for Ageing Better, 2017). At the core of working to be an age-friendly city is a commitment to seeing older people as a resource to be utilised and enhanced, not a burden to be carried.

Creative and resilient ageing in place: an alternative viewpoint

As noted earlier, Fange et al (2012) suggest that ageing in place also encompasses adapting to changing needs as we age. Being able to adapt may be described as being resilient. Driven by the discipline of psychology, but made fashionable by increasing ageing populations unsupported by adequate resources (for example, see Timonen, 2016 for a robust challenge to the successful ageing paradigm), there has been a growth in the literature on resilience (see Bennett, 2015 for a review). As Windle (2011, p 152) suggests, resilience is 'the process of effectively negotiating, adapting to, or managing significant sources of stress or trauma'. Older people, it is argued, use a range of strategies to protect their self-esteem and well-being (Collins and Smyer, 2005) and deploy different sources of strength to adapt constructively to stressful life events (Janssen, Van Regenmortel and Abma, 2011; Bailey et al, 2013).

The majority of research on resilience in adults has focused on identifying individual characteristics and the individual's ability to mobilise assets, suggesting that we have complete control over our lives and can exercise unlimited agency. This view has been criticised for obfuscating wider political and social influences. Windle (2011) and Windle and Bennett's (2012) work on the ecology of resilience refocuses this debate by situating the individual within a local physical and social environment in which both are influenced by socio-political and economic factors mainly beyond the control of any one person. Baldwin suggests that our personal narratives, the stories we tell about ourselves, are woven with strands of these wider influences: 'the personal, interpersonal and the institutional/structural are interrelated through the stories we tell and are told about us, whether by individuals or collectivities' (Baldwin, 2008, p 224). Bartlett and O'Connor (2007) expand this to include 'social practice' on the basis of Prior et al's work, in which 'individuals relate to other people, their communities and the state' (Prior, Stewart and Walsh, 1995). Barnes, Auburn and Lea's (2004) work sets out the notion of 'everyday talk and actions', signalling to ourselves and others who we are.

Whether driven by inadequate contemporary solutions or by the baby-boomer generation's expectations for greater autonomy (Gilleard and Higgs, 2008), there is global evidence of new creative practices shaping alternative later-life housing and living schemes, such as co-housing (Brenton, 2013; Riseborough, 2013a, 2013b) and house sharing (Phillipson, 2011 Baker, 2017). Nesta, an innovation foundation, has supported some innovative ageing-in-place projects, including Shared Lives Plus.[1] This family-based and small-scale placement scheme, which is an alternative to institutional care, is targeted at older people and those living with a disability.

There has also been an interest in understanding more about how older people experience ageing in place. Research at the local level has been working to encourage small-scale actions that work with older people as active change agents, valuing older people's knowledge and experience of the places in which they live and environmental changes they may need to get on with their lives (Handler, 2014). One example is community-led auditing. Two of the authors of this chapter (Douglas and Nichols), as part of Newcastle Elders Council, have been involved in 'as lived' assessment of a local area, using tools such as participant-led mental mapping, similar to the work of Kilburn Older Voices Exchange (KOVE) and Lewisham's Mobilizing Knowledge initiatives.[2] Handler (2014) suggests that community-led audits, gathering accumulated and common experiences, are more likely to find an audience with local policy makers and planners that might, in turn, lead to change that can be monitored, maintained and sustained over time (Handler, 2014, p 33).

A citizen consultation about 'ageing well in place'

Community-led auditing is familiar territory to the Elders Council. As the voluntary older people's forum in Newcastle upon Tyne, the Council works with agencies, organisations and individuals to ensure that the views of the over-50s are taken into account by decision makers in Newcastle upon Tyne. In 2014, the Elders Council engaged with Northumbria and Newcastle Universities and Skimstone Arts,[3] a Newcastle-based, multi-disciplinary arts organisation, to facilitate public conversations about growing older in homes and neighbourhoods. The aim was to gain a better understanding, from an older person's perspective, of how older people support themselves and others in local neighbourhoods. The conversations were intended to gather information on the range of wider activity and support available, and to raise important issues for those working in housing, care and health in later life about what needs to happen in the future to support ageing well in place.

Northumbria University led the eight-month project consultation and the Elders Council set up a steering group with representation from project partners and Elders Council Housing and Health interest group. The project proposal was shared widely with colleagues in housing, health and social care for comment, input and support, and to ensure that all partners gained maximum value from the work. Ethical approval was obtained from Northumbria University.

Our research method: a World Café approach

The World Café is a global consultation, data collection and co-analysis tool based on 'round robin' principles (Brown, Isaacs and

Wheatley, 2005) that encourage all participants' contributions in order to discuss questions pertinent to them, connect diverse responses and perspectives and agree workable solutions. The World Café Community Foundation,[4] has produced a freely available set of principles that echo these, notably emphasising a hospitable ambience where individual and collective ideas are shared, with all participants treated as experts and diverse perspectives encouraged and included in the summarising co-analysing and prioritising of responses and points for future action. The World Café approach has been used in primary care research in Ireland and the US (MacFarlane et al, 2016).

The consultation included participants from two adjacent Newcastle electoral wards representing a median mix of older households and minority ethnic communities. Sampling was purposeful in that we drew on Elders Council's considerable networks in the area and invested time in making contact within and across diverse community groups, as well as talking with individuals. In total, 22 participants, aged 55–90, joined our World Café events which were held in local community centres.

Participants included three people from Black, Asian and minority ethnic communities, one of whom was accompanied by her daughter who acted as her interpreter. Participants were affected by a range of health issues; some described their health as good, being active, and carrying out grandparenting and volunteering activities. Other participants lived with chronic health conditions such as diabetes or heart conditions. One had suffered an acquired brain injury following a fall and had a speech impediment and mobility issues. Others had spousal/family caring duties. This group therefore represented a wide range of different life experiences.

Three participatory World Café events were planned, each lasting between two and three hours (with lunch). The first two events were guided by four questions, which were drafted by the project team and finalised in consultation with the stakeholder group:

- What is your favourite and least favourite place in your home or neighbourhood?
- Who are the key people in your lives?
- Whom would you like to have in your neighbourhood?
- What are the five facilities in your area that are important to you, what might be missing, and how might existing facilities be improved?

These questions came from our understanding of the ageing-in-place literature as presented earlier in this chapter and also from our previous work on creativity, ageing and resilience (for example, Bailey et al, 2017).

The purpose of the third and final World Café event was to co-analyse and prioritise issues of importance to the group so that potential future actions could be identified and reported upon. A priority decided by the research team was that participants should have the opportunity to consider the issues that the four research questions identified (set out above) and vote for the most important three issues. These activities represent World Café data co-analysis and, although messy and challenging, maximise participation in large-group discussions (MacFarlane et al, 2017). The final event also provided a 'taster session' of the arts activities that were likely to be used within a planned week-long arts residency facilitated by Skimstone Arts. The purpose of the residency was to give participants the opportunity to co-create a performance that, although fictionalised, would nevertheless draw on key consensus issues agreed and prioritised within the World Café events. The authors have experience of co-producing arts outputs that have immediacy beyond the written page of a report (Clarke, Bailey and Gibb, 2016). Through performance, audiences – including invited local policy planners commissioners and providers of older people's services – are immersed in participants' lived experiences.

Ageing in two areas of Newcastle, England: our public conversation

Of the 22 participants, 19 came to the first workshop and we were joined by Martin Gollan, our visual artist, who produced drawings of our conversation, and Claire Webster Saaremets, the Artistic Director of Skimstone Arts, who made notes of the shared stories and ideas for our planned collaborative performance. Participants were invited to sit at four tables, in small groups of six to eight people. At each table a facilitator posed one of the questions and participants were invited to reflect on, and then write down responses directly onto a paper table-cloth. Each facilitator managed one of the four questions as outlined above and moved from table to table with the table-cloth, adding to the material and reflections already gathered. Participant responses were then visually interpreted by the artist (Figures 7.1a and b). These are also presented in Table 7.1, which illustrates the agreed and prioritised responses about significant people, places and facilities.

Figure 7.1a and b: Visual representations of group conversations

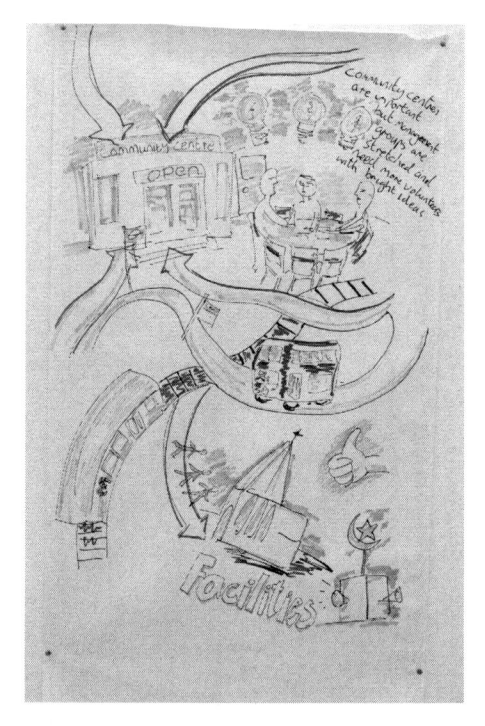

Table 7.1: Workshop 1: conversations about significant people, places and facilities

Component	Consensus	Gaps
People	You! Relying on yourself is key	People who 'know how to'/'what's on'
	Family are very important	Buddy schemes can work well if living alone; we need men as well as women
	Neighbours, this is reciprocal but there are degrees of what feels comfortable and the relationship can and does change	More volunteers, and that includes getting in touch with younger people
	People in church and faith groups as well as community and interest groups and the doctor and dentist but there can be access issues	Contact with community police
	People doing their everyday job (the milkman, 'Ringtons tea man', street wardens) can make us feel connected, it's about routines and familiarity	We are not always sure what we want, as attitudes to what's acceptable (to ask for) change, as do relationships (with family, friends and neighbours for example)
	Care workers and sheltered housing officers and sometimes just a person regularly encountered, they may have good local knowledge, and know what's happening	
Places	Home is by far the most important and favourite place and it provides security. However, planning for the future so that home doesn't become a burden, can be an issue	Places for younger people to go and a place where younger and older people can meet
	For those of us who have one, a garden is also a favourite place. For those who haven't, a garden scheme would be welcome but takes a lot of collective planning	
	Local Community Centre as a meeting and activity place	
	The library and local swimming pool	
	Within sheltered accommodation, the lounge as meeting place	

(continued)

Table 7.1: Workshop 1: conversations about significant people, places and facilities (continued)

Component	Consensus	Gaps
Facilities	The local shops, the butchers, greengrocers, that's where there's life	Need greater variety of local shops, supermarkets are a car or bus journey away (not everyone has cars!)
	Doctor surgeries, dental practices, pharmacies, post office but they all need to be easily accessible	Need a local pub and there are fewer post offices
		More flats for single/older people (lack of provision for this group)
		More facilities for young people in the evenings to prevent vandalism
		Community buses and direct bus routes to key places (such as supermarkets)
		A Register/Handyperson Scheme
		Advertising of activities in locality
		Litter, uneven pavements and back lanes

The second World Café event moved from identifying the significant people, places and facilities deemed important to ageing well in local neighbourhoods, to asking why such people, facilities and places are important. To capture the significance of both individual and community resources, and with the support of our visual artist, we used the concepts of kit bags (individual resources) and washing lines (community resources) and asked the following questions:

- What five things do I have in my kit bag that help me cope with change?
- Choose three to five tea-towels and on each one write about something that you know is happening your area that is a way of helping people to get the things they need.

Within each group, participants first filled their kit bags (that is, made a list of their resources within the drawing) and then each bag was hung on a washing line (drawn on a large piece of paper). In addition, tea-towels that represented a community resource, such as a community centre, were hung on the line. Also, named community workers who signposted people to services were represented on the line. The washing line items were then discussed to identify and agree upon the common individual and collective resources. For example, the following bullet points listed in bold below reveal resources that help each participant to cope with change. The following snapshot of comments recorded from one of the group's conversations illustrates further examples of the resource (verbatim quotes indicated with quotation marks).

- **Inner strength:** "Often we don't realise how strong we are until we have gone through something."
- **Support from others:** "Sometimes you can tell strangers more than close relatives."
- **Communication:** Someone to talk to.
- **Security:** Help from people around. From trusted people. There will always be people who will gossip, so it's important to have trusted confidantes. Change can be frightening.

This exchange led to a reflection on trust more generally, for example:

- **Trust:** "This is broken with my GP." Need more time with the GP, not just 20 minutes. Need longer time to discuss things.

And more generally the consequences of not feeling listened to:

- **Confidence:** "You're not so taken notice of by others when you're older". "When you're old, people think your brain doesn't move as fast." "They treat you as though you're stupid."

Older participants saw themselves in relationship to other generations. Relationships with family, friends and neighbours of different generations were reflected upon, sometimes directly in relation to age: "Young people don't realise what we've gone through 'til they've gone through it themselves." Simultaneously, participants acknowledged that ageing well in place also means working together as a neighbourhood, "You can't do anything on your own, you need to do it as a body."

Participants shared individual resources with each other, from setting up emergency contact numbers on mobile phones to sharing information about local facilities. The tea towel exercise facilitated conversation about community resources and led to consensus about collective responsibility for keeping 'community, living and thriving'. This was considered through everyday small actions, as this exchange between three participants illustrates:

>   Man 1:   It's the feel of the place; get your bins out and put them back and everyone picks up litter.
>   Woman 1: But it's also being friendly [to others], just say hello and have a smile …
>   Woman 2: … community spirit.
>   Woman 1: Yes we could meet up, there must be free spaces around here in [local church], well here too [community centre].
>   Man 1:   Yes but not everyone wants to come out. In bad weather my neighbour, she doesn't like going out so I always ask if she needs anything when I'm shopping.

Conversations also focused on changed communities: "everyone had nothing and shared their nothing", and now "there's too much of a must-have attitude". This was also challenged by one participant: "Whose past, whose history are we talking about and can we share our cultural experiences?"

The final World Café event was planned with the aim of reaching consensus on the prioritisation of the key responses to the four questions and also to introduce the arts residency. The themes participants had prioritised were revisited through discussion during the two events. For example, within the first World Café there was consensus that the most important person is oneself and that being self-reliant is a positive resource for ageing well in place. The second World Café identified individual 'inner strength', but also that there are times when there is a need to call on others for a little bit of help. This led the group to agree a 'statement' that places self-reliance, inner strength and needing a little bit of help within everyday life, such as unexpected change (for example, an illness, accident, house repair) that needs timely and appropriate 'outside help' to avoid longer-term implications.

The group used the language of 'statement' to emphasise that this is what they had generated from the consultation. Seven statements were developed and agreed through initial questioning: 'Have we captured all the dimensions and perspectives of our agreed response or is there something we need to add?'; 'Have we conflated or misinterpreted a point of view?' These statements are presented in Table 7.2, along with examples of participant conversation that relate to each statement.

Following the three World Café events, Skimstone Arts facilitated the arts residency. Throughout five half-day sessions, between five and eleven participants took part and up to six members of the Skimstone Young Artists Collective, aged 16–25 years, joined in. This was in response to the World Café consultation prioritising the need to strengthen multi-generational neighbourhoods, to share skills and expertise and to recognise common issues across all ages, such as social isolation and loneliness, wherein mutual support might be beneficial (see statement 5, Table 7.2). Personal storytelling was achieved through techniques of rap, sound poetry and improvised composition, using images of doorbells and doorsteps as an artistic provocation. Participants actively engaged in collectively forming and performing songs and poems, and crafted, rehearsed and performed their work. Their feedback was positive:

> "Totally barmy group, never been to something like this, but feel inside it."

> "Enjoyed it, no pressure, you took part in what you wanted to."

> "Doing something creative, you can be yourself."

Table 7.2: Distilling the findings of the conversations

	Statement	Participant feedback
1	Getting the balance right between being a good neighbour and helping those around you, but also not doing so much that it becomes a burden.	Your neighbourhood is so close to you. Then your 'far brothers' (family living further away), so you need to look after them (your neighbours).
2	'Getting up and getting on with it' and being self-reliant is important, but there can also be changes in circumstances, such as a short illness or longer-term change, like becoming a little less mobile. Adapting to change can be challenging, but others such as family, friends, good neighbours and others around you can make it easier.	If it's short-term, people can help. If it's long-term change, we need to encourage people to find other solutions, such as extra care. If we had more conversations about ageing we might recognise for ourselves when we need to change. *But* we need good information and advice to help to make decisions and avoid panic decisions. Options must be discussed beforehand, so that people understand and are comfortable with the services/offer.
3	It's good to get out and help people but it's not always easy to ask for help for yourself and it can be hard accepting that a little help is needed. It can also be hard knowing what sort of help is available and how best to get it.	If it were someone else you would be first to offer, so please ask for yourself. You fear losing your independence; you want to keep doing things. Interaction, reciprocity is important, such as Sunday lunch in exchange for lifts.
4	Having places to go and community groups to get involved with keeps you in touch and makes our neighbourhoods vibrant places. Keeping busy and feeling useful gives you a sense of purpose.	Because of cultural differences, sometimes it is hard to access facilities, for example sports centres, swimming pools. Also, there might be language barriers.
5	There is some talk about young people hanging about in the streets but more talk about wanting spaces and places where older and younger people can meet. There are also concerns that younger people do not have the same opportunities as you had.	There are greater expectations on younger people and this puts pressure on them. Yes to opportunities for younger and older people to meet. Contact with older people outside of family networks may help younger people to understand ageing, and mutual expertise and experience may be shared.
6	Taking care neighbourhoods is up to everyone, from picking up litter, to tidying the garden, to getting involved. There are issues that need some outside help too, such as cyclists using pavements and lack of dropped kerbs.	We can do a bit more about sweeping our own paths and collecting litter from immediate area.
7	Planning for the future should happen earlier in life. It's not easy knowing when, how and why to plan.	We need to be able to access advice, help to assist us with planning/having conversation about our plans.

"I enjoyed doing the choreography; I didn't think I'd get the opportunity to do that again."

A 40-minute performance, 'Doorbells of Delight' was collaboratively produced (Box 7.1). It was performed to an audience of 55 people including participants, their friends and family, and representatives from third sector community and arts organisations. Post-performance discussions suggested a need for a stronger intergenerational focus and some further character development. A revised version, 'Doorbells', was performed, with attendees including representatives from the public sector, such as the police services and local authority, and also voluntary and arts sectors, funding organisations and young people.

Designed and managed by one of the authors (Laura Warwick) and hosted by Elders Council, we also developed a project blog to keep our conversation live, share it within and beyond the participant group and keep people updated and in touch. Elders Council also gave updates through their newsletter.

Box 7.1: Synopsis of 'Doorbells of Delight'

The central metaphor was a doorbell. The audience were taken on a journey, into a neighbourhood, a street and over thresholds of homes and gardens. Different tales of change, connections and tensions, such as, on the one hand, being overburdened with the 'doing for everyone else', and on the other, the loneliness of a silent doorbell and the hope that it may ring, emphasised differences in experiences of neighbourhood. 'Hoodie teen dragons' signified participants' tensions with younger community members, but this stereotype was challenged by a 'Hoodie' and his warm relationship with his much loved 'Granny'. The audience also met a disagreeable older neighbour who seemed more dragon-like than the stereotyped 'hoodie'. Suitcases of varying sizes signified 'downsizing', and dancing plastic bags of rubbish brought neighbours together to keep the streets clean. A final scene of a dance within archways, choreographed by one of the project participants, depicted neighbourliness and a sense of shared belonging and connection to a place.

Discussion

By holding open conversations with simple prompts, we were able to gather a wide range of stories and insights into growing older in local communities. Our consultation fits with Handler's (2014) outline of 'small scale action' that works with older people as active change agents who can and do make positive changes to their lives and those of others. We found within the workshops and arts residency that people exchanged ideas and information and, in some cases, this led to immediate action. For example, one participant living in community housing formed a tenants' group and received encouragement and advice to seek funding and open a community bank account to support a programme of social activities.

By using a variety of research, media and creative tools, such as performance and a project blog, people were able to contribute in different ways. For example, the participant with an acquired brain injury and speech impediment, while finding conversation challenging, became very animated through mime and music. Another, who did not speak English and who invited her daughter to accompany her to support her language needs, added to stories of 'free and roaming' childhoods in local neighbourhoods. By drawing simple outlines of a sun, a courtyard, a large shady tree and family members 'gossiping', this participant perhaps reminded other participants that their neighbourhood is very diverse, with a pool of different lifecourse stories. Yet another participant noted commonality, suggesting that the 'gossiping' scene was not so very different from his childhood memories of accompanying his 'Mam' to the local 'steamie' (public laundry).

The example above supports Baldwin's (2008) notion of telling our story from within wider structural givens. In this case, in this exchange between the two participants, there was a sense of shared and familiar memories of a childhood, despite their having been experienced in very different places. Barnes et al (2004) describes such moments as enabling us to signal who we are, in relation to others. Despite the two participants sharing childhood memories from a very different place, 'social practice' weaves a common thread through the difference. This is important when considering what is meant by ageing in place and how we can respond creatively and at a human scale to the complexity of autobiographical, physical and social attachment to place (Rowles, 1978, 1983).

Our conversations highlighted that older people are a considerable asset to communities but that this can feel fragile. From within this consultation, older people were aware of the impact of the ageing demographic on their communities, as well as of cuts to health and social care, resulting in loss of services. They are also aware of some of the media coverage of an ageing population depicting older people as burdensome and requiring resource-intensive health and social care at a cost to younger generations. In common with other research (see, for example, Buffel, Phillipson and Scharf, 2013), the loss of meeting places that had been run by local charities is also notable.

Some participants also shared concerns about the unsuitability of their own and others' homes in relation to adapting to changing needs as they age. Neighbours, both young and old, can attempt to be neighbourly towards someone who has very complex needs and this can be challenging. While participants talked about their 'kit bags' of resources that help them to "look in on a neighbour who can't do as much", there was also frustration at the lack of formal recognition from the state for all that they offer and for their informal supporting role. It was suggested that there needs to be acknowledgment of the way in which "good neighbours" save resources for service-provider organisations, and that this informal support could not continue indefinitely.

Some of the frustration was not focused on cuts to services but, rather, about inflexible systems that cannot rally when "that little bit of help" is needed on the day that the "good neighbour is not available". It was felt that professional advice that provides reassurance or, failing that, signposting to available and suitable help and support, was not available. Securing help was felt impossible, due to a "maze of bureaucratic twists and turns". Our conversations illustrated how resilient people are. Many do have, and are able to, mobilise assets for themselves and others. However, it was argued that such good will and motivation may be worn out by obstructive or ill-fitting, wider structural and political influences.

Our participatory creative tools opened up the complexity of creative and resilient ageing in place. While it drew on the experiences of only 22 people aged from mid-50s to early 90s living in Newcastle upon Tyne, England, we suggest that our conversations have wider resonance for thinking about ageing well within intergenerational communities. We would like these findings to provide a starting point from which to develop a more flexible community infrastructure that supports optimum quality of life as people age.

We already have good processes to realise participatory engagement, such as the World Café model demonstrated here. Other participatory tools include UDecide[5] and the use of collective spaces for intergenerational story sharing and creative activity. Findings presented here suggest that we need to create more opportunities for community conversations that enable people to collectively review what they have and what they need to develop. Within this consultation, we heard people talking about not being valued and being viewed as old and slow, both of which negatively impact on resilience. However, the World Café consultation not only illuminated to individual participants their individual resources, but also provided a community platform from which to share such resources. For example, people made suggestions such as swapping information about, and trialling, walking and security aids. Another suggestion was sharing contact details of trusted joiners or handy-persons. This seems to echo Windle (2011) and Windle and Bennett's (2012) notion of social resilience, with people themselves realising their individual and shared resources. However, in agreement with the authors, this chapter also stresses the need to find appropriate ways to support individual resources to promote longer-term sustainability.

Secondly, we need to have the infrastructure to respond through arts-, health- and community-based organisations that, we argue, encourage and facilitate self- and mutual help within communities. We need to recognise and build upon individual and collective emotional resilience, and to provide opportunities for older people to develop and deliver models of mutual support. We also argue for the need for community facilitators, who can signpost and guide pathways through – to draw from this project – the setting up of constitutions and bank accounts and applying for grants and assistance.

Finally and critically, our conversations highlighted the need to recognise individual and collective responsibility for preparing for older age. Many of us do not like to think that we are getting older, let alone plan for future need. Collectively, there should be the opportunity to work with planners on the design of neighbourhoods to encourage a choice of housing and local amenities. Our ageing demographic is changing the shape of our communities. We need to have more of a dialogue about what it means for all of us, not just older people, to age well in place. We need to decide how to go about planning for an evolving city, so that we have the infrastructure and services to ensure we are ready for ageing.

Conclusion

Creative engagement is adding to the 'talking tools' used to consult with people about issues that matter to them. Artistic interventions such as storytelling and song writing are drawn upon to give participants opportunities to explore their own and others' narratives around a given theme. In our case, our theme was what is needed to enable us to 'stay put' and 'stay well' in our neighbourhoods. There is a move towards initiatives that listen to, and engage, with older people (Buffel, Phillipson and Scharf, 2013). Creative participatory engagement can help to translate public conversations into public policy and practice. We argue that solutions cannot all be created within the neighbourhood. The notion that ageing and living well in neighbourhoods is down to individual capability, or can be managed collectively at a local level, is, we argue, an abdication of state responsibility. If resilience is built from the situated self, then neighbourhoods need to be 'ready for ageing' and to recognise that older people wish to remain involved, connected and engaged with all generations. Such resilient neighbourhoods should enable all of us to age well in place, particularly if influenced by a responsive policy landscape and strong lobbying for appropriate resources.

Notes

[1] See http://sharedlivesplus.org.uk/.
[2] KOVE, www.kove.org.uk; www.cubittartists.org.uk/category/education/elders-and-community/public-wisdom and Alison Rooke and Gesche Wuerfel, *Mobilizing Knowledge – Solving the Interaction Gap between Older People, Planners, Experts and General Citizens within the Thames Gateway: Guidelines, Toolkit and Findings* (Urban Buzz and Goldsmiths CUCR, University of London: 2007).
[3] See http://skimstone.org.uk.
[4] See www.theworldcafe.com/.
[5] UDecide For more detail about this participatory engagement tool please see: www.newcastle.gov.uk/communities-and-neighbourhoods/where-you-live/udecide

References

Age UK (2017a) *Briefing: Health and care of older people in England 2017*, London: Age UK. Available at: www.ageuk.org.uk/Documents/EN-GB/For-Professionals/Research/The_Health_and_Care_of_Older_People_in_England_2016.pdf?dtrk=true.

Age UK (2017b) *Later life in the United Kingdom*. Available at: www.ageuk.org.uk/Documents/EN-GB/Factsheets/Later_Life_UK_factsheet.pdf?dtrk=true.

AWOC (Ageing Without Children) (2017) 'Ageing without children – Why does it matter?' Available at: https://awoc.org/definition-of-ageing-without-children (accessed 19 October 2017).

Bailey, C., Clarke, C., Gibb, C., Haining, S., Wilkinson, H. and Tiplady, S. (2013) 'Risky and resilient life with dementia: Reflections from the literature', *Health Risk and Society* 15(5): 390–401.

Bailey, C., Reynolds, J., Hearne, C., Gavin, C. and Iftkhar, N. (2017) 'Falling on your feet: Dance and holistic wellness in later life', *Gerontological and Geriatric Research*, 3(1): 1028.

Baker, B. (2017) *With a little help from our friends: Creating community as we grow older*, Nashville, TN: Vanderbilt University Press.

Baldwin, C. (2008) 'Narrative, citizenship and dementia: The personal and the political', *Journal of Aging Studies*, 22(3): 222–8.

Barnes, R., Auburn, T. and Lea, S. (2004) 'Citizenship in practice', *British Journal of Social Psychology*, 43(2): 187–206.

Bartlett, R. and O'Connor, D. (2007) 'From personhood to citizenship: Broadening the lens for dementia practice and research', *Journal of Aging Studies*, 21(2): 107–18.

Beard, J., Biggs, S. Bloom, D., Fried, L., Hogan, P., Kalache, A. and Olshansky, S. (eds) (2011) *Global population ageing: Peril or promise*, Geneva: World Economic Forum.

Bennett, K. (2015) *Emotional and personal resilience though life*, London: Foresight, Government Office for Science.

Brenton, M. (2013) *Senior cohousing communities – an alternative approach for the UK?* York: Joseph Rowntree Foundation.

Brown, J., Isaacs, D. and Wheatley, J. (2005) *The world café approach: Shaping our futures through conversations that matter*, Oakland, CA: Berrett-Koehler Publishers.

Buffel, T., Phillipson, C. and Scharf, T. (2013) 'Experiences of neighbourhood exclusion and inclusion among older people living in deprived inner city areas in Belgium and England', *Ageing and Society*, 33(1): 89–109.

Campaign for Better Transport (2015) *Buses in crisis: A report on bus funding across England and Wales 2010–2015*, London: Campaign for Better Transport.

Centre for Ageing Better (2017) *UK network of age-friendly communities*. Available at: https://www.ageing-better.org.uk/our-work/area/age-friendly-communities/.

Clarke, C., Bailey, C. and Gibb, C. (2016) 'On the inside or on the outside of physical and social places – an analysis of resilience and citizenship living with dementia in rural and semi-urban communities', *Dementia*, 15(3): 434–52.

Collins, A. and Smyer, M.A. (2005) 'The resilience of self-esteem in late adulthood', *Journal of Aging and Health*, 17(4): 471–89.

Commission on the Future of Health and Social Care in England (2014) *A new settlement for health and social care: Final report*, London: The King's Fund. Available at: www.kingsfund.org.uk/publications/new-settlement-health-and-social-care.

Edwards, T. (2015) *Bank branch closures*, House of Commons, Briefing Paper No 385 SN00385.

Fange, F., Oswald, F. and Clemson, L. (2012) 'Aging in place in late life: Theory, methodology, and intervention', *Journal of Aging Research*, 2012: article ID 547562. Available at: https://www.ncbi.nlm.nih.gov/pubmed/22619718.

Gilleard, C. and Higgs, P. (2008) 'The third age and the baby boomers: Two approaches to the social structuring of later life', *International Journal of Ageing and Later Life*, 2(2): 13–30.

Gilroy, R. (2008) 'Places that support human flourishing: Lessons from later life', *Planning Theory & Practice*, 9(2): 145–63.

Handler, S. (2014) *An alternative age-friendly handbook (for the socially engaged practitioner)*, Manchester: Manchester University Press.

Humphries, R., Thorlby, R., Holder, H., Hall, P. and Charles, A. (2016) *Social care for older people: Home truths*, London: The Kings Fund.

Janssen, B., Van Regenmortel, T. and Abma, T. (2011) 'Identifying sources of strength: Resilience from the perspective of older people receiving long-term community care', *European Journal of Ageing*, 8(3): 145–56.

Mackintosh, S. and Leather, P. (2016) *The Disabled Facilities Grant: Before and after the introduction of the Better Care Fund*, Nottingham: Care and Repair England.

Newcastle City Council (2012) *Background evidence paper, Fairer Housing delivery plan 2013–2016*, Newcastle-upon-Tyne: Newcastle City Council.

Newcastle City Council (2017) *Newcastle housing statement 2017–20*, Newcastle-upon-Tyne: Newcastle City Council.

ONS (2017) *Overview of the UK population: July 2017*. Available at: https://www.ons.gov.uk/releases/overviewoftheukpopulationjuly2017.

Parkinson, J., Hunter, W. and Barac, M. (2013) *Silver linings: The active third age and the city*. London: RIBA (Royal Institute of British Architects). Retrieved from : https://www.architecture.com/-/media/gathercontent/silver-linings/additional-documents/silverliningstheactivethirdageandthecitypdf.pdf

Phillipson, C. (2011) 'Developing age-friendly communities: New approaches to growing old in urban communities', in R. Settersten and J.L. Angel (eds) *Handbook of the Sociology of Aging*, New York, NY: Springer, pp 279–93.

Phillipson, C. (2012) 'Globalisation, economic recession and social exclusion: Policy challenges and responses', in T. Scharf and N. Keating (eds) *From exclusion to inclusion in old age: A global challenge*, Bristol: Policy Press, pp 17–32.

Pickard, L. (2012) *Public expenditure costs of carers leaving employment*, LSE Health and Social Care Blog, London School of Economics and Political Science. Available at: http://blogs.lse.ac.uk/healthandsocialcare/2012/04/25/dr-linda-pickard-public-expenditure-costs-of-carers-leaving-employment.

Prior, D., Stewart, J. and Walsh, K. (1995) *Citizenship: Rights, community and participation*, London: Pitman.

Riseborough, M. (2013a) *Work on the wild side: Briefing document 1: For developers and architects*, London: Housing Learning and Improvement Network. Available at: https://www.housinglin.org.uk/.

Riseborough, M. (2013b) *Work on the wild side: Briefing document 2: For commissioners and housing and social care providers*, London: Housing Learning and Improvement Network. Available at: https://www.housinglin.org.uk/.

Rowles, G. (1978) *Prisoners of space? Exploring the geographical experience of older people*, Boulder, CO: Westview Press.

Rowles, G. (1983) 'Geographical dimensions of social support in rural Appalachian community', in, G. Rowles and R. Ohta (eds) *Aging and milieu: Environmental perspectives on growing old*, New York: Academic Press, pp 231–9.

Shanks, D. (2016) *Hatching a plan for older people's housing*, London: Housing Learning and Improvement Network. Available at: https://www.housinglin.org.uk/_assets/Resources/Housing/Support_materials/Viewpoints/HLIN_Viewpoint_78_PlanningforOPHousing.pdf.

Timonen, V. (2016) *Beyond successful and active ageing: A theory of model ageing*, Bristol: Policy Press.

United Nations Population Fund (2017) World population trends. Retrieved from: https://www.unfpa.org/world-population-trends

WHO (World Health Organization) (2017) *Ageing and life-course: Global financial crisis and the health of older people*, Geneva: World Health Organization. Available at: www.who.int/ageing/economic_issues/en/.

Windle, G. (2011) 'What is resilience? A review and concept analysis', *Reviews in Clinical Gerontology*, 21(2): 152–69.

Windle, G. and Bennett, K.M. (2012) 'Caring relationships: How to promote resilience in challenging times', in M. Ungar (ed) *The social ecology of resilience*, New York: Springer, pp 219–31.

Woodhouse, J. and Dempsey, N. (2016) *Public libraries*, House of Commons, Briefing paper No 5875 SN05875.

EIGHT

Crafting resilience for later life

Jackie Reynolds

Editorial introduction

This chapter explores the role of long-running craft activities in the lives of older women. The craft activities are understood as both creative and social experiences, and both aspects are seen as supporting resilience responses to the challenges of later life. Resilience is here understood as both individual and communal. The practice of making craft objects also forms the basis for narratives and meanings that contribute to resilient responses to later life.

Introduction

In this chapter, I draw upon my doctoral research, which examined the meanings that older people attach to their participation in group arts activities throughout their lives. The study (Reynolds, 2011) explored participation in a range of activities and focused on understanding the relationship between arts participation and social capital in later life. Social capital is increasingly recognised as a resource for resilience, and can be a characteristic of individuals or communities. The concept was popularised by Robert Putnam, who defines it as 'connections among individuals – social networks and the norms of reciprocity and trustworthiness that arise from them' (Putnam, 2000, p 19).

Commentators have since noted the lack of qualitative insights into how social capital is actually *experienced* (Blackshaw and Long, 2005) and the tendency to ignore gender differences (O'Neill and Gidengil, 2006). The social capital of older women in particular is largely neglected in the literature. While arts activities are recognised as a potentially valuable means of building social capital (Better Together, 2000), our knowledge of the nature of arts-generated social capital has previously been limited. Similarly, the relationship between arts-generated social capital and later-life resilience is also largely unexplored.

In order to address these issues, I focus in this chapter on the findings from ten interviews with female participants who take part in craft activities in groups. I will highlight the ways in which these women's relationships, widowhood, ill-health and a range of other factors have impacted upon their later-life participation. I will also discuss the networks of support and reciprocity arising from their arts engagement. In doing so, I provide insights into the distinctive nature of arts-generated social capital and the implications of this in terms of resilience. Moreover, I demonstrate the value of approaching the topic from a lifecourse perspective, with key aspects of these women's biographies providing useful insights into the importance of their crafts in terms of their identities and the various roles that they have fulfilled at work and at home.

Resilience in later life

The concept of resilience is most strongly associated with the field of developmental psychology, but in recent years has been an increasingly popular topic among social scientists more widely. Moreover, while early resilience research focused mainly on the experiences of children, it is increasingly seen as relevant to all stages of life. There is, however, no common understanding of the potentially distinctive or unique nature of resilience in later life (Wild et al, 2013). There are no universally agreed definitions or measures of resilience, and so the factors associated with the concept are a matter for on-going research and debate. There are, however, some broad and widely accepted understandings of what it entails. Resilience in later life has been defined as 'the ability to stand up to adversity and to "bounce back" or return to a state of equilibrium following individual adverse episodes' (Centre for Policy on Ageing, 2014, p 2). As Langer notes:

> Aging brings many types of changes. It is a challenging period in people's lives that often includes sudden and multiple losses and unforeseen physical, emotional, social, economic, and spiritual assaults to their person. (Langer, 2012, p 459)

Langer observes that, despite such adversity, some older people are able to adjust and to address the challenges that they face with determination and enthusiasm, noting that 'the extent to which they accept and adapt to changes directly affects the quality of life they can achieve and maintain as they grow older' (Langer, 2012, p 459). In cases where adversity is on-going, resilience may also involve having (or developing) the ability to cope with such challenges in the longer term. This includes being able to 'derive meaning from experiences and the realization that life has a purpose, *meaningfulness*' (Langer, 2012, p 462). The meanings are derived from life-themes that people regard as important, and that can include creativity. As Zautra et al (2008, p 44) express it: 'the greater a person's capacity to stay on a satisfying life course, the greater their resilience'. As well as providing a sense of purpose, this is also important for maintaining self-identity. We can observe these processes in the ordinary and everyday events in people's lives, including engagement in arts and creativity.

Researchers of resilience have tended to focus on identifying 'risks', although as Wild et al (2013) note, there is much debate about what constitutes adversity or 'risk', and it can be seen as a subjective, or at least a relative, issue. They draw upon a wide range of research about later-life resilience in identifying the following 'risks' or adversity that might affect older people: socio-economic disadvantage, elder abuse, bereavement, health challenge and changing social roles. They also highlight that more recent research has used the concept of resilience in exploring 'how people cope with "negative life events", and even the more ordinary upheavals associated with normal "life transitions"' (Wild et al, 2013, p 138).

Increasingly, however, work on later-life resilience has been influenced by the movement of gerontology beyond a problem-focused orientation and towards a focus on the strengths of older adults and their contributions to society. Resilience is thus viewed as a key element in 'ageing well' (Resnick et al, 2010), and the focus is on mechanisms through which resilience is developed (Windle, 2010). Understanding these mechanisms includes identifying assets or protective factors (for example, supportive social networks) that can help to mitigate the negative effects of a risk (Wild et al, 2013). To some extent, these assets can be identified as individual characteristics or 'traits', but we have also seen the growth of environmental perspectives on resilience. On a collective level, there is the potential for community resilience to be generated by informal networks within civil society that may help groups or communities to withstand the pressures of social, political and environmental change (Windle, 2010; Wild et al, 2013). This is where we see an explicit link between the concept of resilience and that of social capital.

Such a focus on strengths and assets has resulted in links between resilience research and the positive psychology movement. Resilience has thus become viewed as an important aspect of a person's well-being, enabling them to thrive and flourish, rather than simply surviving:

> Resilience researchers have also argued for further expansion of the concept to incorporate the potential for 'growth' as a *result of*, not just *in spite of*, the experience of adversity – i.e. the idea that new skills are learnt and insights gained through coping with difficult circumstances. (Richardson, 2002 cited by Wild et al, 2013, p 139)

My interest is in the development of social capital assets in the context of craft groups as a mechanism for resilience.

Linking resilience and social capital

Social capital is generally viewed as having originated in the work of Pierre Bourdieu, and was popularised by the work of Robert Putnam (2000). While it is beyond the scope of this chapter to provide an in-depth analysis of the concept, John Field (2008, p 1) sums up its essence in the words 'relationships matter':

> By making connections with one another, and keeping them going over time, people are able to work together to achieve things they either could not achieve by themselves, or could only achieve with great difficulty. People connect through a series of networks and they tend to share common values with other members of these networks; to the extent that these networks constitute a resource, they may be seen as forming a kind of capital. (Field, 2008, p 1)

A strong relationship exists between the concept of resilience and that of social capital. Indeed, Zautra et al (2008) see examinations of social capital as being at the forefront of research into community resources that foster resilience. Just as we have seen that resilience has both individual and collective dimensions, the same is true of social capital: it can be viewed as a benefit that can be accumulated by individuals, or as lodged in social structures, 'a resource that exists only because of the mutual or reciprocal relations or interactions that exist between a group of people' (Sapiro, 2006, pp 157–8).

Wild et al (2013) point to an emerging body of research on social or community resilience, (with the terms tending to be used interchangeably). Drawing on the work of Sapountzaki (2007, cited by Wild et al, 2013), they identify social capital as one of the types of community capital that underpin social resilience (the other types being natural, financial, human and physical). Networks, affiliation, reciprocity, trust and mutual exchange are given as examples of social capital resources. Again, the key point to recognise here is that resilience is much more complex than an issue of individual psychology, and that we need to consider the broader structures and resources that may affect an individual's resilience. Social connectedness (and therefore social capital) is clearly therefore a highly important factor in understanding both individual and collective resilience. There is currently a lack of research that explores resilience from both an individual *and* a community perspective, and there is arguably an '(over) emphasis on personal qualities and experiences within debates on resilience and ageing' (Wild et al, 2013, p 147). Examining the issue from a social capital perspective can contribute towards addressing this deficit.

Within gerontology, both social capital and resilience are concepts that engage with and emphasise the strengths of older people, thus challenging the more common deficit approach to researching later life. Moreover, as Wild et al (2013, p 142) note, much of the work on successful ageing (citing Rowe and Kahn, 1998) can be seen as focusing on overcoming or avoiding problems, whereas 'the resilience literature is more explicitly focused on exploring the *experience of* rather than the *avoidance of* vulnerability'. My research exemplifies this focus on 'what works', as opposed to a deficit approach, by engaging with people who are actively engaged in their community through membership of at least one group (and in some cases belonging to more than one group and/or in a leadership role).

About the research

The study explored the meanings that older people attach to their participation in group arts activities throughout their lives. Reflecting a narrative approach and a lifecourse perspective, it involved qualitative interviews with 24 participants linked to a case study town in the English Midlands (with the pseudonym Greentown). Greentown is a small town with a population of around 25,000, and a lower than average black and minority ethnic population. It lies in a high, shallow valley, surrounded by arable fields and countryside and is about 10 miles from the nearest city conurbation. It contains both the most affluent and the most deprived electoral wards in the local authority area. In the early to mid-20th century it was rich in heavy industry, mainly coal and steel, and also in the production of fabrics. Since the demise of these industries, and the resulting lack of employment opportunities, the town has an ageing population, although in recent years building programmes have encouraged some young families to move into the area.

For many of the older population, the town tends to be characterised by a sense of locality. Most of the arts and cultural opportunities in the town are led by volunteers. There is little in the way of purpose-built accommodation, so venues include the town hall, the library, community centres, churches and schools. There is a branch of the University of the Third Age (U3A) in the town, established in 2005, and a variety of other arts activities and organisations, often typically attracting older participants. Participants for this study were recruited through a range of groups, including choirs, dancing, amateur dramatics and arts and crafts groups. The interviews took place between March and October 2008. A total of 24 participants took part, including 8 men and 16 women, and aged between 60 and 87. This chapter focuses on the findings from interviews with 10 women who were recruited through craft groups, including a U3A Patchwork and Quilting group, hand-made cards and parchment craft. There are also informal groups where people take along a range of individual craft projects to work on in a social setting. The women who took part are listed in the Table 8.1. While the main groups that they attend

Table 8.1: Craft group participants

Name (pseudonyms)	Age	Craft group
Alice	69	U3A Patchwork and Quilting (previously U3A Calligraphy)
Dorothy	73	Leads a general craft group
Edith	87	General craft group (focusing on card making) U3A Parchment Craft
Heather	64	U3A Patchwork and Quilting Several general craft groups
Joan	75	Card making, sewing, tapestry and embroidery – mainly individually but previously U3A Calligraphy and has attended residential craft courses
Margaret	62	U3A Patchwork and Quilting
Marion	66	General craft group (focusing on card making) U3A Parchment Craft
Penny	63	U3A Parchment Craft
Rebecca	75	U3A Patchwork and Quilting
Sandra	62	U3A Patchwork and Quilting

are identified, most of them are avid participants in a range of crafts, often practised individually as well as in groups.

The semi-structured interviews were developed around a number of open-ended themes including: the nature of people's arts participation (past and present); the impact of key lifecourse transitions; what role people's arts participation plays when they deal with life's challenges and setbacks; motivations and barriers to participation; whether creativity changes over time; and the impact of belonging to particular communities or neighbourhoods. While the shortest interview lasted 45 minutes, they were typically much longer, up to around three hours. Interviews were fully transcribed and thematically analysed using NVivo software. In writing this chapter, I have re-analysed the ten interviews identified earlier, examining the data with a specific focus on resilience. While this was often an implicit focus in the original research, re-examining with this lens has further enhanced the understanding and insights gained through the research. It is important to note that participants were not asked to explicitly focus on their engagement in group arts activities in terms of social capital or resilience: the questions of meaning were far more open than this. It is therefore highly significant that their accounts frequently focused on issues relating to these concepts.

Findings

Crafting resilience throughout life

In setting the scene for the ways in which people's involvement in craft activities relate to social capital and resilience in later life, it is important to understand their involvement from a lifecourse perspective. The study's findings highlighted the key roles played by people's childhood experiences at home, school and church – as well as in some cases their employment experiences as adults – in shaping their arts engagement. This was evidenced clearly in the 10 interviews with women crafters. Their experiences were highly gendered, and influenced by cohort factors. Crafting skills were learned from the earliest stages:

> "We used to sit in the evenings cutting up old coats, rag pieces and auntie used to sit pegging rugs on sugar bags, you know and those were our times in the evenings – we used to say, 'Can we get the box out with the bits in?' and we used to sit cutting these little bits of material up and watching her do this – she taught me how to knit, she sat

with me knitting and I had a little toy sewing machine." (Alice)

There were also flower and craft festivals at churches, which again was significant for this cohort who grew up in a time of higher levels of church attendance. This informal learning at home and church also continued at school; Edith, for example, learned how to knit at infant school, and craft education was a big focus of all her school life, which continued until she left school at the age of 14. Margaret specialised in studying dress making at school from the age of 13, and Alice also attended evening classes in embroidery when she was in her teens. Once they left school, the craft skills that were learned were then utilised as part of people's home-making roles, often as a strategy for dealing with poverty:

> "Well when I first got married, we had nothing so to speak and if I hadn't have got the material and stuff or the embroidery silks to do – I don't know what we'd have done – or what *I'd* have done." (Marion)

> "I think then people *did* make a lot more things; they made things for their home, you know, the curtains and the furnishings – and they made things for themselves; there was lots of crafts and there was the knitting and everybody made things and they all had a go at doing it." (Sandra)

As well as making clothes for all her family, Sandra also used to do the same for work colleagues, again as a way of earning some extra money, and Alice went into tailoring after she left school. In this study, people's involvement in craft activities could invariably be traced as a coherent path throughout their lives, with a sense of adaptation in response to varying levels of financial necessity, domestic responsibilities, prevailing fashions and a desire to learn new techniques.

Hence, when people engage in craft activities in later life they are often using skills and resources that they have acquired throughout their lives. Margaret, for example, feels that without her involvement in the patchwork and quilting group, her dressmaking skills would be redundant, as clothes are now much cheaper to buy. And similarly, Sandra talked of her excitement at getting her sewing machine out and serviced upon her retirement, looking forward to utilising and further developing skills that had long been unused due to work and caring commitments.

The findings highlighted in this section have created a context for people's later-life participation and have further demonstrated the importance of the themes that develop during people's lives that may contribute to positive ageing identities. In the next section, we look in more depth at some of the ways in which involvement in crafts can be linked to a sense of meaning and purpose.

Meaning and purpose

A number of key themes emerged from the 10 interviews around the importance of people's craft activities for maintaining a sense of meaning and purpose throughout life, and particularly in later life. As in the previous section, these findings also link strongly to the issue of self-identity; again, adopting a lifecourse perspective is valuable. First, several of the women talked about the ways in which negative experiences at school had undermined their confidence throughout life, but that the craft skills that they had gained had in some way compensated for this, and/or provided a positive self-identity and self-esteem. Dorothy, for example, was clearly resentful that her head teacher had refused to allow her to sit the 11-plus exam and had steered her directly into sewing work:

> "Our headmistress, Miss W, said, 'Ooh no, Dorothy'll never do anything, she'll only sew for her living.' So I always felt a bit miffed that I never had the opportunity to fail, you know. I couldn't sit me eleven plus, she wouldn't let me. And it was up to her." (Dorothy)

However, being "clever with me fingers" is clearly an important part of Dorothy's self-identity, and she makes a direct link between the denial of opportunities at school (involving herself and others) and the talents and resourcefulness of older women in Greentown:

> "Miss W just wouldn't let you go anywhere, she just wanted you to leave school and go in a mill, that's all girls did of my age, they used to go down the mills ... And they got a lot of skills from there cos of the sewing and making things and I think that's why people in Greentown – I mean you put a craft fair on, it's beautiful. The stuff that they make is beautiful. And I'm sure it's just through what they've done at work really. They've taught themselves in a way

because there certainly wasn't the opportunities that there are today." (Dorothy)

As well as taking pride in their skills, there was also a strong sense for these women that they needed to be constantly active and productive. For some, this had been a constant theme throughout life. Marion, for example, links it to having been brought up on a farm where everyone is "always busy". She also talks about always having had to "make her own entertainment", due to her husband long working hours through self-employment. Similarly, for Dorothy the need to be busy is explained very much in terms of continuity:

> "I couldn't do without it, let's put it that way. I *really* couldn't do without it. Sometimes I feel as if I don't want to do anything but I *really* couldn't do without doing something. Me fingers are never still. But – I don't know why that is, I suppose it's because you've been busy all your life, see, and you come to retire and I've just kept going, I've just kept on and on and on." (Dorothy)

However, for some participants, such as Rebecca, who is widowed, this need for achievement and productivity has become more important to her as she has become older:

> "I think it's become more important as I've got older. I still like trying different things. If I didn't have something on the go as it were, or if I didn't have several things on the go, I think I would be, well not exactly lost but I don't think I'd be as contented. You've got a sense of achievement, you've created something, you've made something which you can feel pleased with, and I don't know – no, it's a bigger part of my life now." (Rebecca)

Discussions on the theme were also not limited just to the times that people spent at home, but were also related to their group participation. Heather, for example, values both being productive as a group and also the opportunities to learn from one another:

> "I think you're all learning off one another, you've all got something to put in, whereas if you're just meeting up with a group of friends just for a chat, you're not really developing anything from each other ... I think all life is a learning

curve. And I wouldn't go, like say to just – like some people meet up every week or every fortnight or whatever just for coffee or something, I couldn't do that, as I say, I've got to be doing, I've got to be achieving something." (Heather)

As in Rebecca's case, this desire for challenge and achievement has become more important to Heather as she has become older:

"I think when your children are very little your time is limited, and I think it's only since I retired and I've had loads of time on my hands and I can't bear to do nothing, that I wanted to branch out ... I've always been into the craft side, but it hasn't been until I retired that I've sort of spread me wings and thought, 'Oh yeah, I'll do this, I'll do that. I'll try that.'" (Heather)

Thus, for Heather, a focus on continued learning, setting herself goals and embracing challenges helps her to maintain a positive self-identity in negotiating the upheaval of retirement. Her quotes reinforce the important point that resilience has both individual and collective dimensions, thus highlighting the key role of social capital in understanding resilience. Networks and mutual support are core elements of social capital, and in the following section we turn our attention to these aspects of participants' experiences.

Networks and mutual support

Again, to begin this section, it is useful to draw attention to some of the highly gendered experiences that have shaped the lives of some of these women. People's group involvement could often be traced back to their cohort experiences in terms of the kind of close-knit communities that they grew up in. Several of the women clearly identified themselves as being a "people person", or someone who liked being part of a group, and their desire for social interaction is realised through a long history of joining groups, including arts-related groups. For some, working with others as part of a team was a strong aspect of their identity, and this tended to include nurturing and supporting others' talents.

During their interviews, participants discussed at length the different aspects of emotional and practical support that they had experienced through the groups, and the ways in which this had helped them to address particular challenges in their lives. Mutual support was significant at every stage of people's involvement in the groups. Several women talked about losing confidence in later life, often related to retirement and/or loss of caring roles:

> "It's funny when you retire cos you feel as though, 'Well I've done it now. And I've finished me job. I've brought me children up. I'm no good now.' But you are – really – and you've got a lot of experience and things that you've done, haven't you?" (Sandra)

There was recognition that even for those who were relatively confident, joining a group in the first place could be a significant challenge:

> "It's quite difficult to go into a new group on your own; *I* found it quite difficult and I've got a lot of confidence, as you can tell [laughter], but you know, like I found it quite difficult." (Penny)

However, the local nature of the craft groups, and the ways in which they draw on people's existing skills and experiences, accumulated throughout their lives, make them a relatively accessible opportunity to connect with others. This is exemplified in Heather's account, as she made the decision to join a craft group following a period of mental ill-health. She recalls deciding to go to the local library at a lunch time to look for information on local groups, and how a chance meeting while there led to a new friendship focused on involvement in crafts. Neither woman felt able to go to the group (which also met at the library) on her own, but they agreed to meet outside and go in together.

Even when participants had strong family relationships, they had sometimes faced issues in later life that had left them feeling isolated. Alice, for example, experienced a loss of social contacts due to old friends leaving the area and her grandchildren growing up. She had previously been involved in a church choir for many years, but this eventually folded as members died and no one came forward to replace them. Her husband had experienced a prolonged period of mental ill-health, which resulted in a further loss of social activities. Joining the U3A Patchwork and Quilting group was a means of trying to adjust to all these changes by 'doing her own thing' in a local setting, from where she could quickly return home if her husband needed her.

Marion also had a limited social network, especially since her children had grown up. She had no work-related networks, as she had always worked for her husband, based at home. She relied mostly on the craft groups that she attends for her social relationships. These groups are, in effect, Marion's community, and she becomes isolated at the times when the groups do not meet:

> "I don't mind being on my own at all but I must admit I *do miss* – if the classes are shut for a week or two in the summer or anything you do miss that social, you know, you really enjoy going back, even if it's just for chit chat ... I've got friends there which I wouldn't have ... if I didn't go out to these classes I wouldn't meet anybody, so it's a great outlet for me to go." (Marion)

In Edith's case, it is her social relationships that have developed through attending craft groups that enable her to sustain her involvement. Since she no longer drives and cannot walk far, she relies on group members for lifts to the activities. She also referred to having recently visited a craft centre and cafe at a nearby garden centre with one of the group members with whom she had developed a friendship, and who had driven her there. This further illustrates the social capital mechanisms related to joining these groups, and how they may be experienced in people's everyday lives.

As well as the practicalities of joining and attending the groups, participants also highlight ways in which they experience emotional and practical support once they are regular members of the group. Feeling valued by the group was clearly and deeply meaningful to some of the participants. The patchwork and quilting group seemed to be a particularly close and supportive network. Alice contrasted their understanding and support of her husband's illness with her less positive experiences in a different type of group, and Sandra was moved to tears as she talked about feeling valued by the group:

> "The hard part for me ... is the people that I don't know. And will they think I'm silly? Will they think, 'She's no good'? Will they think this, will they think that? But do you know, they're so lovely and you go and they're, 'I've missed you, you've been away for two weeks' cos the children have been off, you know, I haven't been going – 'Oh, you know we've missed you, you know and we've said "I wonder how Sandra's going on?"' and you think, 'That's really nice',

you know ... it's nice that they're there, that the groups are there that you can join and it is nice to feel you're still wanted." (Sandra)

As well as this emotional support, the groups also tended to be mutually supportive environments in relation to encouraging the development of each other's craft skills, both through positive affirmation and through learning new techniques from each other:

"I would never have attempted the patchwork or anything like that if I hadn't have been – and the encouragement, and when you've done something and you take it in and everybody, oh they're over the moon that you've finished it, that is very important to me. And like the beading and that, if you get stuck there's always somebody there who will show you and guide you and help you. So I wouldn't have done that on my own, not the making the necklaces side of it." (Heather)

Several participants referred to the ways in which they were able to contact each other between group meetings if they were stuck on a particular craft project, and that they would on occasion go to each other's homes to demonstrate a particular skill, for example on a sewing machine. They would also sometimes lend each other expensive equipment, or share a magazine subscription to reduce costs. This was important, as it was recognised that while the groups tended to involve minimal membership costs, the craft activities themselves could be expensive – although this varied depending on the types of project undertaken and from where people sourced their materials.

So far, we have seen examples of the ways in which these women's involvement in craft activities supports the development of social capital and resilience both in their normal, everyday lives and also in relation to particular challenges, such as coping with caring responsibilities, transition to retirement and loss of networks and self-confidence. Ill-health was also an issue for some. We have seen that taking up craft activities could be part of a strategy for dealing with ill-health (for example, in the case of Heather), and while Edith saw her craft activities as simply a continuity, she also made reference to having had to give up other group memberships due to her lack of mobility. Similarly, Marion's involvement in crafts had increased as she had become less able to walk any distances (although it should be noted that for both Marion and Penny, their involvement in crafts also caused them physical discomfort, due to neck and shoulder problems).

Another challenge that was referred to by several participants (although not always in relation to personal experience) was that of bereavement, especially the loss of a partner. Margaret, for example, felt that belonging to a group was important in terms of not relying exclusively on one's partner for social interaction. As a group leader, she also expressed a strong commitment to providing support for bereaved people within the group:

> "if one of us was left on our own you've already got a system in place where you know you're welcome, you can go back at whatever point in time you want to go back and you're not somebody new and you can find that uncomfortable to start joining a group, especially if something's happened then people do become isolated. You need a network of people around you ... I would do that for anybody that something had happened to; I would be there for them. And I just think that's really important. You've got to make them welcome." (Margaret)

Similarly, Dorothy referred to a member of the group that she leads who had been suddenly widowed two years previously, and who had seemingly gained new confidence and craft skills through involvement in the group, which Dorothy found "ever so rewarding". While three of the women (Rebecca, Edith and Joan) were widows, Joan was the only one who discussed this aspect of her involvement in crafts. Joan had attended various arts and crafts groups since being widowed (having been persuaded to do so by a friend). While she values the "good friends" that she has made at some of the groups, some of whom she has been out with outside of the groups (for example, visiting craft fairs), she is generally ambivalent about the commitment involved in friendships, and it seems that the craft activity is of greater importance than the social aspect. She also places emphasis on the ways in which her crafts (and other arts activities) help her to manage her time when she is alone:

> "Time goes quickly ... And when it's winter and cold and dark and wet, it's just nice to get all your bits out and get cracking and stick onto doing something and that's two hours gone before you know where you are ... it's time for

a cuppa, you know. So it's good for that and I think that's needed when you're on your own and you're retired." (Joan)

While this section has focused mostly on some of the strengths that people perceived in relation to their engagement in craft groups, through accessing supportive networks, Joan's account reminds us that we should not make assumptions about people's desire for social relationships, nor ignore the complexities of people's motivations and the way that they may feel ambivalent about particular aspects of their participation. One of the distinctive aspects of crafting activities is that they can be practised both individually and within a group, and both aspects are significant in examining resilience.

Community resilience

It has been argued that there is a need for greater understanding of the relationship between individual and community resilience, and that even when the role of the community is considered, it tends to be in terms of impact on individual resilience (Wild et al, 2013). This chapter has highlighted the interdependence of individual and social resilience. There are three further themes that demonstrate the contribution made by this group of older women to building up and maintaining community resilience. These are: passing on skills, developing leadership and community activism.

The passing on of skills occurs not only within the actual groups, but often more widely, and sometimes with the expressed aim of ensuring that skills do not disappear over time. Margaret, Rebecca and Heather had all been involved in leading Guides or Brownies over time. Rebecca has also helped to run a craft session at a local care home, doing card making. Margaret talks about teaching groups of Brownies to sew buttons onto fabric, noting that they are often no longer taught these skills at school or home. She also worked with Guides from different groups to make friendship bracelets, encouraging them to connect with each other. Alice and Heather also talk about passing on their skills to their grandchildren:

> "My youngest granddaughter is doing textiles, now she's very very interested in what I do because she's sort of making things at school and she said, 'When I tell them my Nan's done this or my Nan can do that' you know and she says, 'I feel at a bit of an advantage over a lot of them

because they've not done, they haven't seen it done in the family'." (Alice)

The leadership of the craft groups is another area requiring recognition in terms of community resilience. Groups in Greentown often struggle to keep going, due to a lack of people willing to lead them:

> "The U3A is pretty good but the groups there, you've got to find somebody from within the group who belongs to the U3A who's prepared to instruct or to be in charge, you know, sort of keep it going. So if there isn't somebody in what you want to do who's prepared to do that ... People get ill or they get tired." (Rebecca)

However, for the craft groups that featured in the research, there seems to be a particular style of informal, collaborative leadership that can support people who do not see themselves as leaders and are perhaps more generally lacking in confidence to take on a leadership role. Drawing upon long-established skills and attending sessions in a local environment also seems to support leadership development. Several participants with longer histories of group leadership described how they had encouraged friends to become co-leaders, to the point where they were confident enough to take on sole leadership. On the one hand, there is a sense that no one is the overall leader, but on the other, there is some recognition of the sacrifice that group leaders do make in terms of their own engagement:

> "Nobody leads them, nobody leads, it's all general. If nobody's there at the parchment [craft group], if the teacher can't come, then I'm the one that tries to show them, because I'm the one that's done it the longest because last week the teacher couldn't come and I said, 'Do you want to carry on?' and they said 'Oh yes, you're there, you can show us'. But when you're the leader, you don't do anything yourself – that's the drawback – because they want to know, so you might as well not take anything." (Marion)

As well as group leadership, other types of volunteering that could be seen to support community resilience more widely include fund raising and supporting charities through craft making. This is a key focus of Dorothy's involvement in leading a craft group. The aspect of her voluntary activities that she focuses on mostly is her commitment to fund raising. Not only does she make a lot of goods to sell and raise funds for causes such as the church, but she also involves the whole group in making items to give away to other charitable causes:

> "But I do take the crochet class down at church, done that about 20 years, but now it's turned more into a craft class because all the ladies that come I think have got more crocheting than they know what to do with really so now they knit, and we take on projects, we've done blankets for the babies in the orphanages in Romania, and – we just take on a project and try and do it." (Dorothy)

A common theme between this and other projects referred to by participants is the sense of joint purpose that results from group efforts in such projects. All of the volunteering activities highlighted in this section can be seen as contributing to community resilience. Yet, such contributions tend to go unrecognised, due to the small-scale, local nature of the groups, and arguably also the gendered and low-status nature of the activities.

Discussion and conclusion

This was a small-scale research study, and this chapter has focused on just ten of the interviews. The women all lived in the same small town and attended some of the same craft groups. Caution is therefore needed in drawing generalisations from the findings. There is much scope for future research into resilience and ageing, including understanding inequalities in accessing resilience resources and the complex interplay between individual and community resilience. In particular, there is still significant potential to further develop our understanding of the relationship between arts participation, social capital and resilience. In discussions of social capital in relation to different types of groups, arts groups are generally not included (see, for example, Gray, 2009). This is a significant gap, since arts and craft groups arguably blur the lines between formal civic participation and informal ties.

This chapter has contributed to addressing this gap by presenting some detailed analysis of the ways in which mechanisms of social capital and resilience can be understood in the everyday lives of these 10 women in relation to their involvement in crafts. Some of the distinctive aspects of craft groups have been emphasised, such as the continuity of skills and experiences; the links to previous employment;

the ability to participate even when in ill-health; and the potential for lifelong learning and personal challenge. Along with the local nature of many of the groups, these aspects of people's engagement challenge the potentially exclusionary and aspirational focus that is often seen in discussions of 'successful ageing'.

The findings have emphasised the importance of adopting lifecourse perspectives when considering processes of resilience, as suggested by Zautra et al:

> we need to study resilience over time. People develop themes in their lives that offer them hope, optimism, purpose, emotional clarity and a wisdom built on a complex and accepting view of their social relationships. But they do not do so all at once. Resilience takes time to unfold. (Zautra et al, 2008, p 50)

All of the women in this chapter were drawing in later life on skills that often dated back to early childhood. They had experienced highly gendered lives, where developing craft skills was a key part of their expected role in a number of contexts including home, school and work. In other areas, they had often been denied opportunities (for example, for educational achievement), but had used their crafting skills to their advantage, both in terms of building positive self-identities and in the ways in which they had applied their craft skills (for example, in making their homes with limited financial resources). While participants would not directly refer to themselves as 'resilient', it was certainly an important message in the biographies of participants. This links directly with the ways in which 'older people use storytelling or "life review" and, in particular, narratives about loss and coping in the "construction or reconfirmation" of a sense of self as resilient' (Wild et al, 2013, p 144, with reference to Gattuso, 2003).

The findings also challenge the academic discourse around the role of class in shaping the nature of people's social capital. Gray (2009, p 15) discusses arguments that membership of organisations is dominated by 'middle-class joiners', and that working-class elders rely more on family contacts and are disadvantaged in terms of making non-family contacts that might generate friendship and support. However, for some participants in this research, issues of class are blurred. Their lifecourse experiences often included working-class childhoods and young adulthoods, but as their lives progressed they apparently achieved relative affluence and class identities became relatively submerged (Gilleard and Higgs, 2005). Again, the craft groups seem to provide continuity of skills, interests and experiences through such transitions, as well as informal, locally based routes into joining and leading groups and making non-family contacts.

It is clear overall that continuity is a key issue for the women in this study. As Langer observes:

> Many older people rely on continuity in their lives because it appears necessary for their security and survival. Continuity of activities and environments concentrates the individual's energies in familiar domains of activity where learned routines can minimize the effects of aging. (Langer, 2012, p 460)

However, focusing on continuity does not always give adequate recognition to people's enthusiasm for adapting their skills, sharing learning, problem solving and developing new craft skills and techniques. It is clear from the findings that such challenges, along with being active and productive, offer a sense of meaning and purpose to participants.

The sense of purpose and meaning, and in particular the supportive networks that are accessed through membership of craft groups, can be seen to help people to deal with a range of challenges, some of them linked to later life. The findings highlight the wide range of emotional and practical support that is generated through craft groups. They also emphasise the value of volunteering as a component of resilience from both an individual and community perspective (see also Morrow-Howell et al, 2010).

Examining older people's resilience through a social capital lens goes some way to identifying the gaps in understanding that are identified by Wild et al (2013) regarding the relationship between individual and collective resilience. We cannot view the resilience of individuals in isolation, and one of the strengths of qualitative research is that it helps us to unpick the everyday, simple interactions in people's lives. This further enables us to identify the 'hidden resilience resources' among low-income and marginalised populations, which are often missed in traditional accounts of resilience (Wild et al, 2013, p 153). This includes unrecognised contributions by older people to building up and maintaining community resilience.

References

Better Together (2000) 'The arts and social capital', Saguaro Seminar on Civic Engagement in America, Cambridge, MA: John F. Kennedy School of Government. Available at: https://www.creativecity.ca/database/files/library/better_together.pdf.

Blackshaw, T. and Long, J. (2005) 'What's the big idea? A critical exploration of the concept of social capital and its incorporation into leisure policy discourse', *Leisure Studies*, 24(3): 239–58.

Centre for Policy on Ageing (2014) *Resilience in older age*, London: CPA. Available at: www.cpa.org.uk/information/reviews/CPA-Rapid-Review-Resilience-and-recovery.pdf.

Field, J. (2008) *Social Capital* (2nd edn), Abingdon: Routledge.

Gilleard, C. and Higgs, P. (2005) *Contexts of ageing: Class, cohort and community*, Cambridge: Polity Press.

Gray, A. (2009) 'The social capital of older people', *Ageing & Society*, 29(1): 5–31

Langer, N. (2012) 'Who moved my cheese? Adjusting to age-related changes', *Educational Gerontology*, 38(7): 459–64.

Morrow-Howell, N., O'Neill, G. and Greenfield, J. (2010) 'Civic engagement: Policies and programs to support a resilient aging society', in B. Resnick, L. Gwyther and K. Roberto (eds) *Resilience in aging: Concepts, research, and outcomes*, New York: Springer, pp 147–62.

O'Neill, B. and Gidengil, E. (2006) (eds) *Gender and social capital*, London: Routledge.

Putnam, R. (2000) *Bowling alone: The collapse and revival of American community*, New York: Simon & Schuster.

Resnick, B., Gwyther, L. and Roberto, K. (eds) (2010) *Resilience in aging: Concepts, research and outcomes*, New York: Springer.

Reynolds, J. (2011) 'Creative ageing: Exploring social capital and arts engagement in later life', unpublished PhD thesis, Keele University.

Sapiro, V. (2006) 'Gender, social capital and politics', in B. O'Neill and E. Gidengil (eds) *Gender and social capital*, London: Routledge, pp 151–83.

Wild, K., Wiles, J. and Allen, R. (2013) 'Resilience: Thoughts on the value of the concept for critical gerontology', *Ageing & Society*, 33(1): 137–58.

Windle, G. (2010) 'What is resilience? A review and concept analysis', *Reviews in Clinical Gerontology*, 21(2): 152–69.

Zautra, A., Hall, J. and Murray, K. (2008) 'Resilience: A new integrative approach to health and mental health research', *Health Psychology Review*, 2(1): 41–64.

NINE

Oral histories and lacemaking as strategies for resilience in women's craft groups

Anna Sznajder and Katarzyna Kosmala

Editorial introduction

This chapter is based on an ethnographic study of a women's lacemaking network in Kraków, Poland. As such, the chapter has much in common with Reynold's chapter discussing women's craft activities in the English Midlands. Indeed, this chapter confirms the value of craft work as both a creative and social activity and as contributing to the participants' resilience. However, it also highlights how the place of creativity is understood in historic craft traditions in a manner that is distinct from understandings of creativity that draw on theatre or fine art. Furthermore, the project reported on here encouraged the women in the lacemaking groups to become amateur ethnographic researchers and advocates for the cultural value of their traditions – processes that had consequences for their identities and resilience.

Introduction

Resilience – when contextualised in relation to older age – can be understood as a process leading to successful adaptation to stresses, difficulties and disturbances associated with ageing and change. It is seen as an important component of ageing and the accompanying decreases in personal autonomy, decline in cognitive functions and coping with the loss of significant others (Tomas et al, 2012). Resilience can be understood as 'a process of recovery (how well individuals are able to bounce back from adversity), sustainability (the capacity to continue to move forward in the face of adversity), and growth (the ability to further develop as a response to adversity)' (Manning, 2013, p 569). It is also seen as a 'dynamic interaction between an individual and his or her social and material environment'

(Janssen et al, 2012, p 344), happening in a particular time and place and in relation with others.

In this chapter, the concept of resilience provides a framework for reflecting upon the ability of individuals to withstand adversities related to old age through engagement in creative craft activity and told through oral stories. The opportunity to express oneself through creative means has been said to promote a sense of control and strengthens social ties (McFadden and Basting, 2010), to create a meaning (life has a purpose) and perseverance (a will to remain involved and active) (Alex, 2010), so that the individuals become more aware and engaged in their everyday life activities.

The chapter offers insights from a research project carried out with the group Charming Threads (in Polish: Czar Nici) and demonstrates the importance of the history of lacemaking in the city of Kraków, Poland for the members of the group. Kraków is situated in the province of Lesser Poland and the group drew in older people from the peripheral areas of the province, with the aim of improving their well-being. The women were encouraged to join the workshops through their promotion as an opportunity to update the knowledge they either learned as teenagers or, more recently, through accessing online craft forums (Brzezińska, 2010).

Lacemaking can be, and was, done alone at home, but the focus here is on the activities carried out in and by the groups that were formed out of the workshops. Meeting up regularly in person was seen by members as important. As engagement in creative activity 'appeared to enable the creation of connections with regard to a larger sense of being oneself' (la Cour, Josephsson and Luborsky, 2005, p 13), hence a physical presence in the group was necessary, as this allowed participants to experience making craft in the 'here and now' with input from other group members.

As well as a space for sharing skills and an opportunity for creative activity, the workshops should be understood as a social environment. Participants shared oral narratives that established connections between people's past and present lives. The narratives functioned at different levels: personal memories, collective memories of the narrative community and official master-narratives (historical politics). Sharing vernacular historical narratives and personal memories facilitated insights into the value of one's own creative work while immersed in the social life of the group meeting. This also allowed group members to rework a (potentially) difficult past. As will be argued later, this is interpreted as contributing to ageing-related resilience through a process of meaning-making for individuals and for the group.

The group moved beyond traditional craft activity to deliberately explore the wider history of women's craft in the city of Kraków, facilitated by academic partners. The Charming Threads group investigated the history of lacemaking workshops, focusing on the development of lacemaking in Kraków in the 20th century. They also collated genealogies of local lacemakers by collecting documents, interviewing former group members, organising exhibitions, reconstructing old patterns and designing laces. Their role as the guardians of local lacemaking heritage is now well documented by them (Węgorek, 2017a,b; Haftkoronka, 2017; Połubok, 2017) and is linked with the city's heritage (Narodowy Instytut Dziedzictwa, 2017).

In our resilience-driven project, combining oral stories with craft making allowed participants to explore how contemporary forms of tradition present in informal craft groups consolidated and developed skills, disseminated knowledge and generated new experiences for individuals making women's crafts either in their homes or collectively. By encouraging participants to undertake their own research, leading to publicly recognisable achievements (such as exhibitions, lectures or registration on the list of national intangible cultural heritage (Narodowy Instytut Dziedzictwa, 2017)), the group were able to formulate discourses of Kraków's history as alternatives to those established by academic historians. The outputs were able to highlight lacemaking as a valued cultural phenomenon.

The chapter is structured as follows: First, we discuss the research methods used in the project. Second, the lacemaking group will be considered as a source of ageing-related resilience. Third, starting with a brief presentation of the Charming Threads 15th anniversary in 2014, we will explore personal identity and the function of lacemaking circles in the context of past and present. Fourth, the relationship between masters and apprentices will be presented through the research conducted by group members and their role in building individual and group resilience. Finally, we will comment on how actions taken by the group and their result – the exhibition Return to Tradition in 2015 – can be interpreted in relation to the broader heritage of Kraków's cityscape and the continuation of women's handicrafts history there.

Methods

In relation to 'hand-made' theory and practice (Hackney, 2013a, 2013b) the chapter draws on participatory methods in ethnographic research. Ethnography, as a method for studying lacemaking circles, allowed for the collection, description and interpretation of multiple materials generated during the project in the forms of craft items, oral stories, written accounts and observations. The complexity of the methodological position included constituting, managing and resisting particular boundaries between researcher and research participants while negotiating otherness. Participant observation relies on tensions between objective and subjective, as well as merging the role of observer and participant, ethnographer and group member (O'Reilly, 2009). There is a complicated relationship dynamic between researcher and participants – the researcher needs to avoid a one-sided interpretation of an 'alien' culture and observing a parallel culture from a self-imposed distance.

Active participation meant integrating the roles of researcher and research participant within the established rules of the group and with the consent of all parties. This enabled dialogue and fostered trust between the researcher and the participants, making the space for participants' empowerment through words, images, objects and actions. The privilege of the research position included also positioning the researchers as a group of advisors for planning activities and writing documents. At the outset of the project, the women perceived themselves as being invisible and unrecognised by official cultural institutions or academic research. When approached, they were therefore keen to seize the opportunity to record their own collective history on their own terms, to document their lives and claim their worth.

Techniques from sensory and visual ethnography were also applied (Pink, 2007, 2009) in order to capture the experiences of lacemaking workshop participants, while at the same time it was accepted that narrative methodologies would be the main medium for sharing experiences. As professional ethnographers, we grounded the project in the participants' recent history, allowing the lacemakers to determine how they would represent themselves. We therefore validated the role of lacemaking as way of performing a life story. The lacemakers became visible and active co-creators of the ethnographic research.

Bauer and Park (2010, p 61) argued that by 'interpreting themselves as having grown in their narratives of the personal past, adults of all ages construct a personally meaningful self-identity'. For this reason, individual and group interviews with selected workshop participants (leaders, instructors, those engaged the most in the group activity) were conducted by researchers to complement the participatory methods. These revealed multiple meanings of material culture that had accumulated over time.

The project activity prompted the lacemakers to make plans for the future promotion and development of lacemaking skills. New goals play a central role in making strategies for self- and life management and 'should be selected on the basis of effective preferences, needs, interested and existing motivations, and of these underlying motives one must become aware in a process of self-understanding' (Dittmann-Kohli and Jopp, 2007, p 288). We argue that involvement in narratives supports personal motivation and legitimises individual and collective memory. Thus the research process itself could be seen as further supporting resilience.

Being and working together: lacemaking workshop as space for discourses of ageing

The first workshops for Charming Threads were organised in 1999, under the direction of Jadwiga Węgorek. Since that time, the group has been recruiting girls and women of various ages (9–84 years old) and professions. Many participants travelled far, from neighbouring villages and towns, attracted by the growing interest in women's handicrafts, as well as the personality of the instructor.

A handicrafts instructor with over 20 years of experience, Jadwiga Węgorek (b. 1952) is a recognised lacemaker and a national and international award-holder in lacemaking. In the mid-1990, she found a way to transform handicraft skills, which were then culturally and economically undervalued, into a sustainable income. She started lacemaking workshops as a response to unemployment and an age-related illness. The decision to start workshops represents a personal, resilient response to her circumstances, grounded in the desire to share her own passion and skills with others. Thus, from personal experience, Węgorek clearly understood the positive psychological aspects of engaging in craft work. In order to make the workshops a viable practice, Węgorek needed to develop a variety of abilities: from the technical, creative and artistic skills of lacemaking, through to organisational and pedagogical skills. Her involvement culminated in the successful establishment of her group and her position as the leader and craft master (Sznajder, 2014).

The concept of the workshop was transformed over time as a result of on-going changes in approach to handicrafts and redefinition of their value by ethnographers, regionalists and cultural activists, who organised contests and markets (Sznajder, 2014). Foremost, the workshop was a place where participants could study and practise various craft skills. It also fostered an environment wherein an atmosphere of sympathy, mutual understanding, optimism despite life difficulties and the desire for systematic learning and improvement could be found. Features of the workshop were: local patriotism (towards Kraków's laces and instructors); loyalty to the group; a sense of duty to contribute pieces to the exhibitions; cooperating (meeting and working together in one place, but also working independently); and the school-like structure of meetings, based on a master with apprentices/followers. These should be seen as the invented practices of a tradition (Hobsbawm, 1983, p 12), and contributed to the growth of the group's identity.

One participant reflected upon the workshops:

> "When I come here, Jadwiga just shows how to make things, at home I struggle alone. All here are kind, there is no hidden knowledge. I come regularly to the advanced group.[1] I make handicrafts at home, and I am here for socialising and some theory, some practice. Home is to practice too. I participate in group exhibitions. Patterns can be bought, we also have an impressive collection of them, so we can share within the group." (Lidia, age 67, Kraków, 2011)

Jadwiga's workshops have become a space for constructing the craft biographies of her students, which then become part of their life narratives. Making the lace and embroidery supports students' self-knowledge. The construction of personal biographies connects together memories of making lace during different time periods. Students reflected on the function of craft during the Second World War, Socialism, and under subsequent neoliberal transformation (see also Makovicky, 2009). From the students' oral recollections, it appears that for a long time craft activities created a space for personal agency: women's handicrafts were part of school programmes; a response to the shortages of consumer goods under socialism; or a way to impress school mates or work colleagues with their creativity. Craft allowed people to compose individual biographies, drawing on family histories, and to see the relationship between their recounted life experiences and similar stories shared by other women in the group:

> "[My daughter] was once here. Now she is sitting in home and also making it. My grandmothers made beautiful embroidery, my mum's cousin was embroidering images from her imagination, without patterns. My father was

Figure 9.1a and b: Charming Threads workshop

trained in England to knit and crochet. He was injured in Monte Cassino battle in 1944. Severely injured, taken to England, was trained in craft, as they had to keep the severely injured in hospital busy. He had patience and he taught me, when he came back to Poland in 1948. I embroidered a bit, copied from mum or granny serviettes at home. There were also women's handicraft classes in school – they were teaching basic things. In People's Republic of Poland as there was a lack of everything, one unstitched a serviette or cardigan and made another one. [...] Necessity is the mother of invention, so as everything was the same, if you want to be original you have to make things yourself."
(Beata, age 68, Kraków, 2011)

As noted earlier, resilience can be construed as a process of successful adaptation to life's difficulties. These processes are reflected in the microcosm of the group work that established new goals and perspectives for self-development. Social resources created through relations within the group include the giving and receiving of emotional support. Involvement in craft making helped participants in times of disruption in their daily life due to illness or disability, by allowing them to focus on growth and establish personal goals.

Adjustment to the group is a necessary part of the didactic process. The workshops took place in school-like rooms prepared for group work and under the instructor's supervision. This set-up is described in the following quotation from Irena, recalling courses led by another lacemaking instructor (Zofia Dunajczan, 1904–85) working in Kraków in the 1980s, and in the field notes from one of Węgorek's group meetings:

"We used to sit at the desks. The room was rectangular. Dunajczan was not a big [person], rather little, when I met her. She was already an old woman. She used to sit next the entrance door, with all her patterns. Always had a register, where she noted our presence and topics of the classes. [...] She approached us if we had any trouble, helped and in free time she worked over her own pillow (...) I participated in these workshops with joy and a will to learn."
(Irena, age 58, Kraków, 2015)

Today workshops are organised in small room on 7th floor of the 'Nafta' Building in Lubicz 25 Street. The main workshop room has windows with a panoramic view on the Kraków city, with tables close to each other making an oval shape. Women are bending over the bobbin lace pillows or embroidery hoop, discussing about the news or woollen shawl brought by the neighbour. […] Next to the entrance there is an office table where Jadwiga sits in her black and grey dress with lace collar around her neck keeping vigilance over the work of trainees. (Field notes diary, 2015)

The school-like system – participants' presences and absences noted in a register, the assignment of homework, set tasks, the insistence on discipline through comments and corrections – allowed the girls and women to improve and develop their skills. This also provided a sense of security and comfort for students.

The figure of the lacemaking instructor and the master–student relationship is a key to understanding the group dynamics, as well as the process of creating a tradition of lacemaking in Kraków. The personality of the instructor provided a psychological comfort for participants, some of whom used the group meetings as an escape from everyday duties and responsibilities. The instructor should, besides being a master herself, support the progress of her students through the effective evaluation of their results.

The status of master is established over decades rather than years. Węgorek's observations suggest, however, that the nature of the master–student relationship is being undermined by other, contemporary cultural factors. During the interview in 2015, she complained that access to the internet influences the relationship between master and student – the level of expert knowledge seems to be "equalised" and democratised through access to information. Additionally, Węgorek felt that the payment of a participation fee resulted in some students taking the approach of 'I pay so I have a right to demand', leading them to expect individual treatment and to resist the rhythm of the group work.

Despite this, the group and the instructor were necessary for many participants to develop their skills. While they learned for themselves, they exchanged knowledge with others, celebrated individual successes within the group and became visible and recognised as members of the group during exhibitions. Meanwhile, Węgorek's role as the creative instructor was demonstrated by the solutions to technical problems she generated. Although participants also satisfied their curiosity by learning new patterns independently.

Systematic creative engagement in workshops (as well as practising techniques at home) had supported the development of personal styles and ideas among the group members. For example, while participating in embroidery workshops in the 1980s, Jadwiga Węgorek, following advice from her instructors, started keeping notebooks recording embroidery techniques, collected samples of embroidery and completed regular homework tasks. Through establishing and reaching goals by realising projects, and expressing creativity within the group context, the women developed skills which they could not have done alone or through learning via the internet. The women also valued aspects linked to belonging to a particular group, such as exchange of experience and making new friendships.

The group identity was constructed in relation to elements from history, and its sustainability relied on participants feeling responsible for sustaining the group genealogy. This sometimes developed into new sub-groups in different locations, which allowed them to replicate the master–students pattern in other places.

Contextualising self in the past and presence: the 15th anniversary of Charming Threads

On 7 November 2014, an exhibition celebrating the 15th anniversary of Charming Threads was opened in a cultural centre in Kraków. The exhibition was dedicated to current and former group members, with the aim of attracting new members through displays rich in different craft techniques. Apart from family members and friends, visitors included passers-by who had come to the cultural centre for other activities. The exhibition included works in lace and demonstrations of embroidery techniques by 28 group members, including three women who had started at the first workshops in 1999 and were still members.

The 15th anniversary exhibition was closely related to Jadwiga Węgorek's own biography. During the celebration, apart from pieces of lace, Węgorek also presented documents to remind participants about the past achievements of the group and the place of individual members in its history. For many years, she had been writing an account of her workshops, in which she photo-documented the group's achievements, distinctions and certificates, press articles recording successes, and comments and reflections from people studying the group's laces during the exhibitions.

Knowledge of craft history allowed participants to reflect upon the strategies worked out by their predecessors and to plan their own development in the context of their contemporary lifestyles (Hackney,

Figure 9.2: Fifteenth anniversary of Charming Threads, November 2014

2013b, p 171). An exhibition of personal work also has implications for one's self-understanding of creative practice, including: a perception of an evolving creative self in the broader context of crafts; interpreting oneself as having grown in the narratives provided by words, objects and people; or participation in creative and timeless actions constituting a backdrop for future new stories and autobiographical memories. The exhibition could also be interpreted as a transitional space between public and private domains. In this way, the creativity displayed through the work can be read as a sign of healthy, successful and productive ageing. It also contributes to a fundamental sense of existence and symbolic independence for the participants by demonstrating their retention of creative capacities through the display of their work. This too becomes a resource for a resilient response to ageing.

Craft making is an embodied as well as intellectual activity – counting eyes, twists, moves, starting work again and again if it was incorrect, selecting colours for patterns. These rhythms aid contemplation and meditation, and resemble forms of prayer. During craft making, memories and emotions are evoked over the bobbin pillow or crochet; the act offering a concentrated escape from worries and everyday duties. These cognitive processes constitute forms of knowledge that are not readily captured through verbal discussion. Thus the exhibition highlighted ways of knowing and making that we argue can only be accessed via the medium of handicrafts. Group members and other individuals who were engaged in craft knew the difficult path from idea to final outcome – these people became the privileged ones, who had been trained in, and had access to, craft knowledge.

The women's efforts placed personal works in the broader context of the group and its history, which was actively and continuously constructed through creative activities. Węgorek deliberately made the group members aware of the importance of their own history and belonging. She did this by displaying portfolios of participants' work alongside biographies. In a broader sense, the awareness of historical significance allowed participants to connect lacemaking biographies over time, where lacemaking technique became a medium for dialogue between master and student.

The outcomes of the exhibition included participants developing an understanding of themselves in relation to others, which led to a growing awareness of the importance of others for the development of their own skills and achievements. In contributing to the success of the exhibition, there was a wider recognition of the strength of the group. There was also an exploration of the embodied aspect of lacemaking via performative acts, which gave value to experiential ways of knowing. Finally, the participants exhibited perseverance in the way they were continually aiming to develop more complicated designs and patterns.

The 15th anniversary exhibition was a turning point for Jadwiga Węgorek and her group. Conversations at the exhibition and questions about techniques or designs, along with reflections over the handmade chronicles noted earlier, became the ground for a new project, Powrót do Tradycji (Return to Tradition). The project leaders wrote:

> The idea appeared to step back in time and search for the person, who had trained our master. This is how we discovered the craft and patterns of Zofia Dunajczan and Olga Szerauc. Thanks to that it was possible to reconstruct many laces from old patterns, or redrawn damaged-by-time forms. It was about searching relations between teachers and students through their works. (Powrót do Tradycji, 2015)

This represented a new direction in the resilience-promoting process of the group: from being amateur craft lovers searching for learning, development and support, they went on to take responsibility for grounding the workshops' identity within a historical narrative.

Masters and apprentices: constructing group and individual identity through dialogue with tradition

Through the Return to Tradition project, the members of the group decided to take on the role of amateur ethnographers to research the early history of the group through the lineage of recognised masters. Zofia Dunajczan (1904–85) and Olga Szerauc (1908–2017) were two such instructors. The process of finding earlier generations of lacemakers began when Jadwiga created a list of 27 people who had participated in Olga's lacemaking and embroidery courses in 1986–2002 in Kraków. Group members conducted interviews, as well as collecting and reconstructing laces and patterns. Support for the amateur researchers came from professional ethnographers and academics, who helped with the construction of the questionnaires, facilitating interviews and discussions about laces and patterns, and providing ideas for an exhibition reviewing the project. The initiative attempted to implement respect among workshop participants for the skills and knowledge of their masters, while preserving the memories of lacemakers by honouring group members' oral stories. The meaning that the women attached to their experience as amateur ethnographers resulted in pen-portraits of lacemaking instructors.

For the purposes of Return to Tradition project, we visited Olga at her home, together with two of her apprentices, Jadwiga Węgorek and Zofia Sienicka. We saw Olga's enormous collection of patterns (kept in drawers, boxes or rolled in a basket), along with pieces of lace and embroidery kept on shelves, in suitcases and in chests. Zofia Sienicka (b 1930) led the interview. The questions were prepared beforehand. However, the interview developed into a more spontaneous chat, in line with the friendly atmosphere that lacemakers are used to creating around their work.

The master–apprentice relationship (between Olga and Zofia) was observed to (re-)emerge through the conversation. Collaborative discussions, reviewing and evaluating handicrafts, discussing the teachers' past and how they coped with changes in their lives, constructing a positive life-review, were prompted by handling laces and patterns (Figure 9.3). Olga also engaged in personal reflections regarding the crafts stored under her bed, which demonstrated her mastership in the art of lacemaking. Stories about lacemaking workshops, repeated in front of former students, provided a sense of biographical continuity for the speaker as well as for the group members listening to the conversation:

"After the war, I started a lacemaking course (…) in Kraków Main Square. Did you know about Piwnica pod Baranami? Amazing Cultural Centre! I have been participating there in lacemaking course. (…) And since then I have been teaching laces. I had so many groups. Students are visiting me in my flat in Kraków (…). I trained many, many people in laces. All of them are my students. Węgorek, her mother – all my students (…) And now we are like lacemaking family. They are all coming to me everyday. Sometimes, as I have only a room and a kitchen, I don't have a place to accommodate them. They come three, four. (…) I have large drawers, boxes with patterns. I used to tell them: Do you want something? Please sit down and search what you need. This is a mine of patterns. (…) You know, when we have a meeting, all are friends of mine. All know me and I know them since years. And you know, lacemakers are friends with each other." (Olga, age 100+, Bobowa, 2011)

These resources (laces, patterns and stories) symbolically represented the subjective meanings of apprentices' creative and personal lives, emphasising multiple correlations between memory and material

Figure 9.3: Zofia Sienicka and Olga Szerauc discussing a lace pattern during an ethnographic interview/conversation

culture in the home (Makovicky, 2007). Setting the interview in Olga's personal space, and being surrounded by objects that were the fruit of her skills and imagination (developed in relations with others), unveiled the social identity of the lacemaker.

The work of the amateur ethnographers in Węgorek's group unveiled a common language and commonality of experiences specific to Olga's and Zofia's generation. Both of them were war survivors, their mutual trust and understanding were grounded in similar experiences, leading them to share memories in common during the conversation. Apart from mutual sympathies and enthusiasm for handicrafts, they shared similar sentiments for the Eastern Borderland (now incorporated into the western territories of Belarus and Ukraine, and south-eastern Lithuania), from which they both originated. Their lacemaking memories were contextualised through the background of bygone noble families' histories, a culture that, after the Bolshevik revolution, was lost forever. Both Olga and Zofia were descended from nobility and witnessed the war crimes of this period. Olga's war experiences supported the processes of Zofia's self-understanding. Zofia, in attempting to search for correspondences in their biographies, emphasised Olga's role as a witness to history:

> "Olga, all which you have taught us on bobbin blocks, on embroidery, on net lace, tulle, you taught us life as well! To give your heart to another human being! Olga taught us also to be humans, has survived herself Siberia, war and seen all of this ... Is same like me when I talk about Ukraine, East, they say to me 'You really have been there, survived all!'" (Zofia, age 80+, Kraków, 2015)

Women's activities such as making, creating and collecting, have psychological value (Hackney, 2013b, p 180): they serve as talismans against unexpected events and express hope for better times. From that perspective, Olga's narrative, revealing her attachment to craft, can be understood as giving a sense of coherence to her biography. Her creative passions, continued until now with the support of family as well as friends/lacemakers, are underpinned by her heroic story as a war survivor. The experience of war 'constitutes a major source of stress, whose traumatic effects endure in many cases a long time after its termination' (Kimhi et al, 2012, p 392). Sharing stories about their passion for lacemaking evoked narrative identities focused on stories from the past. Craft making emerged as a thread of continuity linking and sustaining Olga and Zofia through various periods of hardship and struggle. Thus, Olga and Zofia are able to talk of overcoming their histories of war experiences and cumulative adversity, leading to well-being outcomes in later life. Observing the ethnographic interviews thus provided further insights into how these individuals and, by extension, other lacemakers were able to develop and sustain resilience over the lifecourse. The ethnographic interview provided an opportunity for Olga's own meaning-making.

Olga's story as a master of lacemaking with an extraordinary biography provided a foundation for the extended history of Węgorek's workshop. The activity of Dunajczan and Szerauc, reconstructed by lacemakers involved in the Return to Tradition project, is also a ground for a wider narrative about the place of lacemaking in Kraków's history. As noted earlier, collecting memories and connecting the lacemakers was enabled by studying the old patterns and laces. Looking at the lace and patterns was what appeared to engage the lacemakers, as they were able to apply their embodied expertise as makers to the reflective discussion.

Laces in legendary Kraków's cityscape: co-constructing heritage as an act of resilience

Prats (2009) defines heritage as a socio-cultural construct appearing in a particular historical moment, within which characteristic elements are sufficiently clear that they can be analysed. Heritage appears where society can look at itself as a historical subject, where cultural inheritance is passed from one generation to another. In this context, we ask whether we can talk about the craft group's heritage as emerging as a result of the women's resilience?

The identity of the Charming Threads group developed out of the weekly workshops and the collective exhibitions of laces made by participants. The laces, inspired by a variety of styles and patterns, allowed participants to experience a sense of community and realise the need for emotional solidarity between craftswomen. Individuals winning prizes in contests or being invited to become members of associations, as well as going off to establish their own groups, is testament to the workshop's influence on members' personal and career development.

The Return to Tradition project, discussed above, resulted in an exhibition presented at two events in the autumn of 2015, first in Bobowa and later in Kraków. The comparison of lacemaking in the two places is instructive. The (re)discovery of a lacemaking tradition in Kraków by Węgorek and her group could be seen as creating and identifying with an invented tradition, rather than a tradition that had an established, historical continuity. Whereas in Bobowa, which is in the same voivodeship (administrative area), laces have been perceived as that place's regional product since the end of 19th century. Lacemaking skills, laces and patterns in Bobowa, understood as a heritage transmitted between generations and within a community, acquire their unique and local character from being maintained by a group living in a particular place that, in the past, was a centre for a bobbin-laces cottage industry.

The historio-cultural image of Kraków's city, constructed over centuries, has had an important influence on individuals and group histories. The group emphasised their place-based identity through the workshop's logo (Figure 9.4), which was designed and made from lace by the lacemakers – a letter 'K', imitating the monogram of King Kazimierz the Great from the doors of the Wawel cathedral, now one of the main tourist attractions in Kraków. Mini versions of the monogram were pinned to participants' clothes during lacemaking events in the form of 'visiting cards'. In this way the lacemakers asserted that lacemaking is an important part of Kraków's cultural heritage, and also a source of continuing dialogue with tradition. The role of Kraków as a heritage city for locating lacemakers' identities helps in understanding their embodied experiences, expressed also by other symbols used by group, such as wearing regional dress during important events.

For participants of Węgorek's group, the move from craft making at home to participating in the workshops, to contributing to exhibitions, meant that their craft-based identities moved from private to increasingly public spaces, where they could see their work from different perspectives. One of such perspective was gained by contributing to historical narratives regarding women's crafts in Kraków.

Participants gave presentations during the Return to Tradition exhibitions. They shared the findings of their research with others, and explored new directions for the interpretation of lacemaking. This integrated lacemakers' stories and stimulated a new generation of individual and group narratives. In Bobowa, lacemakers presented how Kraków lacemaking workshops are connected with Bobowa's cottage industry and lacemaking school through the person of Zofia Dunajczan. They also revealed how simple laces, local patterns and specific materials influenced practices in both places, thanks to the instructor.

Figure 9.4: Charming Threads logo in 2015, incorporating the monogram of King Kazimierz

These presentations carried special meanings both for Kraków's lacemakers as well as for Bobowa's craftswomen, as they connected them and distinguished them in front of participants in the International Bobbin Lace Festival in Bobowa. The same festival also exposed them to the wider European history of lacemaking presented on other stalls (Sznajder and Kosmala, 2014). Placing one's own work within a broader discourse of the history of women's handicrafts is the basis for categorising handicraft activities as important and having timeless meaning in sustaining, interpreting and disseminating the tradition for current and future generations. For the Kraków lacemakers, occasional lectures for exhibition visitors (family members, craft makers, craft lovers, also professionals working in cultural institutions and academics) prepared by one of their members allowed them to showcase the rich history of the city's lacemaking groups and provided a ground for understanding the importance of their own actions. Retaining responsibility for decision making in these exhibitions (for example, the subject of display, items for display, arrangement of the exhibition space) allowed the group to challenge the hegemonic discourses dictated by cultural institutions. This decision making fostered resilience by developing personal and group agency. Previous discourses created by ethnographers and museologists tended to focus

Figure 9.5: Collected laces of Zofia Dunajczan during the exhibition in Kraków, 2015

on the skills of regional artisans (Kożuch, 2005) or on the functions of lace in interior decoration and clothing (Turska-Skowronek, 2002). These interpretations had not highlighted the importance of Krakow as a place. The history of Kraków's lace had remained undiscovered because the documents and artefacts were kept in private individual collections, and not in institutional archives. The narratives that the women created through the data and from their embodied knowledge as craft makers form original interpretations of the role of craft for people in Kraków. Besides the importance of master–apprentice relationships or workshop dynamics, we argue that the craft practices gained value through their association with place.

Conclusions

Hackney (2014, p 1) points out that handicrafts, made as a hobby and a source of pleasure, are also sources of new, creative possibilities that strengthen the group and shape its values through skills, knowledge and opportunities, but they are often under-valued. However, if they become recognised, they can be developed and applied in practice by volunteering activities, community activism, entrepreneurship and cooperative practice. In the case of Charming Threads, the group nurtured and sustained such a set of values, including: solidarity in supporting the group leader during the organisation of exhibitions by contributing pieces; regular attendance at classes; participating in contests; and applying the knowledge and experience of the group members to the creation of new handicraft groups outside of Kraków. The emergence of new groups allowed the history of lacemaking to spread. Their activities, projects and workshops allowed various new, local narratives to be developed while providing support, development and growth for new members. Handicraft stories were also perceived as forms of escape from the shadow of anonymity. In displaying their lace in their local parish, gaining entry into recognised craft organisations, or by gathering data, participants can be seen to be actively engaged.

The amateur research driven by Jadwiga Węgorek unveiled novel data on women's handicraft heritage as specific to Kraków. Local heritage lace making practices have only been recently recognised by official institutions. Documents, patterns and laces collected and preserved by Węgorek and other lacemakers, gained value after being contextualised as part of a wider body of women's crafts. Documentation, patterns and laces, collected and preserved by Węgorek and by other lacemakers, became valuable after being linked to the historical context of women's crafts. Furthermore, participation in events and activities linked local and international traditions. By promoting a dialogue between present and past, by creating the discourse of master–student, the group established its place on the cultural and heritage map of the city.

For researchers and research participants, participation in this project allowed the discovery of the mechanisms by which craft groups support older people's resilience. Individual experiences during the workshops demonstrated the therapeutic function of handicrafts. Additionally, participation informed researchers' understanding of how promotional activities shaped entrepreneurial skills and how the need for competitiveness was linked to the craft market (Sznajder and Kosmala, 2018). Besides constructing a new meaning for material culture, the older people in this group fulfilled their need of accomplishing a social role and becoming active agents – co-constructing a contemporary understanding of the importance of oral history and craft in developing the resilience of older people.

Older people choosing to practise arts and crafts resulted in enhanced personal expression and self-esteem. Lace making as part of a group strengthened social connectivity, increased confidence and improved the group's perception of their social status. It gave participants a better sense of the relationship between mind and body and a greater mastery of manual skills. Sharing stories while making craft allows for memories and experiences of the past to be intertwined and simultaneously performed in the present. This project led towards reflection upon the ways craft making can be combined with oral history, constructing the space for formulation of new discourses of ageing. Regional identities, enriched by the history of objects, practices and places, allow people to locate themselves in the context of narratives about craft making.

Acknowledgements

The authors would like to thank the reviewers and the editors for their helpful comments.

Note

[1] Approximately 20 women participate in each course, among whom 5–10 attend the workshops during any given meeting. In 2010 the schedule included a beginners' group, a 'two-year' group and an advanced group. Between 1999 and end of 2015, 202 women participated in the courses; during the same period, the workshop groups organised 41 individual exhibitions.

References

Alex, L. (2010) 'Resilience among very old men and women', *Journal of Research in Nursing*, 15(5): 419–31.

Bauer, J. and Park, S. (2010) 'Growth is not just for the young: Growth narratives, eudaimonic resilience, and the ageing self', in P.S. Fry and C.L. Keyes (eds) *New frontiers in resilient ageing: Life strengths and wellbeing in late life*, Cambridge: Cambridge University Press, pp 60–89.

Brzezińska, A. (2010) 'Wakacje z koronką. Oferta kształcenia w zakresie rękodzieła (wybrane przykłady)' [Holidays with lace. Offer of handicrafts education (selected examples)], pp 272–8, https://repozytorium.amu.edu.pl/bitstream/10593/5255/1/Wakacje%20z%20koronk%C4%85.pdf.

Dittmann-Kohli, F. and Jopp, D. (2007) 'Self and life management: Wholesome knowledge for the third age', in J. Bond, S. Peace, F. Dittmann-Kohli and G. Westerhof (eds) *Ageing in society: European perspectives on gerontology*, London: Sage, pp 268–95, doi: http://dx.doi.org/10.4135/9781446278918.n13.

Hackney, F. (2013a) 'CAREfull or CAREless? Collaborative making and social engagement through craft', in K. Raney (ed) *engage 33: Critical Craft*, London: The National Association for Gallery Education, pp 23–37.

Hackney, F. (2013b) 'Quiet activism and the new amateur. The power of home and hobby crafts', *Design and Culture*, 5(2): 169–94.

Hackney, F. (2014) 'Taking CARE: Building community assets through creative-making', *Making Futures Journal*, 3: 1–7.

Haftkoronka (2017) https://haftkoronka.wordpress.com/category/powrot-do-tradycji/.

Hobsbawm, E. (1983) 'Introduction: Inventing traditions', in E. Hobsbawm and T. Ranger (eds) *The invention of tradition*, Cambridge: Cambridge University Press, pp 1–14.

Janssen, B., Abma, T. and Van Regenmortel, T. (2012) 'Maintaining mastery despite age related losses. The resilience narratives of two older women in need of long-term community care', *Journal of Ageing Studies*, 26(3): 343–54.

Kimhi, S., Hantman, S., Goroshit, M., Eshel, Y. and Zysberg, L. (2012) 'Elderly people coping with the aftermath of war: Resilience versus vulnerability', *American Journal of Geriatric Psychiatry*, 20(5): 391–401.

Kożuch, B. (2005) 'Koronkarstwo' ['Lacemaking'], in A. Rataj (ed) *Dzieła rąk, umysłu, serca* [*The works of hands, mind and heart*], Kraków: Muzeum Etnograficzne im. Seweryna Udzieli w Krakowie, pp 82–7.

la Cour, K., Josephsson, S. and Luborsky, M. (2005) 'Creating connections to life during life-threatening illness: Creative activity experienced by elderly people and occupational therapists', *Scandinavian Journal of Occupational Therapy*, 12(3): 98–109.

McFadden, S. and Basting, A. (2010) 'Healthy ageing persons and their brains: Promoting resilience through creative engagement', *Clinics in Geriatric Medicine*, 26(1): 149–61.

Makovicky, N. (2007) 'Closet and cabinet: Clutter as cosmology', *Home Cultures* 4(3): 287–310.

Makovicky, N. (2009) '"Traditional with contemporary form": Craft and discourses of modernity in Slovakia today', *The Journal of Modern Craft*, 2(1): 43–58.

Manning, L.K. (2013) 'Navigating hardships in old age: Exploring the relationship between spirituality and resilience in later life', *Qualitative Health Research*, 23(4): 568–75.

Narodowy Instytut Dziedzictwa (2017) *Krajowa lista niematerialnego dziedzictwa kulturowego* [*National list of intangible cultural heritage*], http://niematerialne.nid.pl/Dziedzictwo_niematerialne/Krajowa_inwentaryzacja/Krajowa_lista_NDK/.

O'Reilly, K. (2009) *Key concepts in ethnography*, Los Angeles: Sage.

Pink, S. (2007) *Doing visual ethnography. Images, media and representation in research*, Los Angeles: Sage.

Pink, S. (2009) *Doing sensory ethnography*, London: Sage.

Połubok M. (2017) 'Koronka klockowa – tradycyjne rękodzieło' ['Bobbin laces – traditional handicraft'], in Z. Noga (ed) *Małopolska. Regiony – regionalizmy – małe ojczyzny* [*Lesser Poland Province. Regions – regionalisms – small homelands*], Kraków: Małopolski Związek Regionalnych Towarzystw Kultury i Wojewódzka Biblioteka Publiczna w Krakowie, 19: 297.

Powrót do tradycji [Return to tradition. A leaflet] (2015).

Prats, L. (2009) 'Heritage according to scale', in M. Anico and E. Peralta (eds) *Heritage and identity. Engagement and demission in the contemporary world*, London and New York: Routledge, pp 76–90.

Sznajder, A. (2014) 'Jadwiga Węgorek – krakowska koronczarka' [Jadwiga Węgorek – Kraków's lacemaker'], *Twórczość Ludowa* [*Folk Crafts*], 29(3–4): 36.

Sznajder, A. and Kosmala, K. (2014) 'Capturing entrepreneurial lacespaces: Notes from the field', *International Sociological Association. Visual Sociology Working Group*, 9: 17–20.

Sznajder, A. and Kosmala, K. (2018) '"Let's make laces in the garden." Creative tourism in rural Poland', in S. Owsianowska and M. Banaszkiewicz (eds) *Anthropology of tourism in Central and Eastern Europe: Bridging worlds*, Lanham, MD: Lexington Books, pp 217–37.

Tomas, J., Sancho, P., Melendez, J. and Mayordomo, T. (2012) 'Resilience and coping as predictors of general well-being in the elderly: A structural equation modelling approach', *Ageing and Mental Health*, 16(3): 317–26.

Turska-Skowronek, K. (2002) *Sztuka Koronki. Strój i wnętrze. Komentarz wystawy* [*The art of lace. Costume and interior*], Toruń: Muzeum Etnograficzne im. Marii Znamierowskiej-Prüfferowej.

Węgorek J. (2017a) 'W kręgu krakowskich koronek klockowych – od 2013 r.' ['Among Kraków's bobbin laces – since 2013'], unpublished list of events and achievements.

Węgorek J. (2017b) 'Koronczarka. Wspomnienia o Oldze Szerauc' ['The Lacemaker. Memories about Olga Szerauc'], in Z. Noga (ed) *Małopolska. Regiony – regionalizmy – małe ojczyzny* [*Lesser Poland Province. Regions – regionalisms – small homelands*], Kraków: Małopolski Związek Regionalnych Towarzystw Kultury i Wojewódzka Biblioteka Publiczna w Krakowie, 19: 245.

TEN

Objects of loss: resilience, continuity and learning in material culture relationships

Helen Manchester

Editorial introduction

This chapter explore resilience as a response to the ordinary experiences of loss in later life: loss of relationships, loss of a home and loss of objects. Objects, or their absence, feature prominently here. Material culture studies looks at the role objects have in supporting human relationships and memories. Creativity is primarily discussed in terms of the everyday processes of curating objects (and, hence, curating memories and relationships). However, creativity also appears in the research methods that were used to draw out the participants' stories, revealing this intersection of resilience, material culture and everyday creativity.

Introduction

The discussion in this chapter critically explores resilience, learning (as a process of being and becoming fully human) (Gill, 2014) and everyday creativity through self-curation in the context of the process of decluttering as a response to loss. Although consumer societies' concern with materialism has long been seen as detrimental to the quality of human relationships, Miller (2008, p 1) points out that 'the closer our relationships are with objects, the closer our relationships are with people'. How are our relationships with people, places and things affected through loss over time, and is that resulting absence tangible, emotional or somehow both? How does loss change and transform us as we age? Absence and loss are not merely emptiness or a state of *non-* or *no-longer-being*. Instead, absence is 'something performed, textured and materialised through relations and processes, and via objects' (Meyer, 2012, p 103). Meyer goes on to suggest:

> Although, strictly speaking, absence is a thing without matter, absence is ordered, remembered, evoked and made discussable and sufferable through materialities. And even though absence escapes – and can only ever be partially and temporarily contained in – certain places, it is within these places and through leaving various kinds of traces that absence comes to matter. (Meyer, 2012, p 109)

Within the broader context of this discussion, the constructs of resilience and self-curation are problematic in themselves as descriptors of what happens when lives are lived through profound experiences of loss over time and in particularly resonant places. Windle's broadly comprehensive definition of resilience, states:

> Resilience is the process of effectively negotiating, adapting to, or managing significant sources of stress or trauma. Assets and resources within the individual, their life and environment facilitate this capacity for adaptation and 'bouncing back' in the face of adversity. Across the life course, the experience of resilience will vary. (Windle, 2011, p 163)

This chapter argues that two important variables affecting resilience in older adults include a sense of attachment to place and investment in a personal material culture. 'Investment' here does not refer to monetary value or material worth, but instead to the degree to which the objects that matter in an individual's life are imbued with meanings over time, as expressed in part in complex, private choices about care and display. Relationships end and identities are transformed at a fundamental level when people can no longer think and speak of themselves as spouses, children, siblings, friends or parents except through memories and mementoes. These two things, material objects and intangible memories, share much in common through language, taking on each other's characteristics in imagination and metaphor. Especially when viewed in the context of the possibility of loss near the end of life, the solidity of things and the certainty of self-identity that we have known all our lives become equally mutable and fragile. We keep, preserve and display our memories with care, 'curating' both our past and potential selves primarily for ourselves as an act of personal continuity, learning and creativity. As Hallam and Hockey have suggested:

> The immaterial aspect of an inner world, like thoughts emotions, dreams and imaginings that are unavailable to any direct case, is fused metaphorically with material objects which possess distinct structures and boundaries (for example rooms and shelves). (Hallam and Hockey, 2001, p 27)

They go on to point out that immaterial memories are often 'contained' within a vessel or structure that can help to keep certain memories alive. They suggest that these 'metaphors of memory' act to 'connect the intangible with the material' (Hallam and Hockey, 2001, p 27). While oral storytelling has been seen as featuring strongly in learning lives, helping people to navigate change and transitions over time (Goodson, 2013), much less attention has been placed on the significance of material 'metaphors of memory' in enabling autobiographical learning and critical reflection.

Moving from 'my home' to 'a home'

Taking those memories and moving from 'my home' to 'the Home' or 'a Home' at the end of years of busy adult life can be life shattering, especially for those who may feel that, by making such a move, their sense of independence has been compromised and diminished. Confronted by the permanence of loss, people may not so much 'bounce back' or learn to navigate these changes, as continue in response to incontrovertible change. They can never return to where they were before loss and absence altered their lives. At best, they may find that they can accommodate it and live around and through it, like an immutable feature of the emotional landscape. However, having one's things ordered and perhaps ultimately devalued by an outsider, even a close relative or well-meaning friend, and removed from their meaningful contexts during a stressful move to an institutional setting can compound feelings of loss and displacement.

The objects on display in an individual's parlour or living room may be collected and arranged to portray a certain public face as a statement of what a person is willing to display to potential strangers. After a significant change in status, such as widowhood, the public space becomes as much a culturally acceptable way of expressing emotions around the bereaved and reconciled state as a record of past family life together (Cristoforetti, Gennai and Rodeschini, 2011).

However, there is often, though not always, no deliberate intent to showcase this or that, or communicate a particular public message, even if the selection of objects and the privately determined hierarchy of their display or displacement does provide a channel for what Miller (2008, p 2) calls 'an authentic other voice' of personal expression. Sometimes, though, the 'stories we tell ourselves about ourselves', to draw on Geertz's (1973, p 448) iconic definition of culture, are not intended as public performances, until someone asks because he or she needs help in interpreting our material narrative. Sometimes, the stories are for us alone, whispered reminders and silently shouted assertions of who we were, where we went and with whom and why we together might never pass that way again – but didn't we make an impression when we did? While the display of objects may be significant in enabling reflection on lives lived, this may not necessarily involve storytelling for others.

In their everyday lives the accumulated material culture of a person's life, whether active, inactive, or even unrealised as things presently held, previously lost or possibly acquired in the future, reflects a person's relationships with others and the world. Over the course of our lives, we experience many types of constantly changing and developing relationships and we afford them different levels of significance. While this may be easy to differentiate with our personal associations and significant *others*, doing so with our significant *objects* may often require the mediating association of meaningful places and moments as well. We may unconsciously categorise people in terms of their significance to us. Because for the most part people, unlike objects, 'never stay where we last left them'. Generally we don't have to make relationship decisions in terms of the impact on our immediate lived environment. By contrast, the ways in which we understand our personal material culture require an active and dynamic association with place and a qualitatively different set of emotional choices, whether conscious or not. An acquaintance is valued, but not as closely as a long-time friend. A family member's memory may be deeply cherished, but not in the same way as that of a spouse or lover. Where and how we keep objects associated with them is literally embodied in the choices of what we do in our space with the 'stuff' that signifies them to us. As Miller (2010, p 136) observes, 'it is through the medium of things that we actually make people' – particularly the ways in which we may make them profoundly present over time and place through our daily experience with objects.

The parlour is not a blank canvas devoid of memoires of value attachment. A room may be the repository of gifts from work colleagues, souvenirs, pieces acquired through choice or obligation and innumerable masterpieces of bricolage engineered by devoted younger generations. However, in the corner facing our favourite chair might be a photograph of a loved one or an heirloom on a special shelf that only we notice. We don't mind if a given room is primarily a 'public' or private space, but few are ever always exclusively so. The kitchen might be a practical space except for a few whimsical prints or gadgets. Our bedrooms might contain our most beloved objects, some carefully displayed for our pleasure. But many objects are kept in boxes and drawers – except for that one tasteless knick-knack on the dresser that we keep as a deliberate reminder that we cannot take ourselves too seriously, or the well-loved dolls that *must* be kept in reach of marauding grandchildren each time they invade. In each space, there are decisions governing what objects go where and why. Places and objects interact with our emotions to the extent that necessary exceptions to our 'rules' are constantly being negotiated, challenged and changed.

Rather than being spaces of intentional self-curation, then, many of these decisions around care and display are made subconsciously as the complex and organic result of the way we see ourselves over time, in place, and through our relationships. These aspects that make up our interrelated patterns of meaning are always changing and evolving, and the only constant is loss. When we inevitably lose someone or something, we have to adapt to absence. What we do is continue despite absence, and what remains constant is objects, real or remembered, which remind us of how we lived our lives before loss. These objects can be a positive tool for adaptation and reflection, whether an individual relocates to a care home setting or continues living alone for a time in the family home (Kleine and Baker, 2004, p 160). They may never be constructed into an oral account with a narrative structure, in the ways suggested by theories of narrative learning (Goodson, 2013; Goodson and Gill, 2014), but this does not make them less significant. For some people, place attachment in later life, even after many years of established living in the same familiar environment, may be more transferable than we think. Providing that a sense of independence and comfort are maintained in the new surroundings, which may involve bringing cherished possessions, or deciding when and how to dispose of them, place attachment can be transferable (Leith, 2006, pp 326–8).

Resilience and repertoire

Resilience, then, is understood here as a response that is less about a return to a previous condition than as a kind of *context-dependent, embodied, emotional response* that individuals may develop in order to move on with their lives in the face of loss. As such, the ability to develop or maintain resilience when confronted with profound change is significantly affected by situations that result in disruptions to a person's meaningful relationships *and* places, such as many seniors experience with a move to a care home situation after the death of a spouse. The concept of *repertoire*, rather than curation or narration, may capture a sense of the processes at work in the development of an individual's body of expressive material culture because it does not presume any intended public dimension. Broadly speaking, a repertoire refers to the dynamic stock of what a person possesses with respect to a particular genre, with *possession* encompassing knowledge as well as material ownership (Georges, 1993). People may have multiple repertoires. An individual may have a collection of handmade embroideries, be able to sing 200 popular songs from memory and have a wickedly funny but judiciously shared set of 'adult-themed' jokes and anecdotes. All of these collections represent different repertoires within a person's larger, context-dependent expressive culture and all are likely to change in multiple directions over the lifecourse, subject to periods of active expansion, forgetting, occasional disinterest, serendipity and renewed enthusiasm. With regard to artefacts, Kirschenblatt-Gimblett (1989) has identified what may be thought of as several kinds of collection emphases within consumer material culture repertoires, including: *material companions* (which may be inherited but are used regularly rather than displayed, often as a way of maintaining a link with past owners and users, such as an old wooden spoon); *souvenirs*; *mementoes*; and *memory objects*.

Repertoire also encompasses a broader sense of the creative processes involved in developing a personal material culture and assumes making, collecting, borrowing and adapting from a wide range of sources, including tradition and popular culture. For older generations, popular culture as a key source of mass-mediated tradition can be especially important, particularly with respect to long-running radio and television programmes. As discussed in greater detail in this chapter, one creative intervention designed to encourage reminiscence, storytelling and critical narrative learning (Goodson and Gill, 2014) that met with some success at a care home taking part in this research involved the introduction of small group, object-oriented sessions that played with the well-known *Antiques Roadshow* format.

The Tangible Memories project: people, places and methodologies

Tangible Memories is an Arts and Humanities Research Council-funded interdisciplinary project exploring ways of creating community in elder care home settings by using digital technology to put residents' stories into personal objects using intuitive interface controls – such as resonance-based rocking chairs, fabric lap quilts and cushions that can call up a playlist of favourite music, as well as interactive books. It is hoped that these object-based, bespoke interfaces will encourage enriched communication between residents, carers and families through storytelling and play and support the creation of residents' digital legacies.

The original project team was comprised of academics from education, computing, history and folklore; the community partner Alive! (a charity that specialises in enriched programming for seniors in care homes settings, featuring sessions with music, movement, art and guided reminiscence); local artists and interactive media designers; and residents and care staff from three Bristol-area care settings. The three sites chosen for the study were deliberately varied and included a dementia care ward run by a large charitable organisation; an extra care facility belonging to the local authority but run by a local housing provider with care provided by a locally based care company; and a privately owned and run home.

All of the residents participating in the project fall into what Gilleard and Higgs (2010) refer to as 'the fourth age' to the extent that most are in the seventh to ninth decade of life, with the exception of one woman in her mid-60s who moved into sheltered housing when her epilepsy became too severe and unpredictable. All require some additional daily care or, because of mobility or other issues, live with the possibility of needing such support on very short notice.

Initially, as many members of the Tangible Memories team as possible attended every site visit, and each session was framed as the second half of a familiarly structured, interactive programme by the project's charity partner, Alive! After the Alive!-led sessions ended, it was determined that one researcher would continue to facilitate and document small group sessions at the independent-living site on a regular basis and individual interviews were recorded with all residents who wanted to participate. Individual interviews were also undertaken at another, private care home setting. In the case of one site, a dementia ward, two researchers attended each interview with accompanying care staff.

Because many residents felt that they were neither storytellers nor in possession of their most memorable objects now that they had moved into care, various creative, pedagogical approaches and methodologies were tried in order to help elicit stories. These included creative storytelling techniques using props and images that relied more on imagination than memory, music playlist sessions (*Desert Island Discs*), designing proxy objects and what might be called mediated popular culture forms. The most successful creative intervention was an *Antiques Roadshow*-style series of sessions held regularly at one of the sites, where residents took responsibility to bring an object and tell a story about it, often playfully adding spurious elements or inviting the audience to guess the object's use or provenance. As with the *Desert Island Discs* format for the personal playlist interviews, framing the object-based storytelling sessions around a familiar BBC television show gave participating residents a familiar and consistent structure for their reminiscences that did not rely on any common experience other than programme recognition.

The focus of this discussion will centre on residents and staff from the private and extra care homes and their personal and shared experiences of the process of decluttering and object-related stories of loss and continuity. As mentioned, while many residents did not see themselves as good narrators still possessed of the objects that were of greatest interest to themselves, never mind anyone else, over time their self-perceptions changed, as can be seen in a number of the excerpts that follow.

Sweeping up the heart: things, loss, memory and stories

Our relationships to things and places are in many respects as complicated as our relationships to people. For one thing, we often attribute meaning to places and objects based on the presence – or more often absence – of certain individuals in those contexts. Somewhat paradoxically, we may not realise the significance of a place or thing until the person associated with it is lost to us, and then revisiting familiar places and keeping objects that once were important to us because of those cherished associations may be unbearable, as Tuan notes:

> Things and objects endure and are dependable in ways that human beings, with their biological weaknesses and shifting moods, do not endure and are not dependable ... In the absence of the right people, things and places are quickly

> drained of meaning so that their lastingness is an irritation rather than a comfort. (Tuan, 2001, p 140)

Researchers have noted that older people tend to lose interest in the continued acquisition of material goods as they age, for a number of well-considered reasons, including the feeling that they may have too much and are not interested in acquiring new things that they will just have to look after and dispose of. Often, they don't want decisions around the disposition of their material life to be left to their descendants, in part because they may want to have final, independent control over 'who gets what' (Price, Arnould and Folkman Curasi, 2000; Whitmore, 2001). Decluttering or downsizing may arise with the realisation of a need or desire to exert agency over the stuff of one's life. Over the life span, we acquire and maintain relationships with people, places and things, and as these attachments increase, we may find that we have to create a kind of shorthand so that the story of our life of things is not writ too large. Writing of an elderly woman he calls Dora, Miller refers to this phenomenon as an 'economy of relationships' in which:

> each significant relationship, whether to persons or periods and events in her past, ultimately became reduced to just one or two objects, as the other mementoes made way for other relationships. Clearly the more relationships one has lived through, the more any one relationship has to be pruned back to one or two totalizing mementoes in this thrift of memory. (Miller, 2010, p 149)

Sometimes loss needs the stuff of memory to maintain a connection to the absent loved one or the time and place to which we can never return, even if the things in question are not part of daily encounters because they are packed away. Speaking of her sense of a pressing need to "have a good clear out" so that her children are not left to dispose of her possessions, Beryl, a resident of the independent-living extra care home taking part in the project, specifically included things in storage that were accessible to her but not on display in her reflections on the inherent challenges of decluttering. She stated that she had reduced her belongings significantly prior to moving into sheltered housing with her second husband because of the lack of additional storage. Those things that she felt she couldn't part with but did not have room to display in her much smaller flat found places in cupboards, put away but present:

Beryl: Most of the things that I seem to be hanging on to are – *mean something* they've all been given at times as wedding presents, anniversary presents and that kind of thing. And so, they're more sentimental value than useful. But, I think about what I should do about them, I just think about them and do nothing I'm afraid! [laughs] It's very difficult to know how to dispose of them in a way that I would feel happy with. I'd like to think the children would take some of them but they all have their own homes and I don't really think they'd be interested in my – [laughs] in my things. But short of getting everything out and bringing the family here and saying: 'Look, is there anything you want?' [laughs] So as I say, I'm afraid I think about it but not knowing what to do, I do nothing.

SK: Are there things that you think you would miss if you did get rid of them, at this point in your life?

Beryl: I can't honestly say that because a lot of my things are put away so in a sense I don't *need* them but I just still *like to know they're there*! [laughs] That they, you know, I just sort of hang on thinking they remind me of things and if I part with them I'm parting with memories and the thoughts of the people who gave them to me. I seem to sort of lose that connection once I've got rid of everything.

In their study of the process of household disbandment among older people, Ekerdt et al (2004) cite the particular issue of social reciprocity with respect to the keeping of gifts as a way of honouring the givers that would have been particularly important to older generations. When asked how she felt about having to get rid of things that had been gifts that were of value to her but might not be to others, Beryl expressed her feelings in terms of a kind of betrayal that dishonoured the memory of past relationships:

> "I feel a sort of disloyalty in disposing of things that people thought I might like. And also it takes me back. Having been married before. I mean that cabinet [indicating large dresser behind and to the right] has a lot of silver things in it which were from my silver wedding anniversary in

my first marriage. And I can recall more or less who gave me what in there and I can look at it and remember. And some people are still alive and some are not. But it takes me back, to that time and the people I knew then. I think there would be an awful gap in my life if suddenly things went, because they're still a part of me and the past."

For Beryl, material objects link her back to significant relationships and memories, having them "there" is a comfort even where the relationships are now lost. Although she perceives that it may cause some dilemmas in the relatively near future, Beryl was able to decide on what she wanted to take with her from her home into independent residential care. Many residents, however, do not have the luxury of time and personal choice because of poor physical and/or mental health and these decisions fall to adult children or close friends. Barry, a man in his early nineties who also has a flat in the same extra care home site as Beryl, lost his wife of 72 years and suffered ill-health prior to his move. Accordingly, his children played a major part in sorting through and preparing his belongings for the transition. But in doing so, they elected not to include certain things that he would have liked to retain, like some of his grandfather's farm tools, even if they had long since lost their intended usefulness as working implements. Speaking in a small group of other residents and project members, Barry responded emphatically to Beryl's comment that she thought her family would press her to downsize further, now that she had had her flat redecorated:

> Barry: Well, I've had a bit of this trouble, I'm a hoarder as well. And when I moved from my house [to] here, well, I couldn't do very much about it myself, the family and a friend had to do most of the jobs and also: 'Oh, you won't need that up there, [waves hand dismissively], you won't need that.' [Turning to Helen] I've nothing left! It's horrible! [Beryl laughing] It's horrible! But I had loads of tools, tools for everything. And I had all sorts of – I won't say 'cake decorations'.

[Beryl laughs, she had brought a selection of 'Christmas cake toppers' to show the group.]

Helen: Things like that, yeah, everyday things.

Beryl: It got pushed to the back of the cupboard [the collection of cake decorations]. I'd forgotten about them. And then when I'd thought about the cookery book that I did, and then I thought: 'I wonder what happened to the cake decorations?' And there they were still in the tin. That's it, I got rid of a certain amount of stuff, but not the very personal stuff. [laughs wistfully]

Barry: It's a bugger, you can't keep it all you see, that's the trouble.

Beryl: No.

Barry: I had tools of various sorts that belonged to my grandfather. I had sheep shears, kind of thing, that *he* used to use shearing sheep. [Beryl: That's right.] Not the ones that you buy in the – do-it-all place – now. These were the original things. That's the thing, now they're all gone.

Over the course of his involvement with the project, Barry has specifically mentioned the loss of his grandfather's sheep shears on numerous occasions, including the first day of interviewing in January 2014. Clearly, the loss of this object was emblematic for Barry of greater loss that comes through in many of his stories. He talks of the dispossessing changes that technology has brought to rural life in general and work in particular, and how these changes have spilled over into everything from diet to children's play. The loss of the shears has become an important part of Barry's version of the family story as it relates to his disbandment and move (Ekerdt and Sergeant, 2006).

Although illness prevented Barry from participating fully in the disbandment of his household effects, he tells another story about two knives that are not lost themselves, but whose existence and cherished place among Barry's possessions as *material companions* – things used on a daily basis whose continued utility signifies a link with the past – betoken the more recent loss of his wife of many years and the much earlier loss of the relationship with his father in childhood. In each story, despite the continued existence of the object in its proper place in his life, there is a sense of a lack of closure, since the permanence of the things themselves can offer little comfort, healing or affirmation to the people and the relationships they symbolise for Barry.

As mentioned previously, small group *Antiques Roadshow* sessions were regularly held at the extra care home. At these object-oriented storytelling meetings, residents were encouraged to bring an object and tell its story or to allow the audience to guess the artefact's history and usage. With his usual emphasis on accuracy, Barry told the story of the two knives, inviting listeners to fill in details he wasn't sure of, such as when stainless steel was invented and widely available, as he felt that date had a direct bearing on the history of acquisition of his father's knife. Interestingly, Barry fashioned a replacement handle for this artefact, which linked his work as an adult (printing) with this household tool that his father had purchased for his young family's domestic use.

Barry: We were asked to bring something from the old days a little while ago and I don't know what happened – I either didn't turn up or didn't have it. But of course, having moved from a house to a flat, practically everything I possessed is *gone*. [BC chuckling.] I had loads of old things, old agricultural tools, garden tools, all sorts of things. I don't know where it's gone but I haven't got it now. But I've two little knives here, which are probably worth nothing, but they are to me. Is that a noise outside? Well, for what they are, that's a kitchen knife, there's nothing special about that, except that it was bought just after the First World War, in the '20s. And what interests me is that it's stainless steel. Now does anybody know when stainless steel became available because I didn't realise you could get stainless steel as early as that. [BC, considering: 'No …'] Apparently my father must have bought it in the very early '20s when he came out of the Navy and they were setting up home just after the War and it's been in use ever since. So it must be nearly a hundred years old unless – does anybody know when stainless steel was avail – became available? [LM, BC both say no.]

HH *(project artist)*: I have a feeling it might have been 1913. [unclear, BC: 'Heidi's just telling you Barry.'] I've got a feeling that it there was 100-year anniversary of stainless steel just last year.

Barry: Really?

HH:	I could be wrong but I think that Sheffield had a festival and I think it was 100 years, so that would be 1913, wouldn't it?
Barry:	Just before the War and this was purchased just after the War. [HH: 'New technology.'] It had a black handle originally. It was always known as 'Black Handle' this one, [soft laughter] but over the years the handle eventually got worse for wear, so I made a new handle for it.
Beryl:	You made the new handle?
Barry:	That's a nice piece of mahogany which was made out of a printer's half-tone block.
Beryl:	Ah, lovely.
Barry:	That served us alright.
Beryl:	A special knife, a very special knife.
Barry:	Well, it's special to me because, well I think it's the only thing I've ever had of my father, that he's ever touched, anyway.

As has been discussed, although Barry is not really upset with his family for making some of the decluttering decisions they felt they had to, particularly with respect to space and safety concerns in his new environment, he continues to feel the loss of certain possessions acutely because they connected him directly to the individuals and ways of life that defined his past. In a sense, his grandfather's shears may have become a marker of his past identity and lost way of life; less one of his inherited possessions than part of the identity he inherited from his rural ancestors as exemplified by his grandfather (Ferraro, Escalas and Bettman, 2011, p 170). And, as an object that would have been in his possession for a significant part of his adult life, the shears and similar articles may have acquired additional, deeper meanings for Barry over time precisely because of their connection to an earlier, simpler and nostalgically framed way of life, despite their apparently limited value as a practical tool or aesthetically pleasing display object (Karanika and Hogg, 2013, p 913).

Putting love away

Returning to the experiences of family members in the decluttering process and how their perspectives and memories of that collective event contribute to that chapter of the family story, Bell and Bell (2012) reflexively discuss the process of sorting through their mother's things after she was moved into care at the age of 83, citing the challenges of deciding what should be kept and used, kept and stored, donated or thrown away. These challenges may be compounded by the memories that a grown child may or may not have of an object and his or her ambivalence or attachment to it, particularly when these interactions – or lack of them – are further complicated by the place in which the final decisions are made. The Bell siblings' sorting took place in an uncomfortable and impersonal storage space, rather than in situ, which in fact freed them to concentrate on the objects alone. As such, the setting was ultimately helpful to their shared process (Bell and Bell, 2012, pp 64–5). In contrast, for some adult children, 'putting love away' in the very environment in which it was fostered by displacing and re- or devaluing the things that signified their parents' home may add a level of poignancy to an already stressful activity. Where the process is carried out influences what is kept and what is not.

In moving to a care home setting, some residents bring a selection of meaningful objects, while others leave everything behind. According to Diane, activity coordinator for the private care home, the relationship between residents and what they choose to bring or discard varies greatly from person to person. Furthermore, the value placed on what is taken may be more sentimental than material or aesthetic, and therefore the actual choices may seem incomprehensible, even to close outsiders.

> "Sometimes, people bring things that, to outsiders, seem ridiculous and to some family members: 'Why are you taking that?' But to them it could be really important. It could be just a little thing that was brought back by their child when they went on a school trip. It has no value, but when they look at that item, straight away it's 30 years ago and they are remembering when their small child was eight and just in glancing at that, that period of time can come back. And that happens more and more with people with memory issues and dementia. And we all have noticed that – that it's objects that we can't understand why they've brought [them] but they are very important to them. ...
>
> Some people choose to leave *everything* behind. They want a modern room with everything different. They don't want their old life. This is a different direction and they want to go forward." (Diane)

Time is another key facet of place that relates to decluttering and downsizing in important ways. While household disbandment is a specially marked time because it often relates to the final stages of the life span, it is not necessarily a completely unexpected experience. Rather, it may be one that an older person has considered, planned and mentally revisited in stages several times and possibly rejected as *not the right time* before physical necessity enacts the big move (or moves). When it is finally *the time* to move, 'downsizing evokes and unsettles a powerful sense of place experience; there are places in multiple timelines as downsizing is a major transition that deeply engages in multiple streams of personal, family, social and cultural life' (Luborsky, Lysack and Van Nuil, 2011, p 245).

Another intriguing set of complications in people's object/place relations relates to place and time combined with what may be called emotional aesthetics. People don't always actually like what they keep. Instead, continued possession may be strongly connected to contextual placement and emotional attachment to a person or event that is signified by an object that otherwise provokes ambivalence. Moreover, in their 'proper places' in the home, objects may escape our notice, except when there is an aspect about them that suddenly requires attention, such as the need for cleaning or repair. Tuan describes the relationship between house, home and things in these terms:

> The home place is full of ordinary objects. We know them through use; we do not attend to them as we do to works of art. They are almost a part of ourselves, too close to be seen ... Home is an intimate place. We think of the house as home and place, but enchanted images of the past are evoked not so much by the entire building, which can only be seen, as by its components and furnishings, which can be touched and smelled as well: the attic and the cellar, the fireplace and the bay window, the hidden corners, a stool, a gilded mirror, a chipped shell. (Tuan, 2001, p 144)

Just as particular places and things are likely to be evocative of the memory or presence of significant people in our lives, an object may be cherished as much for where it is *placed* as what it *is*, especially when careful placement demonstrates a valuing of intergenerational continuity (Kroger and Adair, 2008, p 17). To give an example, the granddaughter who hangs her great-grandmother's portrait above the mantelpiece because previous generations did so. When her mother comes to visit, she recognises an expression of familial material tradition and display, even if the younger woman never met her ancestor and knows the identity of the woman in the image only vaguely. As Larsson Ranada and Hagberg observe, generations are literally materialised through things: 'It is as if the objects by their materiality and visibility make the links between people concrete' (Larsson Ranada and Hagberg, 2014, p 115).

Similarly, when the entire locus changes, the object placement of a remembered space may need to be recreated in order to achieve a sense of balance and completion, even if some of the objects were not actually valued for anything other than that they formed part of a particularly situated collection. Speaking of her mother's experience of living for a time in the care home where she works, Diane recalled the temporary loss of one particular object that even her two daughters could not have guessed would figure so prominently in her mother's sense of place in the care home:

> "Six years ago my mother came here. Bit of an awkward situation in the beginning, she came for respite and actually staying two years, two very happy years here and had to move on to elderly and mentally infirm [nursing care]. But after she moved here, both my sister and I, as siblings, couldn't understand why she kept on about a tortoise. We hadn't had a tortoise since we were small children. Yet when she went to her bedroom she would totally mention this tortoise: 'Well, where's the tortoise? Where's the tortoise?' And as a professional care coordinator [D. makes a gesture indicating self] I couldn't understand either. I really couldn't understand it. We brought with her, because she was only here for respite in the beginning, we brought through various pictures, photographs of family, pictures that reminded her of my father's profession – he drove a train and that was quite important to her – so she had all of this around her, even her own armchair.
>
> One particular day she mentioned a mantelpiece. And, my sister twigged: 'You know you keep talking about the tortoise and you keep mentioning – you've mentioned the mantelpiece today? Do you mean the china tortoise that used to sit on the mantelpiece at home?' She said: 'Well, yes! What did you think I was talking about?' And my sister, who had the rest of her contents at home packed up in boxes, found this tortoise, a little weighted ornament that was a tortoise, with a shell. And lots of people in the

60s, 70s used to take the shell off, put their bits of pins, whatever in it and put it on your mantelpiece. My sister brought it in and my mother cried: 'Oh, thank God, I have everything around me now. You see, this is my room, this is my room and everything's complete. Except for the picture of Venice.'" (Diane)

The picture of Venice did not fare as well as the tortoise, however. Diane and her sister made the decision to get rid of it when their mother went into care, based on the knowledge that her mother did not like the picture for its own sake. What they did not realise was that the picture was the final piece needed to recreate her past lived environment in her new surroundings:

"And then we realised, when we looked around, we'd been able to bring most of what was in her lounge on the wall. So to my mother, she was in her lounge, in her own world, except for the picture of Venice, which was a horrible picture of Venice, had no value, like, just rubbish. [voice softens] And we'd thrown it away. And we really wished we hadn't thrown it away, but we never thought she liked it that much. But, she didn't like it that much, but to her, that put the whole room right." (Diane)

Concluding thoughts

This chapter has explored issues around memory and material culture with particular emphasis on decluttering and downsizing as a necessary process over the lifecourse, particularly when individuals move into care. Resilience here is described in relation to attachment to place and investment in a personal material culture that may help older people moving into care to continue with their lives (rather than 'bounce back') in the face of loss. The chapter has suggested the importance of attending to the material lives of older people in providing opportunities for them to reflect on their lives, identities and relationships. Caring practices may need to be developed that offer greater support for the process of materially moving to 'a home' from 'my home'. Drawing on and acknowledging the material repertoires of older people assumes a creative process of making, collecting, borrowing and adapting from a wide range of sources, including tradition and popular culture. Carers and families may need to account for this everyday creativity and design activities and support structures to enable this to continue in care settings.

It is both interesting and perhaps inevitable that one of the outcomes of research with people is that individuals often begin to critically reflect on the very aspects of their lives that researchers question them about because their relationships to the phenomena under investigation are mutually transformed through inquiry. Rather than discourage decluttering over the course of the project, despite the fact that this would certainly result in the loss of more objects and more object-based stories than had already happened through other events in residents' lives, the project took the view that decluttering and loss were themselves important aspects of individuals' personal material cultures and worthy of critical exploration within the larger context of the study. As Turkle writes, we think and feel through objects, even if we don't always realise it, especially things that are lost or that signify absence: 'When objects are lost, subjects are found' (Turkle, 2007, p 10). Sometimes, as this chapter has clearly demonstrated, other objects and their stories are found or rediscovered and people who may have previously thought themselves bereft of tales and things of interest to share with a wider audience may suddenly find themselves possessed of an embarrassment of riches after all.

References

Bell, M.E. and Bell, S. (2012) 'What to do with all this "stuff"? Memory, family, and material objects', *Storytelling, self, society: An interdisciplinary journal of storytelling studies*, 8: 63–84.

Cristoforetti, A., Gennai, F. and Rodeschini, G. (2011) 'Home sweet home: The emotional construction of places', *Journal of Aging Studies*, 25(3): 225–32.

Ekerdt, D.J. and Sergeant, J. (2006) 'Family things: Attending the household disbandment of older adults', *Journal of Aging Studies*, 20(3): 193–205.

Ekerdt, D.J., Sergeant, J., Dingel, M. and Bowen, M.E. (2004) 'Household disbandment in later life', *The Journals of Gerontology. Series B, Psychological Sciences and Social Sciences*, 59(5): S265–73.

Ferraro, R., Edson Escalas, J. and Bettman, J.R. (2011) 'Our possessions, our selves: Domains of self-worth and the possession-self link', *Journal of Consumer Psychology*, 21(2): 169–77.

Geertz, C. (1973) *The interpretation of cultures: Selected essays by Clifford Geertz*, New York, NY: Basic Books.

Georges, R.A. (1993) 'The concept of "repertoire" in folkloristics', *Western Folklore*, 53(4): 313–23.

Gill, S. (2014) 'Mapping the field of critical narrative', in I. Goodson and S. Gill (eds) *Critical narrative as pedagogy*, London: Bloomsbury, pp 13–38.

Gilleard, C. and Higgs, P. (2010) 'Aging without agency: Theorizing the fourth age', *Aging & Mental Health*, 14(2): 121–8.

Goodson, I. (2013) *Developing narrative theory: Life histories and personal representation*, London: Routledge.

Goodson, I. and Gill, S. (eds) (2014) *Critical narrative as pedagogy*, London: Bloomsbury.

Hallam, E. and Hockey, J. (2001) *Death, memory and material culture*, Oxford: Berg.

Karanika, K. and Hogg, M. (2013) 'Trajectories across the lifespan of possession–self relationships', *Journal of Business Research*, 66(7): 910–16.

Kirschenblatt-Gimblett, B. (1989) 'Objects of memory: Material culture as life review', in E. Oring (ed) *Folk groups and folklore genres: A reader*, Boulder, CO: Utah State University Press, pp 329–38.

Kleine, S.S. and Menzel Baker, S. (2004) 'An integrative review of material possession attachment', *Academy of Marketing Science Review*, 2004: 1–35.

Kroger, J. and Adair, V. (2008) 'Symbolic meanings of valued personal objects in identity transitions of late adulthood', *Identity* 8 (March 2015): 5–24.

Larsson Ranada, Å. and Hagberg, J. (2014) 'All the things I have – handling one's material room in old age', *Journal of Aging Studies*, 31: 110–18.

Leith, K.H. (2006) '"Home is where the heart is ... or is it?" A phenomenological exploration of the meaning of home for older women in congregate housing', *Journal of Aging Studies*, 20: 317–33.

Luborsky, M.R., Lysack, C. and Van Nuil, J. (2011) 'Refashioning one's place in time: Stories of household downsizing in later life', *Journal of Aging Studies*, 25(3): 243–52.

Meyer, M. (2012) 'Placing and tracing absence: A material culture of the immaterial' *Journal of Material Culture*, 17(1): 103–10.

Miller, D. (2008) *The comfort of things*, Cambridge: Polity Press.

Miller, D. (2010) *Stuff*, Cambridge: Polity Press.

Price, L.L., Arnould, E. and Folkman Curasi, C. (2000) 'Older consumers' disposition of special possessions', *Journal of Consumer Research*, 27(2): 179–201.

Tuan, Y.-F. (2001) *Space and place: The perspective of experience*, Minneapolis, MN: University of Minnesota Press.

Turkle, S. (2007) 'Introduction: The things that matter', in S. Turkle (ed) *Evocative objects: Things we think with*, Cambridge, MA: The MIT Press, pp 4–10.

Whitmore, H. (2001) 'Value that marketing cannot manufacture: Cherished possessions as links to identity and wisdom', *Generations*, 25: 57–63.

Windle, G. (2011) 'What is resilience? A review and concept analysis', *Reviews in Clinical Gerontology*, 21(02): 152–69.

ELEVEN

Later-life gardening in a retirement community: sites of identity, resilience and creativity

Evonne Miller, Geraldine Donoghue, Debra Sullivan and Laurie Buys

Editorial introduction

This chapter explores the experience of gardening in later life, focusing on how older people who move to a retirement community maintain or reinterpret their gardening identity. The authors discuss how gardening is a site of identity, creativity and resilience in ageing: a strategy for defining and maintaining 'body, mind and spirit' in their new home. Phenomenographic analysis (that is, analysis which explores the variation in people's experiences) revealed that residents experienced later-life gardening in five ways: the productive gardener; the creative gardener; the restricted gardener; the contemplative gardener; and the social gardener. This chapter highlights the significance of designing retirement communities that encourage engagement between residents and the creative leisure pursuit of gardening as a means of supporting individual happiness, pleasure and resilience.

Introduction

Throughout their lives, people often derive great pleasure from participating in creative activities. Whether participation is passive (for example, reading, attending theatre, listening to music) or more active (for example, photography, singing in a choir, creative writing, visual art, dancing, playing a musical instrument), a vast body of research literature confirms what we all intuitively know: engaging with creative activities has multiple psychological, emotional, psychological and physical health benefits, fostering overall life satisfaction and contributing to a higher quality of life, health and happiness as we age (Vaillant, 2002; Cohen et al, 2006; Dupuis and Alzheimer, 2008). Of course, creative activities need not only fit traditional notions of those arts-based examples provided above; rather, creativity can be accessed and practised through a myriad of everyday engagements. For Hallam and Ingold (2007), creativity is a state of being that is embedded in everyday living – a point poignantly made by McFadden and Basting, who argue that older people 'display creativity when they bring something new that has value into the world ... a poem written for a grandchild's birthday, a recipe modified to take advantage of garden vegetables, a song written in celebration of a friend's retirement, or a story told by a campfire' (McFadden and Basting, 2010, p 151). Indeed, while seemingly insignificant, these lived moments of creativity offer rich psychosocial experiences that are meaningful throughout the lifecourse and often take on a special salience in later years (Bhatti et al, 2009). The day-to-day mundane moments that define daily life (working, raising a family, household chores) often impede our inner creativity but may have a 'joyous resurgence in later life', when more time is available (Lamdin and Fugate, 1997, p 63).

Drawing on this notion of the creativity in the everyday, and the particular value of creativity in the lives of older persons, this chapter focuses on older adults' experience of gardening – an everyday creative leisure activity that, we argue, not only offers rich social, temporal and symbolic meaning and dimension to the lives of older people transitioning into an aged care environment, but is also a powerful means of maintaining identity and building personal and community resilience.

The outdoor creative activity of gardening

Simply defined as the care of plants and their environment, the practices, processes and experiences of gardening are visual, multisensory and deeply immersive as gardeners become 'aware of shades and colours, touching a worm, catching the wind; getting hands dirty in the soil, hearing a sprinkle of water; smelling a flower that takes them back to childhood' (Bhatti et al, 2009, p 66). For many, gardening quickly becomes a way of life (Wang and MacMillan, 2013), involving a range of aesthetic and practical decisions about site characteristics, climate and plants, which are built around the goals of individual gardeners: whether to create a lush vegetable garden, beautiful floral (or native) plantings or some combination. Annear et al (2014) categorised home gardens as either pleasure or productive: the pleasure garden, an extension of an individual's creative self-identity, is designed to be restorative, to be enjoyed socially with friends and to be enjoyed visually. In contrast, the productive garden primarily produces fruit and vegetables for consumption. Of course, while some gardens fit one of these neat categories, for many people, their gardens fall somewhere in between: a place that produces both food and a sense of relaxation and pleasure.

Gardening is widely viewed as a valuable pursuit, with many associated benefits, including positive influences on physical well-being (Wang and MacMillan, 2013) and psychological health (see Keniger et al, 2013 for a thorough review). Gardens can be enjoyed actively (potting, planting and weeding) or passively (sitting, walking, smelling and touching), sites of valued connections to nature and time for both individual reflection and social interactions. Centrally, gardening is a powerful outlet for physical and creative activity and, offering what Bhatti et al (2009, p 72) describe as an 'everyday workplace of bodily pleasures; getting hands dirty, being out in the wind, rain and sunshine; or aching from hard digging'. While the gardening activities of planning, digging, weeding, pruning, planting and watering are essential physical and practical tasks, for many the act of gardening goes beyond physical fitness, and is a deeply artistic or creative endeavour. Whether it be moving pots, or adding plants for colour or height variation, or looking through catalogues and planning future plantings for a bare site – the act of gardening is often a creative activity, full of hope and possibility for how a site may change or be changed.

While gardening is often a solitary endeavour, it also offers opportunities for building social connections and interactions. For example, there are growing numbers of community gardens, gardening clubs, workshops, garden trips and tours (local, national and international) that provide opportunities to interact, learn and share a passion for gardens with like-minded people (Clayton, 2007; Nettle, 2016). And, whether it is caring for their own home garden or working in a community garden, many older people view the garden and gardening as a significant part of their self-identity and a source of pride, enjoyment and value (Same et al, 2016). Gardens provide an important means of public self-expression (Clayton, 2007) and can also be sites of reflection and lived memory, with Orr et al (2004) describing the way one man loved his yellow roses because they connected him to the memory of his late wife.

A small but growing body of literature has documented the experience of gardeners as they age. A survey of 331 retired older Australians living in their own homes revealed that they primarily gardened for the aesthetics or beauty of gardens, vividly describing the joy of changing seasons, colours and shapes (Scott et al, 2015).

In adjusting to declining health and reducing mobility, these older gardeners adopted multiple strategies to maintain participation, such as careful task planning, using modified tools, more frequent but shorter gardening sessions, seeking paid or voluntary assistance for difficult tasks (for example, heavy lifting and digging) and downsizing to smaller homes and gardening areas. Same et al (2016) have also documented the positive impact of home gardening services for frail elderly Australians – support that enabled them to better enjoy their homes and age in place for longer as their gardens transformed from 'mess' to 'well-maintained'.

While gardening can bring both joy and challenges throughout the lifecourse, having to leave a garden behind can be especially difficult. This is particularly relevant for older adults who relocate to a retirement community or aged care facility, as they must leave both their home and much-loved garden behind – and often quite quickly, given that residents often report that there can be little time to secure available and suitable accommodation. Interestingly, despite the projected increase in demand for aged care places, and the knowledge that gardening plays an important role in the health and well-being of older people, there is little research that seeks to understand if and how older people maintain or reinterpret their gardening identity when they downsize and move into a retirement village (known as continuing care communities in the United States).

Moving to a retirement community and the role of creative leisure

While the decision to move to a retirement community is generally motivated by declining health and a desire for the additional support, security and services that are associated with life in an age-segregated community, neither the decision nor the transition and adjustment process is necessarily straightforward (Crisp et al, 2012, 2013). Currently, almost 6% (184,000) of older Australians aged 65 years and over live over in 1,750 retirement villages (Property Council of Australia, 2014), with the independent housing (units, townhouses and/or small houses) typically attractively grouped around an array of healthcare, leisure and life style facilities including cafes, swimming pools, a library, gym and access to organised social, physical, educational and creative activities (Miller and Buys, 2007; Nathan, Wood and Giles-Corti, 2013).

Several studies have explored the experience of leisure for retirement village residents, with most focusing on physical activity. For example, in Australia, Miller and Buys (2007) found that older retirement village dwellers reported leading more physically active lives (engaging more in walking, dancing and lawn bowls) than their community-dwelling peers, suggesting that the social and physical environment of retirement communities might make physically active life styles more visible and easier to adopt. Kleiber and Nimrod (2009) explored the constraints and enablers of leisure for 20 American retirement village residents, using the Selective Optimisation and Compensation (SOC) model of successful ageing. SOC argues that success is about making the best of what one has and pragmatically adapting to the losses, constraints and limitations of later life: *selection* is prioritising activities and goals, *optimisation* is maximising resources to achieve those goals and *compensation* is maintaining involvement through alternatives. Indeed, for Kleiber and Nimrod's sample, later-life leisure was about exploration and substitution, swapping jogging and tennis for the lower-impact exercises of yoga, golf and walking. While they generally reported positive adaptation to their health constraints, later life-leisure was a constant process of 'struggle, confrontation and reassertion of purpose' (Kleiber and Nimrod, 2009, p 72).

With little known about gardening in a retirement village context, this chapter explores whether and how older Australians maintain or reinterpret their interest in the creative-engagement leisure activity of gardening when they move into a retirement village – where often they have little private land space for gardening. Conceptually, this research is informed and guided by both an awareness of SOC (Baltes and Baltes, 1990, p 9) and continuity theory, which argues that one way adults successfully cope with life transitions is by maintaining continuity in their life through continued and adapted engagement with core interests (Atchley, 1999). Specifically, we focus on whether and how older retirement village residents maintain or reinterpret their interest and engagement in gardening in this new communal environment.

Method

Consistent with a constructivist theoretical mode, the frame of reference for this research was phenomenology, which aims to interpret 'situations in the everyday world from the viewpoint of the experiencing person' (Becker, 1992, p 7). Our approach was purposely collaborative, with 15 older retirement village residents invited to be active 'co-researchers' exploring their gardening experience in the past, now in their retirement community and into the future.

Participants and setting

Seven men and eight women, with an average age of 77.5 years, participated. All now lived in one not-for-profit retirement community located 40 kilometres from Brisbane, the capital city of the state of Queensland in Australia. As well as an on-site nursing home with 107 aged care rooms, the 230 independent living units (villas and higher-density apartments, ranging from studios to three bedrooms) are set on a flat, attractively landscaped 13-hectare site that includes gardens, walking trails, a creek, fish lagoon, bird aviary, croquet and bocce lawn, and barbeque areas. There are two swimming pools, a small gym and a coffee-shop, as well as a library, community centre and chapel. The facility is in a suburban area, approximately one kilometre from the adjacent beach waterfront esplanade and four kilometres from the nearest large shopping centre. In terms of each participant's garden context, participants live in either a multi-storied apartment unit (n=7) or ground-floor villa (n=8). Those residents living in a multi-storied apartment unit have access to a private large veranda that opens out from each resident's lounge room. The remaining residents living in ground-floor villas each have a small courtyard either at the front or rear of their villa, which is mostly open to other residents to view.

Procedure

After approval was obtained from both the facility and the university ethics committee (Gardening in Retirement Communities: Expectations and Experiences; Ethics Number QUT1500000416), a short recruitment/information letter explaining the project and inviting participation was placed in mailboxes and under doors within the complex. In 2015, interested older people participated in two semi-structured in-depth interviews (up to four weeks apart) conducted in their home in the retirement community, often over a cup of tea. Interviews involved sharing their gardening spaces, both their own smaller space (on a patio or veranda) and, if relevant, a walking tour of the larger facility grounds, where favourite spaces, plants and flowers were discussed. In between interviews, residents were asked to keep a creative and reflective written diary (Broom et al, 2014) and engage in a photo-elicitation task, drawing, reflecting on and photographing their gardening experiences (Harper, 2002). The first in-home interview discussed the role of gardening throughout their lives (as well as diary and camera orientation) for approximately an hour, while the second, shorter interview focused on their diary and photographs.

Finally, in a group workshop, residents reviewed and discussed their photographs, creating a shared narrative and visual understanding of their gardening experience in a retirement community setting. The initial categories for discussion included: 'I eat what I grow', 'Keeping fit', 'Reminders of my past' and 'Adapting the garden as I age'. As a thank you for participating, residents were given a plant. The plants were purposely selected, with residents being given a plant that they did not currently own but that a fellow participating co-resident had grown well in their garden space. The consideration of individual circumstances and thoughtful selection generated a great atmosphere of enthusiasm and discussion of ideas and information, fostering social interactions and connections during (and after) the workshop.

Analysis

Analysis began 'in the field' as participants were interviewed, as well as from later reviewing and coding of the transcriptions and the intentional visual images – including sketches/collages in diaries and photographs. Interviews were audio-taped and professionally transcribed verbatim. Transcripts were read and re-read, coded and systematically analysed using Marton's (1981) phenomenographic approach, which emerged in education and is a second-order perspective that focuses on the *variation* or qualitatively different ways in how people experience, understand or conceive of the same phenomenon. The focus is the relationships between the actors (older people living in a retirement community) and the phenomenon (gardening), specifically the variation and collective 'categories of description' that form the experience of later-life gardening (labelled the outcome space). (For a comparison of phenomenographic and phenomenological analyses, see Larsson and Holmstrom, 2007). In phenomenography, although conceptions originate from individual interviews, the descriptions are made on a collective level and reflect different 'ways of experiencing' gardening. The analysis followed Marton's seven analytic steps: familiarisation, condensation, comparison, grouping, articulating, labelling and contrasting. This coding process was iterative and, at times, simultaneous as similarities and differences were identified, categories developed, labelled and contrasted to understand the later-life gardening experience in a retirement community.

As the season and climate are critical in gardening, a note that the data was collected during winter – generally dry and mild in subtropical Brisbane (average winter daytime temperatures of 11–21 degrees Celsius). Season does determine specific tasks and interactions, with one participant explaining that in spring there are "jobs to do every day, you feel delighted to be out there every day. In the heat of summer, there are some days we just can't go there and the garden doesn't really need more than just watering." Thus, our analysis does not focus on season-specific gardening tasks but, rather, on the differences in overall gardening experiences, decisions and identities.

Moreover, guided by Lincoln and Guba (1985), four key strategies were adopted to maintain methodological rigour and trustworthiness, including: (1) starting with a thorough literature review, understanding of knowledge gaps and the topic under investigation (the authors are social gerontologists and landscape architects, respectively); (2) keeping interview questions open ended, multiple methods of data collection (individual and group interviews, guided walks, diaries and photography) and extensive reflexive memos; (3) fostering a culture of rigorous and reflexive conversations, discussing emergent ideas within the research team and with participants at the last workshop; and (4) fostering credibility, by purposely including multiple excerpts from the raw data in the results that enable readers to judge for themselves the accuracy and representativeness of the analysis. These four steps increase the trustworthiness of the data, helping to ensure that 'interpretations of the findings were not figments of the inquirer's imagination, but are clearly derived from the data' (Tobin and Begley, 2004, p 392).

Results

For these older gardeners, leaving their homes and beloved gardens to start a new life in a retirement community was a significant and challenging life event. Gardening was an important part of their life, with all describing a lifelong interest and passion for creating and working in their garden, taking great pleasure in watching something they had planted and cared for flourish. Indeed, one older man recalled how as a child he had been reluctant to go on holidays because "who was going to look after the garden? [Laughs]". While the creative leisure activity of gardening remained central to their identity, as they aged, an array of individual, social, environmental and relational factors intertwined to impede or facilitate their continuing participation. Thus, our phenomenographic analysis revealed that gardening in a retirement village was experienced in five qualitatively different ways: the productive gardener (growing food); the creative gardener (creative self-expression); the restricted gardener (gardening within confines of health and ability); the contemplative gardener (gardening for soul); and the social gardener (interactions and conversations).

Conception 1: the productive garden

The first conception was 'the productive gardener', with older residents viewing and valuing their garden for its edible 'bounty' of herbs, fruits and vegetables. These gardeners took significant pride in still eating, cooking and creating meals with their own home-grown produce – whether they were growing herbs, vegetables and fruit trees in pots, or in a small patch of garden on their patio or appropriated within the large communal grounds of the facility. Residents described the enjoyment of eating tomatoes they had grown, plucking basil from a pot to add to a meal or snacking on a mandarin from their own small fruit tree. As one woman explained, "the lunch I have almost every day consists of smoked salmon, tomato, onion, lettuce. But I always put a lot of garlic chives, basil, all the fresh herbs. And they are the main things that I grow."

With the exception of one couple, almost all described how their interest in gardening as an adult had its roots in a pragmatic desire to contribute to the household budget, save money and eat healthily through a home vegetable garden. Now, in their early 70s, gardening remained an important part of their self-identity and provided a continuing sense of purpose. Compared to the temporality of flowers, productive gardeners enjoyed the longevity of herbs, fruits and vegetables and took enjoyment in watching their garden change seasonally, planting appropriate plants, watching them grow and eating from their own gardens; as one explained, "I like to eat from my own garden, something twice a day … something to pick for lunch and evening every day … and we more or less do that, and have done, for years." Unfortunately, many felt they had an "awful space" to work with in the retirement community, and creating a productive garden was a challenge, due to the poor condition of the soil and the building orientation, which meant plants simply did not get enough sun to grow. Interestingly, several residents attempted to push back against their site conditions by appropriating empty spaces to grow the plants that did not bloom in their own private garden. One resident was growing five herbs (basil, garlic chives, parsley, onion chives) in a sunny public corner of the retirement complex, with the tacit approval of the facility gardener, who saw the resident gardening there one day and commented that he would "not spray weed-killer there".

Conception 2: the creative garden

This second conception highlights the creative and artistic pleasure that is associated with gardening, through thoughtfully and attractively arranging and layering plants in terms of colour, texture and pattern. In these small, everyday spaces that were a quarter the size of their previous gardens, residents proudly and creatively displayed their unique idiosyncratic gardening histories and habits. From paved areas and balconies overflowing with pots to larger garden spaces filled with fruit trees, Australian native plants, shrubberies, sculptures, bromeliads, ferns and/or flowers, these gardeners used every tiny space (climbing frames, side fences, spaces in the communal gardens) to express their creativity through their garden space. As one explained, creating a garden was the ultimate act of self-expression and expressing love: "love for your house, love for your home, love for your spouse".

Like the interior of a home, these residents felt that their garden spoke to their image "your life's image, how you see your life. It should speak of what you do and what you love. I think our garden does that." Whether it was through the artful arrangement of plants, the use of scale, proportion and height, or simple colour choices, there was great pride in making their garden space as beautiful as it could be – both for themselves and for passers-by to enjoy. As one couple explained, their front yard garden "looks pretty because of the choice; the choice of green and red and purple ... and the zigzag edge". Another resident described how her front garden was designed for "the passing crowd", purposely creative and full of flowers that "brighten your life". In this sense, the garden offered deep symbolic value to the residents in that it continued to express their individuality and their commitment to continued home making.

Conception 3: the restricted gardener

This third conception captures change, compromises and resilience as these older gardeners (in light of declining health and mobility) purposely downsized their gardening aspirations and expectations. All described past home gardens that had been large, wonderfully expressive and creative – ranging from a "rainforest in a gulley" to a purpose-built "fern-house", formally manicured lawns and flower-beds, as well as large raised gardens and vegetable beds.

With age, however, came compromise. All were struggling with the physicality of gardening, explaining that diminishing energy and restricted mobility meant there were certain things they just could not do as well and their body was telling their mind to "ease up a little". As well as finding it harder "getting down, to do gardening", age was affecting the choice of plantings; one resident explained that she no longer grows her own tomatoes because they irritate her mouth. Maintaining gardening participation in later life required adaptation, from taking more breaks to using a stool or choosing only one pot plant, not a whole garden: "I have a step on the bottom of the back and this hip here. So I can't do it on my knees, I can't do it sitting down, and I can't get up if I sit right down on the ground. So I have a little stool about this high, which I sit on." Another explained that she simply did not have the "spare energy these days for all those sorts of things that need doing", while one woman reflected on how her multiple sclerosis limited her mobility and changed her gardening habits. She reluctantly relocated to the retirement community after her husband died and found "it is really just an effort to get out and water the potplant that I have, let alone another garden". Again, building design was a barrier, as the lack of water on the balcony made the simple task of watering the plants a challenge because her balance was compromised and she had to hold on to something all the time: "it is a matter of getting jugs of water, putting them on a trolley, taking it over here, and then I have got a step there. I have got a series of holding points, where I can hang on and go out and take water. So, uhm … a tap would help." As well as health considerations, residents explained that they were often consciously selecting lower-maintenance plants. Once couple described putting in "shrubbytype of things, not so much the flowers" to minimise their own gardening workload and enable them to travel easily, to "just lock the doors and go". That said, the desire to keep gardening also dictated the type of retirement housing residents chose (villa with a garden or apartment with a balcony), with one woman explaining how she "could never go into an apartment, because I love my garden".

Conception 4: gardening as contemplation

The fourth category was the sense of peace, purpose and fulfilment that come from 'being a gardener', whether that was the physical process of gardening or simply sitting in quiet appreciation of the garden. While the physicality of gardening provided valued thinking time, it was enjoyable seeing "things grow and develop and getting some satisfaction about seeing the response and care that you are giving to plants". The garden was also a place of memory, with one woman describing how she brought eight stalks of lavender from her home garden to plant in her new home and she loved "getting down on my hands and knees and going around the edges and just doing it the way I like it and I think about lots of things … about my family, my grandfamily and my siblings". Another explained how, in summer, she and her husband would sit out there and enjoy the place, watching the "birds and butterflies going by".

Conception 5: gardening as social connections

The fifth and final conception was the social act of gardening, and the connectivity between residents strengthened through the sharing of both produce and plants. One woman described how she always gave "half of a punnet" next door and another resident has just given her a "bulb of turmeric and a lime basil". At the time of data collection, there was no formal gardening club or community garden. In part that was due to the work involved – residents were apprehensive to initiate and take on a large project that required significant personal effort, with one explaining he was "not pursuing them. Because unless somebody commits to being involved in a leading capacity, it just becomes hard work." However, despite residents not forming a formal gardening group, it was evident that gardening still acted as a social connector, with gardening often the subject of chatter and conversation between residents. Shared discussions about what is in season, the challenges of each resident's gardening site, and tips and suggestions for gardening queries were some of the examples. The act of sharing tools was also a way in which residents used the garden as a point of social connection, with one resident humorously noting "if you want somebody to remember who you are, borrow something from them".

Discussion

As Butterfield (2014) raises in her work on healthcare and gardens, a question that is often voiced within healthcare design is 'do gardens really matter?' A similar question emerges (frequently in the very late stages) of aged care design. With the emphasis often on the architectural footprint and maximising the number of residents that can be comfortably housed in an allotted space, the question of the role of the garden is often less explored. However, as detailed in this chapter, gardens and the creative act of gardening matter for older people living in a retirement village.

This qualitative phenomenographic analysis provided insight into the various ways that older adults residing in a retirement community experienced gardening, revealing five different yet interrelated 'conceptions' (Marton, 1981) that help us to understand the ways in which older retirement community residents engage in gardening and their experiences of maintaining their gardening identity after moving into aged care: the productive gardener, the creative gardener, the restricted gardener, the contemplative gardener and the social gardener. Of course, these conceptions or categories aren't 'fixed' in that residents' responses often crossed numerous themes; however, they do highlight the five different ways that these residents went about maintaining and nurturing their gardening identity. They speak to ways in which gardens are sites of resilience and adaption, and offer practical/creative and contemplative/social meaning to the lives and identities of older people living in a retirement village.

The first two conceptions (the productive gardener and the creative gardener), emphasise the basic (and different) decisions that the residents made about the primary purpose of the garden space, including: how it is designed, its functionality and the intended purpose of the final product. That is, the residents first sought to identify whether the garden would be primarily ornamental (for example, plants and flowers, such as roses) or bountiful (for example, fruit and vegetables). While other research has highlighted this distinction in whether a garden is for purpose or pleasure (for example, Annear et al, 2014), this study demonstrates that one way that gardeners maintain and adapt their gardening identity is by considering the function of the garden in relation to how they had previously enjoyed and interacted with gardens. For example, those who described large and bountiful vegetable gardens in previous homes still worked toward producing an edible landscape, albeit on a much smaller scale – whether it was pots of herbs in the kitchen sill or growing beans on a patio trellis.

Practically, however, residents described the challenges of maintaining a productive garden space in a retirement community where their interest and desire in gardening had clearly not been a design consideration. From dealing with poor soil comprised of builders' rubble to the lack of an outdoor tap on their balcony, neither the low-rise villas nor the high-rise apartment units had been designed to facilitate later-life gardening, revealing the ways in which outside structural forces can challenge an individual's desire to maintain an integral aspect of their identity in residential community living.

As detailed in the second conception, the connection between creativity and gardening was especially relevant for a number of residents who cherished the ways that they were able to creatively garden to reassert their meaning of home. Residents described gardening and the seemingly simple acts of choosing and layering foliage and flowering colours to be home-making tasks performed not only for public image and impact, but also for private enjoyment and as a creative outlet. The sense that gardening is a means of engaging creativity is a finding consistent with Ashton-Shaeffer and Constant (2006), who listed creativity as one of the seven motivational factors for older adults who garden.

The contemplative aspects of gardening were important for residents, as it provided solace and an opportunity to observe the patterns and rhythms of nature and to engage with quiet thoughts. This finding supports the work of Kaplan and Kaplan (2005), who – building on the work of Olmsted– argue that contact with nature assists cognitive repair and renewal through gaining 'cognitive quiet'. That is, the simple act of observing nature – the activity of the bee or the movement of leaves in the breeze – provides a rest to the mind, allowing it to break away from the clutter of other thoughts (see Ashton-Shaeffer and Constant, 2006 for a rich discussion on this point). As detailed by one participant, the act of kneeling and moving along the ground while weeding provided a quiet solace, which worked to induce almost meditative thoughts of family.

While the intimate and quiet contemplation that arises from the act of gardening was integral to many residents, the social connectivity between residents as a result of gardening also emerged as an important aspect of the gardening identity. For example, residents discussed how the act of gardening opened pathways for easy and good-natured discussion with co-residents, allowing more social residents to tap into new friendships and neighbourly relations. Interestingly, however, the social aspects of gardening were not as strong as the pleasure derived from the contemplative qualities of gardening. Indeed, for the majority of residents, gardening was enjoyed most strongly as a solitary act. Given that retirement villages are uniquely communal environments (both socially and spatially), often with minimal visual boundaries between private and public spaces, the restorative benefits of gardening as a peaceful activity should be recognised and supported.

Finally, it is important to acknowledge the importance of gardening in later life as a creative activity that fosters both identity and resilience. At its core, resilience is associated with a sense of hardiness and personal elasticity – particularly during times of transition such as older age (Bailey, 2015). The importance of resilience, and its relationship with gardening, emerged across all five conceptions; however, it was especially evident in the third conception, the restricted gardener. Residents described an array of compensatory strategies that they employed to manage declining health and mobility in order to continue gardening. Indeed while many older persons are living until the fourth age (75+ years old), and are thus living long lives, they are often doing so with declining physicality. As Bhatti (2006) richly details in his work on homes and gardens in later life, this declining physicality can be especially difficult for gardeners and others who seek to maintain active life styles as they age but are confronted with altered mobility. While a resident may want to perform work in the garden, they often are unable to do so, which can present emotional struggles and frustrations at the mismatch between desire and ability. In response, we found that a number of residents engaged resilient strategies in one of two ways: they used their gardening identity as a means of minimising further bodily decline (that is, using gardening as a means of retaining physical fitness); and/or incorporated altered gardening techniques such as planting low-maintenance shrubs and incorporating more pot plants to save bending down to the ground, as a means of maintaining their ability to care for their garden. In both cases, the act of gardening was closely intertwined with a practice of adapting to losses as a means of maintaining a continued presence in the garden.

The historical Latin meaning of resilience is 'to jump or leap back' (see Bailey, 2015), which speaks to the modern relationship between resilience and the notion of adaption. Indeed, the notion of adaption is central to the life-management strategy of SOC, which argues that adaptive and compensatory strategies are essential for healthy ageing. Its central tenet is that people continue to have great capacity for functioning as they age, and are highly adaptable during times of transition. As Scott et al aptly summarise, SOC proposes that 'healthy adaptation to ageing involves a shifting balance between losses and gains, and the congruence between the individual's goals and behaviour and their personal resources or environmental support for that behaviour' (Scott et al, 2015, p 2181). Thus, both our observation on the ways that older adults employ resilience and our broader findings of how people in retirement villages go about gardening, support the utility of SOC in understanding leisure in later life.

In conclusion, this chapter has highlighted how creative leisure activities, such as gardening, play an important role in the lives of older people who are living in a retirement village. Drawing on interviews, we have highlighted how individual, social and structural factors combine to either impede or facilitate the continuation of a lifelong creative engagement and leisure activity of gardening. While we would not go as far as permaculturist Geoff Lawton in arguing that 'all the world's problems can be solved in a garden' (cited in Maule and Megar, 2016, p 56), gardening was a beneficial and much-valued activity for these older adults and it is our hope is that the results of this study will provide insight into the meaning and importance of gardening for retirement village residents – findings that may enable designers and service providers to better meet the expectations of an ageing population.

References

Annear, M., Keeling, S., Wilkinson, T., Cushman, G., Gidlow, B. and Hopkins, H. (2014) 'Environmental influences on healthy and active ageing: A systematic review', *Ageing and Society*, 34(4): 590–622.

Ashton-Shaeffer, C. and Constant, A. (2006) 'Why do older adults garden?', *Activities, Adaption and Aging*, 30(2): 1–18.

Atchley, R. (1999) *Continuity and adaption in aging: Creating positive experiences*, Baltimore, MD: Johns Hopkins University Press.

Bailey, C. (2015) 'The influence of gardens on resilience in older adults living in a continuing care community', unpublished PhD thesis, Florida Atlantic University.

Baltes, P. and Baltes, M. (1990) 'Psychological perspectives on successful aging: The model of selective optimization with compensation', in P. Baltes and M. Baltes (eds), *Successful aging: Perspectives from the behavioral sciences*, New York: Cambridge University Press, pp 1–34.

Becker, C. (1992) *Living and relating: An introduction to phenomenology*, Newbury Park: Sage Publications.

Bhatti, M. (2006) '"When I'm in the garden I can create my own paradise": Homes and gardens in later life', *The Sociological Review*, 54(2): 318–41.

Bhatti, M., Church, A., Claremont, A. and Stenner, P. (2009) '"I love being in the garden": Enchanting encounters in everyday life', *Social and Cultural Geography*, 10(1): 61–76.

Broom, A., Kirby, E., Adams, J. and Refshauge, K. (2014), 'On illegitimacy, suffering and recognition: A diary study of women living with chronic pain', *Sociology*, 49(4): 712–31.

Butterfield, A. (2014) *Resilient places? Healthcare gardens and the Maggie's Centres* (PhD thesis). University of Arts, London and Falmouth University.

Clayton, S. (2007) 'Domesticated nature: Motivations for gardening and perceptions of environmental impact', *Journal of Environmental Psychology*, 27: 215–24.

Cohen, G., Perlstein, S., Chapline, J., Kelly, J., Firth, K. and Simmens, S. (2006) 'The impact of professionally conducted cultural programs on the physical health, mental health, and social functioning of older adults', *Gerontologist*, 46(6): 726–34.

Crisp, D., Windsor, T., Anstey, K. and Butterworth, P. (2012) 'What are older adults seeking? Factors encouraging or discouraging retirement village living', *Australasian Journal on Ageing*, 32(3): 163–70.

Crisp, D., Windsor, T., Anstey, K. and Butterworth, P. (2013) 'Considering relocation to a retirement village: Predictors from a community sample', *Australasian Journal on Ageing*, 32(2): 97–102.

Dupuis, S. and Alzheimer, M. (2008) 'Leisure and ageing well', *World Leisure Journal*, 50(2): 91–107.

Hallam, E. and Ingold, T. (2007) 'Creativity and cultural improvisation: An introduction', in E. Hallam and T. Ingold (eds) *Creativity and cultural improvisation*, London: Routledge, pp 1–24.

Harper, D. (2002) 'Talking about pictures: A case for photo elicitation', *Visual Studies*, 17(1): 13–26.

Kaplan, R. and Kaplan, S. (2005) 'Preference, restoration, and meaningful action in the context of nearby nature', in P. Barlett (ed) *Urban place: Reconnecting with the natural world*, Cambridge, MA: The MIT Press, pp 271–98.

Keniger, L., Gaston, K., Irvine, K. and Fuller, R. (2013) 'What are the benefits of interacting with nature?', *International Journal of Environmental Research and Public Health*, 10: 913–35.

Kleiber, D. and Nimrod, G. (2009) '"I can't be very sad": Constraint and adaptation in the leisure of a "learning in retirement" group', *Leisure Studies*, 28(1): 67–83.

Lamdin, L. and Fugate, M. (1997) *Elderlearning: New frontier in an aging society*, Phoenix, AZ: Oryx Press.

Larsson, J. and Holmstrom, I. (2007) 'Phenomenographic or phenomenological analysis: Does it matter? Examples from a study on anaesthesiologists' work', *International Journal of Qualitative Studies in Health and Well-Being*, 2: 55–64.

Lincoln, Y. and Guba, E.G. (1985) *Naturalistic inquiry*, California: Sage Publications.

Marton, E. (1981) 'Phenomenography: Describing conceptions of the world around us', *Instructional Science*, 10: 177–200.

Maule, M. and Megar, M. (2016) 'Effects of agriculture on environmental and human health', in M. Singer (ed) *A Companion to the anthropology of environmental health*, Massachusetts: Wiley-Blackwell, pp 44–67.

McFadden, S. and Basting, A. (2010) 'Healthy aging persons and their brains: Promoting resilience through creative engagement', *Clinics in Geriatric Medicine*, 26(1): 149–61.

Miller, E. and Buys, L. (2007) 'Predicting older Australians leisure-time physical activity: Impact of residence, retirement village vs. community, on walking, swimming, dancing and lawn bowls', *Activities, Adaption and Aging*, 31(3): 13–30.

Nathan, A., Wood, L. and Giles-Corti, B. (2013) 'Environmental factors associated with active living in retirement village residents: Findings from an exploratory qualitative enquiry', *Research on Aging*, 35(4): 459–80.

Property Council of Australia (2014) *National overview of the retirement village sector*, Sydney: Property Council of Australia.

Nettle, C. (2016) *Community gardening as social action*, New York: Routledge.

Orr, B., Mattson, R., Chambers, N. and Wichrowski, M. (2004) 'Actors affecting choice for horticultural therapy at the Rusk Institute of Rehabilitation Medicine', *Journal of Therapeutic Horticulture*, 15: 6–14.

Same, A., Lee, E., McNamara, B. and Rosenwax, L. (2016) 'The value of a gardening service for the frail elderly and people with a disability living in the community', *Home Health Care Management and Practice*, 28(4): 256–61.

Scott, T., Masser, S. and Pachana, N. (2015) 'Exploring the health and wellbeing benefits of gardening for older adults', *Ageing and Society*, 35(10): 2176–2200.

Tobin, A. and Begley, C. (2004) 'Methodological rigour within a qualitative framework', *Journal of Advanced Nursing*, 48(4): 388–96.

Vaillant, G. (2002) *Ageing well: Surprising guideposts to a happier life from the landmark Harvard study of adult development*, Victoria: Scribe Publications.

Wang, D. and MacMillan, T. (2013) 'The benefits of gardening for older adults: A systematic review of the literature', *Activities, Adaptation and Aging*, 37(2): 153–81.

Index

Page numbers in *italics* indicate figures, tables and boxes. Page numbers followed by an n indicate end-of-chapter notes.

A

absence 227–228, 231
action-research 113
activities 90
adaption 263
adverse events 30, 31, 32, 33, 183
aesthetic encounter 3, 20, 36, 37, 46–47
aesthetics, emotional 242
affordable housing redevelopment project 130–131
  community-based participatory research (CBPR) 133–136
  conceptual framework *135*
  outcomes and limitations 150–151
  qualitative methods 136–150, *137*
    community 'walk-alongs' 148–150
    deliberative dialogue 145–147, *146*
    narrative inquiry 138–142
    participatory mapping 147–148, 149–150
    photovoice 142–145
  sense of place 131–133
ageing
  global 160
  resourceful 51
ageing in place 132, 157–160
  creativity and resilience 160–162
  see also affordable housing redevelopment project; retirement communities
ageing in the right place 132, 134
ageing well 183
ageing well in place 162
  conclusion 176
  discussion 173–175
  public conversations 164–172, *166–167*, *171*
  research method 162–164
agency 34, 38, 208
  semantic 70
Ages and Stages project 43–44
  academic context 44–47
  creative context 47–49
  creative participatory research 50–53
    benefits and challenges 58–60
    findings 56–58
    participants' reflections 53–56
    research questions *50*
Alzheimer's Poetry Project 73
Antiques Roadshow sessions 234, 238–239
art forms 3–4
  see also cultural forms
art therapies 115–116, 122
arts activities 104
  see also craft activities; visual arts enrichment activities
Arts Council England 39n
arts engagement *see* creative engagement; cultural engagement
arts residency 170, 171
austerity 157–158
Australia 252–253
  gardening research study
    discussion 260–264
    method 253–256
    results 256–260
autobiographical narratives 97–100
autobiographical reasoning 90

B

Bell, M.E. and S. 240–241
Bennett, K. 22
bereavement 31, 32, 38, 195, 229
Bobowa 219, 220
body awareness workshop *116*
Bristol Old Vic 45

C

Canada
  affordable housing redevelopment project 130–131
  community-based participatory research (CBPR) 133–136
  conceptual framework *135*
  outcomes and limitations 150–151
  qualitative methods 136–150, *137*
    community 'walk-alongs' 148–150

267

deliberative dialogue 145–147, *146*
  narrative inquiry 138–142
  participatory mapping 147–148, 149–150
  photovoice 142–145
  sense of place 131–133
care 159, 244–245
  narrative 88, 105–106
care homes
  poetry intervention
    background 67–72
    conclusion 83–84
    discussion 80–83
    methods 72–75
    quantitative results 75
    transcripts and notes 76–80
  Tangible Memories project 233–234
    concluding thoughts 244–245
    personal objects and memories 235–244
  visual arts enrichment activities 87–88
    analysis 95
    baseline characteristics of study sample *96*
    conclusion 106
    discussion 103–106
    methodology and data 92–95
    results 95–103
    theoretical framework 89–91
characterisation 104
Charming Threads research study 204–205
  15th anniversary of workshops 212–214
  Charming Threads logo *220*
  group and individual identity 215–218
  heritage co-construction 218–222
  methods 205–207
  workshop set up 207–212
Chile 112
  psychosocial interventions 112–113
    artistic and cultural expression 115–117
    discussion and conclusions 122–124
    funding 124
    memory 120–122
    methods 113–115
    natural environment 117–120
class *see* social class
Cohen, Gene 44, 69
collage workshop *120*
collective memory 113, 114
communication 66
  poetry intervention
    background 67–72
    conclusion 83–84
    discussion 80–83
    methods 72–75
    quantitative results 75
    transcripts and notes 76–80
  see also theatrical poses
community 139
community activism 197–198
community research *see* affordable housing redevelopment project; Chile
community resilience 115–122, 129–130, 131, 133–134, 146, 183
  craft activities research study 196–198
community 'walk-alongs' 148–150
community-based participatory research (CBPR) 129, 133–136, *135*
community-led audits 162
confidence 192
contemplation, gardening as 259–260, 262
coping 28–29, 38
craft activities 181
craft activities research study 185–187
  discussion and conclusion 198–200
  findings 187–198
    community resilience 196–198
    meaning and purpose 189–191
    networks and mutual support 191–196
    resilience throughout life 187–189
  participants *186*
  see also lacemaking workshops research study
creative engagement 2, 3–5, 249–250
  and resilience 6–7
  and well-being 7–8
  see also cultural engagement; gardening; participatory theatre
creative gardens 258, 261–262
creative participatory research 50–53
  benefits and challenges 58–60
  findings 56–58
  participants' reflections 53–56
  research questions *50*
creative problem solving 5
creativity 1, 3–5, 115
  ageing in place 160–162
  dementia care 81–82
  gardening 262
  in later life 69
  material objects 227
cultural animation method 19, 25, 38–39
cultural engagement 8–9
  and resilience (research study) 19–21
    conclusion 37–39
    interview questions *27*

Index

literature review 21–24
participants 26
research methods 24–27
results and discussion 27–37
  learning 34–36
  older people's conceptualisations of resilience 27–30
  resilience across the lifespan 30
  resilience as specific to old age 30
  social relationships 36–37
  strategies and resources to develop resilience 31–33
and well-being 21
see also creative engagement; participatory theatre
cultural forms 39n
cultural identity 35, 38
cultural resilience 24
cultural value 46–47
culture 114, 116–117, 230
Cyrulnik, Boris 115
Czar Nici *see* Charming Threads research study

D

decluttering 235–238, 240–244, 245
deliberative dialogue 145–147, *146*
dementia 65
  narrative identity 91
  poetry intervention
    background 67–72
    conclusion 83–84
    discussion 80–83
    methods 72–75
    quantitative results 75
    transcripts and notes 76–80
  Tangible Memories project 233, 241
  visual arts enrichment activities 87–88
    analysis 95
    baseline characteristics of study sample *96*
    conclusion 106
    discussion 103–106
    methodology and data 92–95
    results 95–103
    theoretical framework 89–91
Dementia and Imagination project 87, 88
dementia care wards 66
dialogue *see* deliberative dialogue
dislocation of place 131
displacement 132
'Doorbells of Delight' (performance) *172*
downsizing 235–238, 240–244, 258

drama 3, 45–46
see also participatory theatre; plays
Dunajczan, Zofia 210, 214, 215, 219, *221*

E

earthquakes 112
  psychosocial interventions 112–113
    artistic and cultural expression 115–117
    discussion and conclusions 122–124
    funding 124
    memory 120–122
    methods 113–115
    natural environment 117–120
economy of relationships 235
education 21, 28
see also learning
emotional aesthetics 242
emotional support 193–194, 195, 210
engagement *see* creative engagement; cultural engagement; social engagement
ethnography 205–206
Etruria R. 598a (poem by C. Ramsell) 59–60

F

Fals-Borda, O. 113
Fevered Sleep 45
Field, John 184
films 36
'flourishing' 69–70, 83, 84n
folk music 116–117
fourth age 233, 263
fund raising 198

G

gardening 249, 250–252
  research study
    discussion 260–264
    method 253–256
    results 256–260
gender 181
see also women
Glazner, Gary 73
global ageing 160
'go-along' method 148–150
God 119
Golant, S.M. 132, 134
group activities *see* craft activities research study
group identity 214–218, 222

H

Hallam, E. and Hockey, J. 229
handicrafts *see* craft activities research study; lacemaking workshops research study
Harris, Phyllis 68–69
health and social care 159
heritage co-construction 218–222
Hildon, Z. 22–23
hobbies 90
home 139, 229–231, 242
home gardens 250–251
home-grown food 257
homo ludens 71
housing *see* ageing in place; ageing well in place; retirement communities
housing development project 130–131
 community-based participatory research (CBPR) 133–136
 conceptual framework *135*
 outcomes and limitations 150–151
 qualitative methods 136–150, *137*
  community 'walk-alongs' 148–150
  deliberative dialogue 145–147, *146*
  narrative inquiry 138–142
  participatory mapping 147–148, 149–150
  photovoice 142–145
 sense of place 131–133
Huizinga, Johan 71

I

Icarus (poem) 100
identity
 cultural 35, 38
 and gardening 257–260, 263
 group and individual 214, 215–218, 222
 local 117–120, 122
 narrative 90, 91, 97–106, 217
 place-based 219
 self-identity 183, 189, 206
identity projects 90
in-depth interviews 138–139
individual identity 214, 215–218
 see also identity: self-identity
interests 90
International Bobbin Lace Festival, Bobowa, Poland *220*
interview training 50–53
 participants' reflections 53–56
interviewers 51
interviews 94, 95, 138–139
isolation 68, 69, 118–119, 192

J

Jennings, B. 70, 83
Juliet and her Romeo (play) 45

K

Keyes, Corey 70
Kleiber, D. and Nimrod, G. 253
knowledge 213–214, 232

L

lacemaking workshops research study 204–205
 15th anniversary of workshops 212–214
 Charming Threads logo *220*
 group and individual identity 215–218
 heritage co-construction 218–222
 methods 205–207
 workshop set up 207–212
landscape 117–120
Langer, N. 182–183, 200
language 65–66
 poetry intervention
  background 67–72
  conclusion 83–84
  discussion 80–83
  methods 72–75
  quantitative results 75
  transcripts and notes 76–80
 see also linguistic capital
later life 30, 69, 182–184, 203–204
 see also old age
leadership 123, 197
learning 34–36, 37, 190–191, 194, 208, 211
leisure activities 252–253
 see also creative engagement
life events 30, 31, 32, 33
life narratives 208, 210
lifecourse perspective 199
 meaning and purpose 189–191
 resilience throughout life 187–189
linguistic capital 28
literature 35
local identity 117–120, 122
loneliness 118–119
loss 227, 228, 231, 232, 235, 238

M

Machielse, Anja 68
'man the player' 71
mapping *see* participatory mapping
master-student relationship 211

Index

material companions 232, 238
material culture studies 227
material objects 227, 228–229
  in the home 229–231
  resilience and repertoire 231–232
  Tangible Memories project 233–234
  concluding thoughts 244–245
  relationships and memories 234–244
meaning 189–191
media 174
memories 120–122, 173, 204, 229, 242–243
  gardening 259–260
  Tangible Memories project 233–234
  concluding thoughts 244–245
  relationships and memories 234–244
mental ill-health 192
Meyer, M. 227–228
Miller, D. 235
mindfulness 104
mobility 194–195, 233, 252, 258–259, 263
mortality 34
music 116–117, 122
mutual support 191–196

N

narrative care 88, 105–106
narrative foreclosure 90
narrative identity 90, 91, 97–106, 217
narrative inquiry 89, 138–142
narratives 89
  autobiographical 97–100
  life narratives 208, 210
  of local identity 117–120
  oral 204, 205, 215–218
  and resilience 89–91
  textual 100
  see also stories
natural disaster *see* earthquakes
nature 117–120, 262
neighbourhoods *see* affordable housing redevelopment project; ageing in place
Nesta 161
networks 191–196
  see also social capital
Newcastle upon Tyne 158, 160
  ageing well in place 162
  conclusion 176
  discussion 173–175
  public conversations 164–172, *166–167, 171*
  research method 162–164

O

objects 227, 228–229
  in the home 229–231
  resilience and repertoire 231–232
  Tangible Memories project 233–234
  concluding thoughts 244–245
  relationships and memories 234–244
old age 30
  see also ageing; later life
On Ageing (play) 45
oral narratives 204, 205, 215–218
Our Age, Our Stage (play) 48–49

P

Paredones, Chile 112
  psychosocial interventions 112–113
  artistic and cultural expression 115–117
  discussion and conclusions 122–124
  funding 124
  memory 120–122
  methods 113–115
  natural environment 117–120
participation, social 27
participatory arts, dementia care 67, 69
  see also poetry intervention
participatory mapping 147–148, 149–150
participatory methods 10–12, 47, 113
participatory research *see* community-based participatory research (CBPR); participatory theatre
participatory theatre 25, 43–44
  academic context 44–47
  creative context 47–49
  creative participatory research 50–53
  benefits and challenges 58–60
  findings 56–58
  participants' reflections 53–56
  research questions 50
personal identity *see* self-identity; individual identity
personal narratives *see* autobiographical narratives; stories
personal objects 227, 228–229
  in the home 229–231
  resilience and repertoire 231–232
  Tangible Memories project 233–234
  concluding thoughts 244–245
  relationships and memories 234–244
  see also possessions
personhood 71–72
phenomenographic analysis 249, 255
phenomenology 253

photovoice 142–145
physical activity 252–253
physical expression *see* theatrical poses
place 9–10, 131–133, 138–139
  ageing in place 132, 157–160
    creativity and resilience 160–162
  ageing in the right place 132, 134
  ageing well in place 162
    conclusion 176
    discussion 173–175
    public conversations 164–172, *166–167, 171*
    research method 162–164
  and loss 234
  and material objects 242–243
  see also home; housing redevelopment project; retirement communities
place-based identity 219
play (activity) 71, 82
plays (theatre) 36
  see also participatory theatre
pleasure gardens 250–251
poetry 59–60, 100, 104
poetry intervention
  background 67–72
  conclusion 83–84
  discussion 80–83
  methods 72–75
  quantitative results 75
  transcripts and notes 76–80
Poland
  lacemaking workshops research study 204–205
    15th anniversary of workshops 212–214
    Charming Threads logo *220*
    group and individual identity 215–218
    heritage co-construction 218–222
    methods 205–207
    workshop set up 207–212
positive ageing 134
possessions 232
  see also personal objects
Powrót do Tradycji (Return to Tradition) project 214–218
problem solving 5
productive gardens 251, 257, 261
psychological resilience 23, 29
psychosocial interventions 112–113
  artistic and cultural expression 115–117
  discussion and conclusions 122–124
  funding 124
  memory 120–122
  methods 113–115
  natural environment 117–120
public funding 159

purpose 189–191, 259
Putnam, Robert 181

R

race 35
Ramsell, Colin 59–60
reading 34–36
relationships 9, 36–37
  economy of 235
  master-student relationship 211
  networks and mutual support 191–196
  over the lifecourse 228, 230–231
  personal objects and memories 234–244
  and resilience 31–32
  see also social capital
reminding 83
repertoire 232
research interviewers 51
research methods *see* participatory methods
research skills training 50–53
  participants' reflections 53–56
resilience 1–2, 6–7, 19–20, 228
  ageing in place 160–162
  craft activities research study 181, 187–188
  cultural 24
  and cultural engagement (research study) 19–21
    conclusion 37–39
    interview questions 27
    literature review 21–24
    participants 26
    research methods 24–27
    results and discussion 27–37
      learning 34–36
      older people's conceptualisations of resilience 27–30
      resilience across the lifespan 30
      resilience as specific to old age 30
      social relationships 36–37
      strategies and resources to develop resilience 31–33
  and dementia 68–69, 80–81
    narrative construction 89–91, 99, 104–105
  and gardening 262–263
  in later life 182–184, 203–204
  and natural disaster 112
  psychological 23, 29
  and repertoire 231–232
  social 23, 158, 175, 184–185
  and social capital 184–185
  supporting factors 22–23

Index

and well-being 7–8, 183–184
  see also Ages and Stages project
resourceful ageing 51
restricted gardening 258–259
retirement communities 252–253
  gardening research study
    discussion 260–264
    method 253–256
    results 256–260
Return to Tradition project 214–218
Richmond, Canada
  affordable housing redevelopment project 130–131
    community-based participatory research (CBPR) 133–136
    conceptual framework *135*
    outcomes and limitations 150–151
    qualitative methods 136–150, *137*
      community 'walk-alongs' 148–150
      deliberative dialogue 145–147, *146*
      narrative inquiry 138–142
      participatory mapping 147–148, 149–150
      photovoice 142–145
    sense of place 131–133
risks 183
  see also adverse events
rural communities *see* Paredones, Chile

S

Second World War 30, 217
Selective Optimisation and Compensation (SOC) model 253, 263
selfhood 71, 72
self-identity 183, 189, 206
  see also individual identity
semantic agency 70
sense of place 131–133
Share Lives Plus 161
Sienicka, Zofia 215, *216*, 217–218
situational isolation 68
Skimstone Arts 170
small scale action 173
social capital 9, 23, 181, 184–185
  networks and mutual support 191–196
  and social class 199–200
social class 8–9, 21, 199–200
social connections 251
social connectivity
  dementia 68, 69
  gardening as 260, 262
  see also flourishing; social capital
social documentaries 48

social engagement 67–68
social interaction 67–68
social isolation 68, 69
social networks 191–196
  see also social capital
social participation 27
social reciprocity 236–237
social relationships 9, 36–37
  networks and mutual support 191–196
  and resilience 31–32
  role of cultural engagement in 37–38
  see also social capital
social resilience 23, 158, 175, 184–185
stories 89–90, 91, 117–120, 161, 230
  see also narratives
storytelling 21, 138, 139–140, *140–141*, 144, 170, 173
  see also narratives
structural isolation 68
Szerauc, Olga 215–218, *216*

T

Tangible Memories project 233–234
  concluding thoughts 244–245
  personal objects and memories 235–244
textual narrative 100
theatre 45–46
  see also participatory theatre
theatrical poses 101–103, 104
time 139–141, *140–141*, 195–196, 242
tradition, Return to Tradition project 214–218
trauma 115–117
triangulation 132–133
Tuan, Y.-F. 234–235, 242

U

urban studies 130

V

visual arts enrichment activities 87–88, 117
  analysis 95
  baseline characteristics of study sample *96*
  conclusion 106
  discussion 103–106
  methodology and data 92–95
  results 95–103
  theoretical framework 89–91
visual representations of group conversations *165*

visualisation *see* participatory mapping; photovoice
volunteering 197–198
Vorenberg, Bonnie 45

W

Węgorek, Jadwiga 207, 212
well-being 7–8, 21, 183–184
  see also Ages and Stages project
Wild, K. 23, 185, 200
Windle, G. 89, 158, 161, 175, 228
women 181
  craft activities research study 185–187
    discussion and conclusion 198–200
    findings 187–198
      community resilience 196–198
      meaning and purpose 189–191
      networks and mutual support 191–196
      resilience throughout life 187–189
    participants *186*
  lacemaking workshops research study 204–205
    15th anniversary of workshops 212–214
    Charming Threads logo *220*
    group and individual identity 215–218
    heritage co-construction 218–222
    methods 205–207
    workshop set up 207–212
World Café 162–170
World Health Organisation (WHO) 160
World War II 30, 217

Y

Young Vic 45

Z

Zautra, A. 183, 184, 199